Somali - English

THESAURUS

QAAMUUSKA 'TESOORAS'

Soomaali - Ingiriisi

HAAN Associates . London . 1997

ISBN 1 874209 77 4

Published by HAAN Associates
PO Box 607
London SW16 1EB

Printed and bound in Great Britain by The Ipswich Book Company Ltd.

Introduction to the Thesaurus

This Thesaurus lists together words of the same or similar meaning. It is designed to be a word finder. It will help students increase and improve their English vocabulary. It will help the student who wants to find a better or alternative word to replace the one that is not quite right in the context.

When you are writing essays or reports, or if you are preparing an oral English presentation, you will want to be able to express yourself in the best possible way. This Thesaurus will help you to do so. You can think of a Thesaurus as a storehouse or treasury of words. You can use it to find a word that will be just right for what you want to say.

There are many reasons why an alternative word might be needed. Maybe you have been using the same word too often and you want to avoid repetition. Maybe the word you first thought of is not right in some way – maybe it is too formal or too colloquial, or not quite precise enough. Sometimes the word you want will not just come to mind; in this case, you may find the word by looking up a similar one in the Thesaurus.

Arrangement of the Thesaurus

SAMPLE ENTRY

ka tagid. abandon *vb* desert, drop, evacuate, forsake, leave, quit, relinquish yield; cede, forgo, give up, let go, renounce, resign, surrender, vacate, waive.

1 The Thesaurus is arranged, like a dictionary, in alphabetical order according to the Somali headword or key word. Where more than one word is used in the Somali entry, the headword is considered to be the word which carries the root meaning. Therefore, in the example above, **ka tagid** will be entered under the letter T, not under K.

2 A point or full-stop (.) separates the Somali entry from the English equivalents. The Somali entry is followed by the key English equivalent, and both of these are in **bold type**.

3 The different forms or functions of a word are indicated in *italic type* by the following letters: *vb* (verb), *adj* (adjective), *adv* (adverb), *n* (noun), *prep* (preposition), *conj* (conjunction).

4 The list of English words which follow the Somali and English main entry are words which have **the same or similar meaning to the English key entry**; they are synonyms for the English word first listed. Sometimes a particular English word can have several different meanings. In the list of synonyms a slight change in meaning is indicated by a semi-colon (;). You will discover that not all the English synonyms have an identical meaning to the Somali entry word(s), but they do have a related meaning to the key (first) English entry word.

This Thesaurus is to help you access English and improve your command of the English language. Use the words you know as a springboard to explore other words and other meanings.

As you become familiar with using the Thesaurus, you will very quickly discover how it can help you improve your range of written and spoken English. It will lead you on a fascinating trail of words and their uses for all occasions.

Most importantly, always seek assistance from a teacher or an English-speaking friend if you need more help using the Thesaurus or understanding these explanations.

Hordhaca Qaamuuska

Qaamuuskan wuxuu qoraayaa ereyo isku micno ah ama isu micno dhow. Ardayga wuxuu ka caawiniyaa inuu kororsado, hormariyana erayyadda Ingiriisidda ah ee uu yaqaan. Sidoo kale wuxuu kaa kalmayn marka aad rabtid inaad heshid ereyga ugu habboon ee aad meel u isticmaali lahayd.

Marka aad diyaariniso qoraal, warbixin ama khudbadda Ingiriisi ah, waxaad u baahan tahay in aad u qortid ama u hadashid sida ugu fiican ee laguu fahmi karo. Qaamuuskani wuu kaa caawin arrintaas oo kale. Waxaa kale oo uu kuu noqon karaa marjac kayd ee.

Sababo badan ayaa keeni kara in aad u baahatid erey kale. Waxaa dhici karta in hal erey isticmaashay dhowr mar, oo aad jeclaato inaad ka leexato ku celcelinta ereygaa. Amaba ay maskaxdaada ku soo dhici weydo ereyga aad rabtay. Markaas oo kale waxaa laga yaabaa inaad ereygaas heshid aado ka eega Qaamuuska erey la micno ah.

Qaabka uu u habaysan yahay Qaamuuska

TUSAALE

ka tagid. abandon *vb* desert, drop, evacuate, forsake, leave, quit, relinquish, yield; cede, forgo, give up, let go, renounce, resign, surrender, vacate, waive.

1. Qaamuuskan waxaa loo habeeyey, sida ay u kale horreyaan Xarfaha Alfabetikadu. Meelaha dhowr erey ka kooban, ereyga muxurka wata ayaa la qaatay.

   Tusaale: **Ka tagid**, waxaa lagu habeeyey xarafka T, ee ma aha K.

2. Dhibic (.) ayaa u dhexeeysa ereyga Soomaaliga ah iyo kuwa Ingiriisidda ah. Ereyga Soomaaliga ah waxaa ku xiga ereyga Ingiriisidda ah ee ugu micno dhow, labaduba waxay ku qoran yihiin xuruuf waaweyn.

3. Si loo kala qeexo qaybaha hadalka ee kala duwan, waxaa la isticmaalay xarfo oo u dhigma, vb (verb), adj (adjective), adv (adverb), n (noun), prep (preposition), conj (conjunction).

4. Liiska ereyadda Ingiriisida ah ee la socoda ereyga Soomaaliga, waxay la micno yihiin ama u micno dhaw yihiin ereyga ugu horreeye ee Ingiriisidda ah (Ereyga Farta weyn ku qoran ee ku xiga ereyga Soomaaliga ah). Marar waxaa la arkaa in erey kali ah oo af Ingiriisi ihi yeesho micno kala yar duwan amba aan isu dhaweyn oo aad u kala duwan. Sidaas darteed, dhammaan ereyyadda Ingiriisidda ihi lama wada micno ah ereyga Soomaaliga ah, ee waxay la micno yihiin ama u micno dhow yihiin ereyga Ingiriisida ah ee ugu horreeya.

Xasuuso, Qaamuuskani wuxuu kaa caawiniyaa in uu kuu noqdo irid barashadda iyo si fiican ugu hadalka af Ingiriisidda. Marka hore ku bilow inaad isticmaashid ereyadda aad taqaanid, ka dibna isku day inaad heshid ereyo kale iyo micnahooda.

Kolba marka aad sii baratid isticmaalka Qaamuuskan, waxaa kuu caddaan sida dhakhsida ah ee uu kaaga kaalmayn horumarinta awooddaada ku hadalka iyo qoridda Ingiriisidda. Wuxuu kuu hoggaamin taxano ereyo ah iyo isticmaalkooda wakhti walba.

Mar walba la kaasho macallin ama qof Ingiriisidda yaqaan fahmidda sharaxan

A

aad habaysan. pomp *n* magnificence, ostentation, show, splendour.

aad u yar. iota *n* atom, bit, glimmer, grain, jot, mite, particle, scintilla, scrap, shadow, spark, tittle, trace, whit.

aad u yar. scanty *adj* insufficient, meagre, narrow, scant, small.

aakhirka. eventual *adj* final, last, ultimate.

aalad. instrument *n* appliance, apparatus, device, implement, musical instrument, tool, utensil.

aamin ah. trustworthy *adj* dependable, honest, upright, reliable, safe, sure; firm, fixed.

aamin-darro. betray *vb* be false to, divulge, expose, reveal, ruin, seduce.

aaminid la'aan. mistrust *vb* distrust, doubt, suspect;

ku aaminid. entrust *vb* commit, confide, consign.

aaminid. trust *vb* depend, rely; believe, credit. *n* belief, confidence, expectation, faith, hope.

aamusan. absolutely *adv* completely, dead, downright, fundamentally, quite.

aamusan. hush *n* quiet, quietness, silence, stillness.

aamusan. mute *adj* dumb, silent, speechless, still, taciturn. voiceless.

aamusan. quiet *adj* hushed, motionless, still; calm, contented, mild, meek, modest.

aamusiin. silence *vb* hush, gag, muzzle, calm, subdue.

aamusiin. stifle *vb* choke, muffle, muzzle, silence, smother, suffocate.

aamusnaan. silence *n* hush, noiselessness, quiet, stillness.

aan bislayn. rare *adj* bloody, underdone.

aan caadi ahayn. odd *adj* inappropriate, irregular, peculiar, strange, uncommon.

aan caadi ahayn. uncommon *adj* exceptional, infrequent, rare, scarce, unfamiliar, unusual.

aan caadi ahayn. novel *adj* fresh, modern, new, rare, uncommon, unusual.

aan caadi ahayn. irregular *adj* abnormal, anomalous, devious, erratic, exceptional, unusual; fitful, spasmodic, variable; disordered, uneven, unsystematic.

aan caadi ahayn. unusual *adj* abnormal, curious, exceptional, odd, peculiar, rare, remarkable, strange, uncommon.

aan caadi ahayn. freak *n* abnormality, monster, monstrosity.

aan caadi ahayn. peculiar *adj* idiosyncratic, eccentric, extraordinary, odd, queer, rare, singular, strange.

aan caddaalad ahayn. inequitable *adj* unfair, unjust.

aan daahin. promptly *adv* directly, immediately, instantly, punctually, quickly, speedily, straightaway, swiftly.

aan dabeeci ahayn. unearthly *adj* supernatural, uncanny, weird.

aan dan ka lahayn. lukewarm *adj* tepid, thermal; apathetic, indifferent, unconcerned.

aan dan ka lahayn. indifference *n* apathy, unconcern; disinterestedness, impartiality, neutrality.

aan deganayn. unstable *adj* insecure, unbalanced, unsafe, unsteady; changeable, erratic, fickle, volatile.

aan dhamayn. partial *adj* incomplete, limited; biassed, one-sided, prejudiced, fond.

aan faa'iido lahayn. vain *adj* futile, ineffectual, unavailing, unprofitable; conceited, egotistical, self-opinionated, vainglorious

aan ficil ahayn. theoretical *adj* abstract, conjectural, hypothetical, speculative.

aan fiicnayn. unsound *adj* defective, impaired; erroneous, fallacious, illogical, questionable.

aan hadal lagu soo koobi karin. unspeakable *adj* indescribable, ineffable, inexpressible, unutterable.

aan haysan. lack *vb* need, want.

aan is bedelin. immutable *adj* constant, fixed, invariable, unchangeable.

aan is qaadan karin. incompatible *adj* contradictory, incongruous, irreconcilable, unsuitable.

aan la akhri karin. indecipherable *adj* illegible, unintelligible, unreadable.

aan la daweyn karin. incurable *adj* hopeless, remediless; helpless, incorrigible, irreparable.

aan la hubin. changeable *adj* uncertain, unsettled, variable; fickle, vacillating, wavering.

aan la hubin. uncertain *adj* doubtful, indefinite, indistinct, unsettled; insecure, precarious, problematical.

aan la masaxi karin. indelible *adj* fast, fixed, ingrained, permanent.

aan la moodi karin. insuperable *adj* impassable, insurmountable.

aan la qiimeyn karin. invaluable *adj* inestimable, priceless.

aan la qiyaaso karin. unlimited *adj* boundless, infinite, measureless; absolute, complete, full.

aan la raali gelin. fretful *adj* cross, ill-humoured, ill-tempered, peevish, petulant, touchy.

aan la soo celin karin. irreversible *adj* irrevocable, unalterable, unchangeable; changeless, invariable.

aan la tirin karin. untold *adj* countless, incalculable, innumerable, uncounted, unnumbered.

aan la xiriirin. irrelevant *adj* extraneous, foreign, illogical, inapplicable, unrelated.

aan laga maarmi karin. indispensable *adj* essential, necessary, needed, requisite.

aan laga murmi karin. indisputable *adj* undeniable, indubitable, unquestionable.

aan lahayn meel. vagabond *adj* footloose, rambling, roving, roaming, wandering; itinerant, nomadic, vagrant.

aan laysu keeni karin. irreconcilable *adj* incompatible, incongruous, inconsistent.

aan loo baahnayn. superfluous *adj* excessive, needless, redundant, unnecessary.

aan loo baahnayn. undue *adj* improper, excessive, disproportionate, immoderate, unsuitable.

aan loo dul qaadan karin. intolerable *adj* insufferable, insupportable, unbearable, unendurable.

aan micno lahayn. trivial *adj* frivolous, insignificant, light, paltry, petty, trifling, unimportant.

aan mihnad lahayn. amateur *adj* inexpert, lay, nonprofessional.

aan muhiim ahayn. worthless *adj* childish, empty, foolish, frivolous, giddy, idle, light, trivial, unimportant, vain.

aan muuqan. potential *adj* latent, possible.

aan nadiif ahayn. slovenly *adj* unclean, untidy, unkempt, lazy, negligent, slapdash.

aan qiimo lahayn. invalid *adj* baseless, fallacious, false, untrue, worthless; (*law*) null, void.

aan raalli ahayn. unwilling *adj* averse, disinclined, loath, opposed, reluctant.

aan raalli laga hayn. unwelcome *adj* disagreeable, unacceptable, unpleasant, unpleasing.

aan shaki qabin. unsuspecting *adj* confiding, credulous, trusting, unsuspicious.

aan shaqaynayn. void *adj* ineffectual, invalid, null.

aan sharci ahayn. illegal *adj* contraband, forbidden, illicit, prohibited, unauthorized, unlawful, unlicensed.

aan sinnayn. jagged *adj* serrated, ragged, uneven.

aan u culus. unwieldy *adj* bulky, cumbersome, heavy, hulking, large, ponderous, unmanageable, weighty.

aan ula kas ahayn. incidental *adj* accidental, casual, chance, nonessential, occasional.

aan waxba ka jirin. groundless *adj* baseless, causeless, false, gratuitous, unfounded, unwarranted.

aan waxba ogayn. unwittingly *adv* inadvertently, unconsciously, unintentionally, unknowingly.

aargoosi. vengeance *n* retaliation, retribution, revenge.

aargoosi. avenge *vb* punish, retaliate, revenge, vindicate.

aargudasho. revenge *n* rancour, retaliation, retribution, vengeance, vindictiveness.

aargudid. revenge *vb* avenge, repay, retaliate, vindicate.

aasid. bury *vb* entomb, inter; conceal, hide, secrete, shroud.

abaabulid. organize *vb* adjust, form, make, shape; arrange, coordinate.

abaalgud. reward *n* compensation, pay, remuneration; bounty, bonus, fee, gratuity, honorarium, tip.

abaalmarin. prize *n* honours, reward, decoration, medal, laurels, trophy.

abaalmarin. award *vb* adjudge, allot, assign, bestow, decree, grant.

abaalmaris. reward *vb* compensate, pay, remunerate.

abaar. drought *n* aridity, drouth, dryness, thirstiness.

abuur. creation *n* cosmos, universe.

abuure. maker *n* creator, god; builder, constructor.

abuure. creator *n* author, designer, inventor, originator.

abuurmid. originate *vb* begin, create, invent, produce.

adag in la fahmo. complex *adj* complicated, entangled, intricate, involved, knotty, tangled.

adag. laborious *adj* arduous, difficult, fatiguing, hard, irksome, tiresome.

adag. tough *adj* cohesive, hard, inflexible, leathery; callous, formidable, obdurate.

si adag. hardly *adv* barely, scarcely; cruelly, harshly, roughly, severely, unkindly.

adag. harsh *adj* astringent, biting, hard, rough, sharp, sour, tart; discordant, grating, jarring, metallic, raucous, strident, unmelodious; cruel, disagreeable, hard, ill-natured, severe, stern, unfeeling.

adag. difficult *adj* arduous, exacting, hard, tough, uphill.

adag. firm *adj* established, rooted, secure, stable; compact, compressed, dense, hard, solid; constant, determined, loyal, resolute, unshaken; stanch, stout, sturdy, strong.

adag. hard *adj* firm, rigid, solid, resistant, stony, stubborn, unyielding; difficult, intricate, knotty, perplexing, puzzling; arduous, exacting, fatiguing, laborious; callous, cruel, hard-hearted, severe, unsympathetic, unyielding.

adag. strict *adj* austere, inflexible, harsh, orthodox, puritanical, rigid, rigorous, severe, stern, strait-laced, uncompromising, unyielding.

adag. rigid *adj* firm, hard, inflexible, stiff, unbending, unyielding; austere, correct, exact, formal, harsh, severe, stern, strict; cruel.

adag. concrete *adj* firm, solid.

adag. stiff *adj* firm, inflexible, prim. rigid, stark, stilted, unbending, unyielding.

adagtay si loo xallilo. intricate *adj* complicated, difficult, entangled, involved, mazy, obscure, perplexed.

addun. nature *n* universe, world; character, constitution, essence.

adduunka. earth *n* globe, orb, planet, world; clay, clod, dirt, ground, land, loam, sod, soil, turf.

u adeegid. serve *vb* assist, attend, minister, oblige; benefit, promote.

ka adkaan. subdue *vb* beat, conquer, control, defeat, master, overpower; curb, moderate, restrain, soften, suppress.

ka adkaan. vanquish *vb* conquer, defeat, outwit, overcome, overpower, subdue; crush, foil, master, quell.

ku adkayn. accentuate *vb* accent, emphasize, mark, point up, punctuate, stress; highlight, overemphasize, underline, underscore.

adkayn. emphasis *n* accent, stress; force, importance, moment, significance, weight.

u adkaysi. stand *vb* abide, bear, endure, suffer, sustain, tolerate; fix, place, put, set upright.

adkaysi. endurance *n* tolerance, toleration; forbearance, fortitude, guts, patience.

ku adkaysi. insist *vb* demand, maintain, urge.

u adkaysi. endure *vb* bear, suffer, undergo, weather; abide, tolerate, withstand; continue, last, persist, remain, wear.

u adkaysi. withstand *vb* confront, defy, face, oppose, resist.

adke. solid *adj* compact, dense, firm, hard, strong, substantial.

adkeysi leh. hardy *adj* enduring, firm, hale, healthy, hearty, lusty, robust, rugged, stout, strong, sturdy, tough.

u adkeysi. undergo *vb* bear, endure, experience, suffer, sustain.

u adkeysi. cope *vb* strive, struggle.

ku adkeysi. persevere *vb* continue, persist, resolve, stick.

ku adkeysi. persist *vb* continue, endure, last, remain; insist, persevere.

adkeysi. determination *n* firmness, constancy, grit, persistence, stamina, resoluteness, resolution.

adoon ah. servile *adj* cringing, fawning, grovelling, slavish.

adoonsi. enslave *vb* captivate, dominate, master, overpower, subjugate.

af la'. blunt *adj* dull, edgeless, unsharpened; abrupt, plain-spoken, outspoken.

af suuqdi. jargon *n* gabble, gibberish, nonsense: cant, lingo, slang.

afduubid. kidnap *vb* abduct, capture, carry off, remove, steal away.

afka. oral *adj* spoken, verbal, vocal.

afqanbi. overthrow *n* downfall, fall, demolition, defeat.

aftahinimo. eloquence *n* fluency, oratory, rhetoric.

afti. vote *n* ballot, franchise, poll, referendum, suffrage, voice.

afuufid. blow *vb* breathe, gasp, pant, puff, waft.

agaasimid. conduct *vb* direct, escort, lead; manage, operate, regulate.

agagaarka. about *prep* around, encircling, surrounding, round; near; concerning, referring to, regarding, relating to, relative to, respecting, touching, with regard to, with respect to. *adv* around, before; approximately, near, nearly.

ka fakarid. fancy *vb* conjecture, imagine, suppose, think.

la akhari karo. legible *adj* clear, decipherable, fair, distinct, plain, readable.

akhlaaq. conduct *n* actions, behaviour, manners.

akhlaaq fiicni. civil *adj* courteous, gracious, obliging, polite, well-mannered.

aan akhlaaq lahayn. unprincipled *adj* dishonest, immoral, iniquitous, lawless, unscrupulous.

akhlaaq leh. suave *adj* affable, bland, courteous, glib, smooth, unctuous, urbane.

akhlaaq wacan. gracious *adj* affable, civil, courteous, easy, familiar, polite.

akhlaaq xun. impudent *adj* bold, bold-faced, brazen, impertinent, insolent, insulting, rude, shameless.

akhlaaq xun. uncouth *adj* awkward, boorish, gawky, loutish, rough, rude.

akhlaaq xun. insolent *adj* abusive, insulting, rude, supercilious; cheeky, impertinent, impudent, insubordinate.

akhlaaq xun. surly *adj* churlish, cross, ill-tempered, morose, rude, snarling, sour, sullen, uncivil, ungracious.

ka timi xagga alle. divine *adj* godlike, superhuman, supernatural; angelic, celestial, heavenly, holy, sacred, spiritual.

aan la akhriyi karin. illegible *adj* indecipherable, obscure, undecipherable, unreadable.

alaabo. goods *n* merchandise, provision, supplies.

alaabta dibedda laga keeno. import *n* goods, importation, merchandise.

amaahasho. borrow *vb* take and return, use temporarily; appropriate, imitate.

amaahin. lend *vb* advance, give, grant, loan, supply.

amaanid. complimentary *adj* flattering.

amakaag. surprise *n* amazement, astonishment, shock.

amakaakid. nonplus *vb* astonish, bewilder, confound, embarrass, perplex, pose, puzzle.

amar. command *n* order, requirement.

amar diid. insubordinate *adj* disobedient, mutinous, riotous, seditious, ungovernable, unruly.

amar diid. disobey *vb* infringe, transgress, violate.

ambaqaad. resume *vb* continue, recommence, renew, restart.

ammaan. flattery *n* adulation, blarney, cajolery, fawning, obsequiousness.

ammaan. distinction *n* credit, eminence, fame, renown, repute, respectability, superiority.

ammaan. praise *n* acclaim, approval, commendation; eulogy, glorification, homage, tribute.

ammaanid. commend *vb* recommend; applaud, approve, extol, praise.

ammaanid. flatter *vb* compliment, praise; butter up, court, fawn, humour.

ammanid. praise *vb* acclaim, approve, commend; compliment, flatter.

amoomi. unsociable *adj* reserved, solitary, standoffish, taciturn, uncommunicative.

amrid. dictate *vb* command, decree, order, prescribe, require.

amrid. will *vb* bid, command, decree, direct.

amrid. instruct *vb* bid, command, direct, educate, enlighten, guide, indoctrinate, inform, order, school, teach, train.

amrid. boss *vb* command, direct.

amrid. brief *vb* give directions, instruct.

amrid. decree *vb* command, decide, order, ordain.

amrid. command *vb* bid, charge, direct, enjoin, order, require; control, dominate, govern, lead, rule; compel, demand.

an la go'on karin. priceless *adj* precious, inestimable, invaluable.

anaani. selfish *adj* egoistic, greedy, mean, self-seeking, ungenerous.

anshax xumo. indecent *adj* improper, indecorous, outrageous, unbecoming, unseemly, immodest, impure, indelicate, lewd, nasty, obscene, pornographic, smutty, unchaste.

anshax xun. immoral *adj* corrupt, loose, sinful, unethical, wicked, wrong.

anshax. morals *npl* ethics, morality; behaviour, conduct, habits, manners.

la aqbali karo. acceptable *adj* agreeable, gratifying, pleasant, pleasing, pleasurable, welcome.

aqbalid. accept *vb* acquire, derive, get, gain, obtain, receive, take; accede to, acknowledge, acquiesce in, admit, agree to, approve, assent to, avow, embrace.

aqoon leh. academic *adj* collegiate, lettered, scholastic.

aqoon leh. literary *adj* bookish, erudite, learned, literate, scholarly, well-read.

aqoon yahan. academic *n* academician, classicist, doctor, fellow, pundit, savant, scholar, student, teacher.

aqoon yahan. intellectual *n* academic, highbrow, scholar.

aqoon yahan. learned *adj* erudite, literate, scholarly, well-read; expert, knowing, skilled, well-informed.

aqoon. knowledge *n* comprehension, understanding; acquaintance, information, learning, scholarship, science.

aan la aqoon. unsigned *adj*

aqoondarro. ignorance *n* illiteracy, unawareness.

aqoonleh. knowledgeable *adj* aware, conscious, experienced, well-informed; educated, intelligent, learned, scholarly.

aqoonsi. identity *n* existence, individuality, personality, sameness.

aqoonsi. qualification *n* ability, accomplishment, capability,

arag. look *n* appearance, complexion, manner, mien.

arag. spot *vb* discern, make out, observe, see, sight.

aragati dheeri. foresight *n* anticipation, forecast, forethought, precaution, prudence.

aragga. sight *n* appearance, perception, visibility; eyesight, seeing, vision.

aragga. vision *n* eyesight, seeing, sight; apparition, hallucination, illusion, phantom, spectre.

aragti. view *n* outlook, panorama, prospect, scene, vista; belief, idea, judgement, notion, opinion, sentiment, theory.

aragtid. witness *vb* corroborate, note, notice, observe, see.

arbush. inconvenience *vb* annoy, disturb, trouble, vex.

arbush. excitement *n* agitation, bustle, commotion, disturbance, ferment, flutter, sensation, stir, passion, violence, warmth.

arbush. inconvenience *n* annoyance, disturbance, trouble, vexation; awkwardness.

arbushid. unsettle *vb* confuse, disturb, unbalance, upset.

arbushid. bother *vb* annoy, disturb, harass, molest, pester, plague, tease, trouble, vex, worry.

arbushid. molest *vb* annoy, bother, disturb, harass, irritate, trouble, vex, worry.

arday. learner *n* beginner, novice, pupil, student.

arday. disciple *n* learner, pupil, scholar, student; adherent, follower, supporter.

argagax leh. uncanny *adj* eerie, ghostly, unearthly, unnatural, weird.

argagax leh. unearthly *adj* supernatural, uncanny, weird.

argagaxis. terror *n* alarm, awe, dismay, dread, fear, horror, intimidation, panic, terrorism.

argati xumayn. blur *vb* darken, dim, obscure.

arji qorosho. solicit *vb* appeal to, ask, beg, entreat, implore, urge.

arji. petition *n* appeal, application, request, solicitation.

la arkaayo. visible *adj* perceivable, perceptible; apparent, clear, conspicuous, evident, obvious, revealed.

aan la arkayn. unseen *adj* undiscerned, undiscovered, unobserved, unperceived

arrimo fuliye. executive *n* administrator, director, manager.

arrin. affair *n* business, circumstance, concern, matter, office, question; event, incident, occurrence, performance, proceeding, transaction; battle, combat, conflict, encounter, engagement, skirmish.

asaas. foundation *n* base, basis, bed, bottom, footing, ground, support; endowment, establishment, settlement.

asaas. essential *n* fundamental, principal, rule.

asaas. base *n* foundation, underpinning; pedestal, plinth, stand; headquarters, HQ; starting point, basis, bottom, foot, foundation.

asaasi ah. fundamental *adj* basic, bottom, essential, indispensable, principal, primary, radical.

asaasi. primary *adj* first, initial, original; chief, main, principal; basic, elementary, fundamental, preparatory.

asaasi. staple *adj* basic, chief, essential, main, primary, principal.

asaasid. establish *vb* organize, originate, plant, raise; ensconce, install, place, plant, root, secure; prove, substantiate, verify.

asaasid. found *vb* build, construct, erect, raise; establish, institute, originate, plant.

asaaska. root *n* base, bottom, foundation; cause, reason, source.

isku asal ah. kindred *adj* allied, connected, related, sympathetic.

asal ah. authentic *adj* genuine, pure, real, true, unadulterated, uncorrupted, veritable; accurate, authoritative, reliable, true, trustworthy.

asal. origin *n* beginning, birth, commencement, original, root, source, starting point; heritage, lineage, parentage.

askari. martial *adj* military, soldier-like, warlike.

asla ah. original *adj* first, primary.

awood la'aan. impotent *adj* helpless, incapable, powerless, unable, weak; barren, sterile.

awood lahayn. incompetent *adj* incapable, unable; inadequate, unfit.

aan awood lahayn. incapable *adj* feeble, impotent, incompetent, unable, unfit, unqualified, weak.

awood lahayn. helpless *adj* disabled, feeble, impotent, infirm, powerless, weak; defenceless, unprotected.

awood leh. influential *adj* controlling, effective, effectual, powerful, strong; authoritative.

awood leh. powerfully *adv* profoundly; eminently, loftily; luxuriously, richly.

awood siin. enable *vb* authorize, capacitate, commission, empower, fit, permit, prepare, qualify, sanction, warrant.

awood siin. empower *vb* authorize, commission, permit, sanction, warrant.

awood weyn. omnipotent *adj* almighty, all-powerful.

awood. *n* might, power, strength, vigour; coolness, courage, endurance, firmness, fortitude, pluck.

awood. might *n* ability, capacity, force, power, strength.

awood. impetus *n* energy, force, momentum, propulsion.

awood. authority *n* power, sovereignty; control, influence, rule, supremacy, sway; order, permit, sanction, warranty; connoisseur, expert, master.

awood. impulse *n* force, impetus, push, thrust; inclination, instinct, passion.

awood. potential *n* ability, capability, possibility.

awood. faculty *n* ability, capability, capacity, endowment, power, property, quality.

awoodid. afford *vb* furnish, produce, supply, yield; bestow, communicate, confer, give, grant, impart, offer; bear, endure, support.

awoodleh. mighty *adj* able, bold, courageous, powerful, robust, strong, huge, immense.

awoodsiin. authorize *vb* empower, enable, entitle; allow, approve, confirm, countenance, permit, ratify, sanction.

axdi jabin. violate *vb* break, disobey, infringe, invade; desecrate, pollute, profane; abuse, debauch, deflower, outrage, ravish.

axmaq. ruthless *adj* barbarous, cruel, ferocious, hardhearted, inexorable, inhuman, merciless, pitiless, savage, uncompassionate.

axmaq. cruel *adj* barbarous, blood-thirsty, ferocious, hard-hearted, inhuman, merciless, pitiless, ruthless, savage, unfeeling.

axmaq ah. savage *adj* uncultivated, wild; bloodthirsty, ferocious, brutal, barbarous, cruel.

si axmaqnimo ah. beastly *adj* abominable, brutish, low, vile.

axmaqnimo. outrageous *adj* furious, frenzied, mad, violent, wild; monstrous, villainous; excessive, extravagant.

axmaqnimo. austere *adj* ascetic, difficult, formal, hard, harsh, morose, relentless, rigid, rigorous, severe, stern, stiff, strict, uncompromising, unrelenting.

axsaan. favour *n* approval, goodwill, kindness, benefit, dispensation; gift, present, token; bias, partiality, prejudice.

B

baabin. neutralize *vb* cancel, invalidate, offset.

baad. extortion *n* blackmail, demand, exaction, overcharge, tribute.

baadhid. inquest *n* inquiry, inquisition, investigation, quest, search.

baadhid. investigate *vb* examine, explore, follow up, inquire into, look into, probe, question, research, scrutinze, search into, search out, sift, study.

baadhitaan. investigation *n* examination, inquiry, inquisition, study.

baadid. bully *vb* browbeat, domineer, intimidate, overbear.

baahi. need *n* emergency, necessity, want.

baahi. dearth *n* deficiency, insufficiency, scarcity; lack, shortage, want.

baahi. necessity *n* inevitability, unavoidability, compulsion, need, requirement, requisite.

baahi. want *n* deficiency, insufficiency, lack, paucity, scarcity, shortage; destitution, indigence, need, penury, poverty, privation.

baahin. scatter *vb* broadcast, sprinkle, strew; disperse, disseminate.

baahsan. extensive *adj* general, large-scale, mass, widespread.

baahsan. prevalent *adj* extensive, general, rife, widespread.

baarid. probe *vb* examine, explore, investigate, scrutinize, sift, verify. * *n* examination, exploration, inquiry, investigation, scrutiny, study.

baarid. examine *vb* inspect, observe; explore, inquire, investigate, scrutinize, study, test; catechize, interrogate.

baarid. scrutiny *n* examination, inspection, investigation, search, sifting.

baaris. prospect *vb* explore, search, seek, survey.

baaris. check *n* examination, inspection, overhaul.

baaritaan adag. ransack *vb* pillage, plunder, rifle, sack, strip, search thoroughly.

baaritaan. examination *n* inspection, observation; exploration, inquiry, inquisition, investigation, perusal, research, search, scrutiny.

baaxad leh. massive *adj* big, bulky, colossal, enormous, heavy, huge.

baaxad leh. vast *adj* boundless, infinite, measureless, spacious, wide; colossal, enormous, gigantic, huge, immense, mighty.

baaxad leh. large *adj* big, broad, bulky, colossal, elephantine, enormous, great, huge, immense, vast.

baayactan. bargain *n* agreement, compact, contract, transaction

badan. ample *adj* broad, capacious, extended, extensive, great, large, roomy, spacious; abounding, abundant, copious, generous, liberal, plentiful; diffusive, unrestricted.

badan. plenty *n* abundance, adequacy, enough, plethora, profusion.

aad u badan. abundant *adj* abounding, affluent, ample, bountiful, copious, exuberant, fertile, flowing, full, good, large, lavish, luxuriant, rich, liberal, much, overflowing, plentiful, plenteous, replete, teeming, thick.

aadu badan. copious *adj* abundant, ample, exuberant, full, overflowing, plenteous, plentiful, profuse, rich.

aad u badan. profuse *adj* abundant, bountiful, copious, lavish, overabundant, plentiful.

inta badan. majority *n* bulk, greater, mass, more, most; adulthood, manhood.

badan. numerous *adj* abundant, many, numberless.

badan. multitude *n* assembly, collection, crowd, herd, mass, mob, pack, populace, rabble, swarm, throng.

badbaadin. rescue *vb* free, liberate, release, save.

badbaadin. save *vb* keep, preserve, rescue; economize, gather, hoard; prevent, spare.

badbaado. deliverance *n* emancipation, escape, liberation, release.

badbaado. rescue *n* deliverance, liberation, release, salvation.

badeed. naval *adj* marine, maritime, nautical.

badhxid. temper *vb* assuage, mitigate, mollify, moderate, soften, soothe.

ka badin. override *vb* outride, outweigh, pass, quash, supersede, surpass.

ka badin. surpass *vb* beat, cap, exceed, excel, outdo, outshine.

badin. multiply *vb* extend, increase.

ka badin. exceed *vb* cap, overstep, surpass; excel, outdo, outstrip, outvie, pass.

ka badin. transcend *vb* exceed, overstep, transgress; outstrip, outrival, outshine, surpass.

badin. double *vb* duplicate, increase, multiply, repeat.

ka badin. outdo *vb* beat, exceed, excel, outgo, outstrip, surpass.

ka bajin. scare *vb* alarm, frighten, intimidate, shock, startle, terrify.

ka bixin. strip *vb* disrobe, uncover, undress.

badiyaaba. often *adv* frequently, generally, oftentimes, repeatedly.

badqabid. safe *adj* unharmed, unhurt, guarded, secure, dependable, reliable.

badweyn. main *n* high seas, ocean;

bahal. monster *n* brute, demon, fiend, villain, wretch.

is bahaysi. coalition *n* alliance, association, combination, confederation, federation, league, union.

bajin. menace *vb* alarm, frighten, intimidate, threaten.

bajin. alarm *vb* daunt, frighten, scare, startle, terrify.

ka bajin. terrify *vb* alarm, appal, dismay, frighten, horrify, scare, shock, terrorize.

bakhaar. warehouse *n* depot, magazine, repository, store, storehouse.

bakhaar. treasure *n* treasury; storehouse; market, shop.

ballaadhan. roomy *adj* ample, capacious, commodious, expansive, extensive, large, spacious, wide.

ballaaran. gross *adj* big, bulky, burly, fat, great, large; beastly, coarse, indelicate, unbecoming, unrefined, vulgar, rough; aggregate, entire, total, whole.

ballaaran. broad *adj* ample, expansive, extensive, large, spacious, sweeping, vast, wide.

ballan-qaaddid. pledge *vb* bind, contract, engage, promise.

ballan. engagement *n* appointment, contract, obligation; betrothal; action, battle, combat, encounter, fight.

ballanqaadid. promise *vb* pledge, swear, underwrite, vow; assure, attest, guarantee, undertake. *n* agreement, contract, oath, pledge, undertaking, vow, word.

balli. mere *n* lake, pond, pool.

banaaabax. demonstration *n* display, exhibition, manifestation, show.

bandhig. display *n* exhibition, show; pageant, parade, pomp.disposed *adj* apt, inclined, prone, ready, tending.

bandhig. exhibition *n* demonstration, display, exposition, representation, spectacle, show.

bandhig. show *n* display, fanfare, ostentation, parade.

bandhig. exhibition *n* show, spectacle; display, ostentation, pomp, splendour.

soo bandhigid. tender *vb* bid, offer, present, proffer, propose. qandaraas. tender *n* bid, offer, proposal.

bangi. bank *n* depository, fund, reserve, savings, stockpile.

bannaan. plain *n* grassland, plateau, prairie, steppe.

bannaan. plan *vb* arrange, concoct, contrive, design.

dhul bannaan. heath *n* field, moor, wasteland; plain, rangeland.

bannan. blank *adj* empty, vacuous, void.

baqanaya. afraid *adj* aghast, alarmed, anxious, apprehensive, frightened, scared, timid.

baqdin badan. eerie *adj* awesome, fearful, frightening, strange, uncanny, weird.

baqdin leh. tremendous *adj* alarming, awesome, fearful; amazing, extraordinary.

baqdin. alarm *n* panic, shock.

baqdin. dismay *n* alarm, consternation, fear, fright, horror, terror.

baqid. phobia *n* aversion, dread, fear, hatred.

baqid. quail *vb* flinch, shrink, tremble.

bar. spot *n* fleck, mark, speck; blemish, stain; locality, place, site.

u baraarugsan. conscious *adj* awake, aware.

baraarujin. invigorate *vb* animate, brace, energize, fortify, stimulate, vivify.

baraf ah. frosty *adj* chilly, cold, icy, stinging, wintry; cold-hearted, frigid, uncordial.

bararid. swell *vb* bulge, dilate, distend, expand, increase, inflate.

barasho. practised *adj* able, experienced, practical, proficient, qualified, skilled.

baratan. race *n* competition, contest, sprint.

barbarad. amateur *adj* inexpert, lay, nonprofessional.

barbarad. novice *n* apprentice, beginner, initiate, learner, novitiate, probationer.

barid. teach *vb* coach, educate, enlighten, explain, inform, instruct, preach, train.

barkad. mere *n* lake, pond, pool.

barkin. cushion *n* bolster, hassock, pad, pillow.

barroosin. anchor *n* (*naut*) ground tackle; defence, hold, security, stay.

baruur. fat *n* grease, oil; best part, cream.

barwaaqaysi. prosper *vb* flourish, grow rich, thrive, succeed.

barwaaqo. prosperity *n* affluence, good luck, success, well-being; boom, heyday.

baryid. pray *vb* ask, beg, beseech, entreat, implore, petition, request.

baryid. plead *vb* appeal, beg, entreat, implore.

baryid. beg *vb* ask, beseech, entreat, implore, petition, pray, request

basaasid. spy *vb* discern, glimpse, observe, see, spot.

baxsasho. escape *vb* elude, evade, flee from; abscond, bolt, flee.

bedbeddelis. variation *n* alteration, change, modification; deviation, innovation.

beddel. change *n* alteration, shift, transfer.

beddel. change *n* alteration, variation.

beddelid. shift *vb* change, fluctuate, move, rearrange, vary.

beddelid. change *vb* alter, modify, vary; replace, shift, substitute.

beddelid. alter *vb* change, conform, modify, shift, turn, transform, transmit, vary.

bedel. change *n* assignment, conveyance, move, transmission.

la bedeli karo. mutable *adj* alterable, changeable, variable.

isku bedelid. exchange *vb* barter, change, substitute, swap, trade. * *n* barter, change, substitution, reciprocity; bazaar, fair, market.

bedelid. convert *vb* alter, change, transform, transmute; interchange, transpose; convince.

bedelid. modify *vb* alter, change, vary;

bedelid. modification *n* alteration, change, variation;

bedelid. transform *vb* alter, change, convert, translate, transmute.

bedelis. veer *vb* change, shift, turn.

bediil. choice *n* option, preference.

been ah. mendacious *adj* deceitful, deceptive, false, lying, untrue, untruthful.

been ah. falsehood *n* fabrication, fib, fiction, lie, untruth.

been ka sheeg. misrepresent *vb* distort, falsify, misinterpret, misstate.

been ka sheegid. distort *vb* falsify, misrepresent, pervert.

been sheegid. lie *vb* falsify, fib, romance.

been. untrue *adj* false, inaccurate, wrong; disloyal, faithless, treacherous, unfaithful. *n* deceit, deception, error, falsehood, fabrication, fib, fiction, lie, untruth.

been. false *adj* untrue, fictitious, forged, made-up; artificial, bogus, counterfeit, forged, hypocritical, pseudo, sham; erroneous, incorrect, unfounded, wrong; deceitful, fallacious. misleading.

been. lie *n* falsehood, fib, misrepresentation, untruth.

beenabur. forgery *n* counterfeit, fake, falsification, imitation.

beenabur. falsify *vb* alter, adulterate, cook, counterfeit, doctor, fake, falsely, misrepresent.

beenabuur. counterfeit *n* copy, fake, forgery, sham.

beenayn. prevaricate *vb* dodge, equivocate, evade, quibble.

beenayn. deny *vb* refute; disavow, disclaim, renounce; disallow, refuse, reject, withhold.

beerid. plant *vb* sow, establish.

beerid. cultivate *vb* farm, fertilize, till, work.

beri hore. ancient *adj* old, primitive, pristine; antiquated, antique, archaic, obsolete.

bidaar. bald *adj* bare, naked, uncovered, treeless.

biil. bill *n* account, charges; advertisement, banner, hoarding, placard, poster; bill of exchange, certificate, money.

ku biirid. side (with) *vb* befriend, favour, to, join with, support.

ku biirid. enlist *vb* enrol, recruit, register; engage.

ku biirid. join *vb* add, annex, append, attach; cement, combine, connect, couple, link, unite, yoke; amalgamate, associate, confederate, consolidate.

bilaa sharci. lawless *adj* anarchic, chaotic, disorderly, rebellious, wild.

bilaabid. commence *vb* begin, inaugurate, initiate, institute, open, originate, start.

bilaabid. begin *vb* commence, inaugurate, institute, originate, start.

bilaabid. introduce *vb* present, usher in; begin, broach, commence, inaugurate, initiate, institute, start.

bilaabid. begin *vb* commence, inaugurate, launch, open, start.

bilaabid. start *vb* begin, commence, inaugurate, initiate; depart, leave, set off, set out. *n* beginning, commencement, inauguration, outset.

bilaabid. initiate *vb* begin, commence, enter upon, inaugurate, introduce, open; ground, indoctrinate, instruct, prime, teach.

bilaabid. undertake *vb* begin, embark on, engage in, enter upon, take in hand.

bilaabin. induct *vb* inaugurate, initiate, instal, institute, introduce.

bilicsan. magnificent *adj* elegant, grand, majestic, splendid, superb.

bilicsan. gorgeous *adj* brilliant, dazzling, fine, glittering, grand, magnificent, resplendent, rich, shining, splendid, superb.

bilow. beginning *n* initiation, introduction, opening, preamble, preface, preliminary, prelude, start.

bilow. beginning *n* commencement, dawn, emergence, inauguration, inception, initiation, opening, outset, start; origin, source.

bilow. outset *n* beginning, commencement, entrance, opening, start, starting point.

bilowga. initial *adj* first; beginning, introductory, opening, original; elementary, rudimentary.

bini aadmi ah. humane *adj* accommodating, benevolent, benign, charitable, compassionate, good-hearted, merciful, sympathetic.

bir tumid. forge *vb* beat, fabricate, form, frame, hammer; coin, devise, frame, invent; counterfeit, fabricate, falsify, feign. *n* furnace, ironworks, smithy.

bisil. ripe *adj* mature, mellow; fit, prepared, ready; complete, finished.

bislaan. mature *vb* develop, ripen.

bislaan. season *vb* harden, mature; flavour, spice.

aan weli bislayn. immature *adj* green, imperfect, premature, raw, unfinished, unripe, youthful.

bixid. exit *vb* depart, go, leave.

kaa soo bixid. mount *vb* ascend, climb, escalate, scale; get upon.

bixid. departure *n* exit, leaving, parting, removal, recession, removal, retirement, withdrawal; abandonment, forsaking; death, decease, demise, deviation, exit.

soo bixid. appear *vb* emerge, loom; break, open; arise, occur, offer; look, seem, show.

soo bixid. emerge *vb* appear, arise.

bixin. pay *vb* settle, recompense, reimburse, reward.

bixin. give *vb* bequeath, bestow, confer, present; donate, grant, proffer.

kala bixin. stretch *vb* elongate, extend, lengthen, protract, pull.

bixin. fee *vb* pay, recompense, reward.

dib u bixin. repay *vb* refund, reimburse, restore, return; compensate, remunerate, reward; retaliate, revenge.

bocor. mould *n* mildew, mouldiness, rot; fungus, lichen, mushroom.

cunto boobid. guzzle *vb* carouse, drink, gorge, gormandize, quaff, swill, tipple, tope.

boobis. snatch *vb* clutch, grasp, grip, pluck, seize, wrest..

boobsiis. offhand *adj* abrupt, brusque, curt.

booddo awreed. leap *n* bound, hop, jump, leap, skip, spring.

booddo. bounce *n* jump, leap, spring, vault.

boodid. hop *vb* jump, leap, skip, spring; dance, trip; hobble, limp.

boodid. vault *vb* bound, jump, leap, spring.

boodid. gambol *vb* caper, cut, frisk, frolic, hop, jump, leap, romp, skip.

dibusoo boodid. bounce *vb* bound, jump, leap, spring.

boodid. skip *vb* bound, hop, jump, leap, spring.

boodid. bound *vb* jump, leap, spring.

boodin. spring *vb* bound, jump, leap, vault.

boodin. jump *vb* bound, caper, hop, leap, skip, spring, vault.

boodo. spring *n* bound, jump, leap, vault.

boofin. inflate *vb* bloat, blow up, distend, expand, swell; puff up; enlarge, increase.

boofsan. inflated *adj* bloated, distended, puffed-up, swollen; overblown, pompous.

bootin. vault *n* bound, leap, jump, spring.

boqor. king *n* majesty, monarch, sovereign.

boqor. sovereign *n* emperor, king, monarch, ruler.

boqor. monarch *n* chief, emperor, king, potentate, prince, queen, ruler, sovereign.

boqortooyo. dynasty *n* dominion, empire, government, rule, sovereignty.

boqortooyo. empire *n* domain, dominion, sovereignty, supremacy; authority, command, control, government, rule, sway.

boqortooyo. kingdom *n* dominion, empire, domain, province, realm.

botaacid. spurt *vb* gush, jet, spout, stream out.

bucsharo. merchandise *n* commodities, goods, wares.

bucshro. commodity *n* goods, merchandise, produce, wares.

bud. club *n* bat, cosh, cudgel, stick, truncheon; association, company, fraternity, set, society.

budhcad. bandit *n* brigand, gangster, highwayman, outlaw, robber.

budhcad. gang *n* band, clique, company, coterie, crew, horde, party, set, troop.

budhcad. robber *n* bandit, brigand, desperado, highwayman, marauder, pirate, thief.

budhcadnimo. robbery *n* embezzlement, larceny, piracy, plagiarism, plundering, theft.

buka. sick *adj* ailing, ill, indisposed, unwell; nauseated, queasy.

bukaan ah. infirm *adj* ailing, feeble, frail, weak, weakened.

bukaan ah. invalid *adj* bedridden, frail, ill, infirm, sick, weak.

bukaan. patient *adj* meek, uncomplaining, long-suffering.

bukaan. invalid *n* convalescent, patient.

bulaacad. drain *n* channel, culvert, ditch, sewer, sluice, trench, watercourse.

bulsho. society *n* culture, community, mankind.

bulsho. community *n* people, public, society.

ku buquid. crowd *vb* compress, cram, jam, pack, press; collect, congregate, flock, herd, huddle, swarm.

burbur. havoc *n* carnage, damage, destruction, devastation, slaughter.

burburid. disintegrate *vb* crumble, decompose, dissolve, pulverize, separate.

burburid. shatter *vb* burst, smash, splinter.

burburin. quell *vb* conquer, crush, overcome, subdue;

burburin. destroy *vb* demolish, overthrow, overturn, subvert, raze, ruin; efface, kill.

burburin. demolish *vb* annihilate, destroy, dismantle, level, pulverize, raze.

burburin. crash *vb* break, shatter, smash, splinter.

burburin. impoverish *vb* pauperize, ruin; deplete, exhaust.

burin. cancel *vb* erase, obliterate; annul, quash, repeal, rescind, revoke.

burin. nullify *vb* abolish, abrogate, annul, cancel, invalidate, negate, quash, repeal, revoke.

butaacid. gush *vb* burst, flood, flow, pour, rush, spout, stream; emotionalize, sentimentalize. * *n* flow, jet, onrush, rush, spurt, surge; effusion, effusiveness, loquacity, loquaciousness, talkativeness.

buufin. spray *n* aerosol, atomizer, shower, sprinkler.

ku buufin. sprinkle *vb* scatter, spray, strew.sprout vb bud, develop, germinate, grow, put forth.

ku buufin. spray *vb* gush, jet, shower, splash, splatter, sprinkle, squirt.

buunbuunin. exaggerate *vb* enlarge, magnify, overstate, romance, stretch.

buuq. noise *n* clamour, clatter, din, fuss, hubbub, hullabaloo, pandemonium, racket, row, sound.

buuq. uproar *n* clamour, commotion, din, hubbub, pandemonium, racket, tumult, turmoil.

buuqaya. noisy *adj* blatant, blustering, boisterous, loud, riotous, tumultuous, vociferous.

buuqsan. uproarious *adj* boisterous, clamorous, loud, noisy, riotous, tumultuous.

buur. mount, mountain *n* alp, hill, mountain, peak; heap, mound, stack.

buuran. fleshy *adj* corpulent, fat, obese, plump, stout.

buuran. fat *adj* corpulent, fleshy, gross, obese, paunchy, portly, plump, pudgy.

buuran. obese *adj* corpulent, fat, gross, plump, portly, stout.

buuxa. plump *adj* chubby, fat, fleshy, full-figured, well-rounded.

buuxa. full *adj* abounding, replete, well-stocked; overflowing, packed, saturated, stuffed, swollen; adequate, complete, entire, mature, perfect; abundant, ample, copious, plenteous, plentiful, sufficient.

buuxa. plentiful *adj* abundant, ample, copious, full, sufficient.

si buuxda. quite *adv* completely, entirely, precisely, totally, wholly.

si buuxda. fully *adv* abundantly, amply, completely, entirely, largely, sufficiently.

mar kal buuxin. replenish *vb* fill, refill, renew, re-supply.

buuxin. fill *vb* occupy, pervade; replenish, stock; cram, pack, satiate, satisfy, stuff; fulfil, hold, occupy, officiate, perform.

C

caaadi ah. homely *adj* domestic, familiar; inelegant, plain, simple, unattractive.

caabsiin. frighten *vb* alarm, intimidate, scare, terrify.

caabudaad. worship *vb* adore, esteem, honour, revere, venerate. jabin. worst *vb* beat, conquer, crush, defeat, foil, overpower, overthrow, quell, subdue, subjugate, vanquish.

caabudid. adore *vb* worship; esteem, honour, idolize, love, revere, venerate.

caadaysi. addict *vb* accustom, apply, dedicate, devote, habituate. *n* devotee, enthusiast, fan; head, junkie, user.

caadi ah. standard *adj* average, customary, ordinary, regular, usual.

caadi ah. medium *adj* average, mean, mediocre, middle.

caadi ah. common *adj* general, everyday, familiar, frequent, usual; inferior, low, ordinary, popular.

caadi ah. mediocre *adj* average, commonplace, medium, middling, ordinary.

aan caadi-ahayn. extraordinary *adj* abnormal, amazing, distinguished, exceptional, marvellous, peculiar, phenomenal, rare, remarkable, special, strange, uncommon, unusual, wonderful.

caadi. ordinary *adj* everyday, normal, regular, common, frequent, habitual, usual; average, commonplace, undistinguished; homely, plain.

caadi. normal *adj* natural, ordinary, regular, usual.

caadi. regular *adj* normal, ordinary, typical; customary, habitual, periodic, usual, recurring, seasonal, stated, usual.

caadi. frequent *adj* common, customary, everyday, familiar, habitual, persistent, usual.

caadi. usual *adj* accustomed, common, customary, everyday, familiar, habitual, normal, ordinary, wonted.

caadi. passable *adj* ordinary, so-so, tolerable.

caadifi ah. sentimental *adj* over-emotional, romantic, tender.

caadifi. lyrical *adj* melodious, musical, poetic.

caadiga ah. conventional *adj* common, customary, everyday, habitual, ordinary, orthodox, regular, standard, traditional, usual.

caadiga ah. norm *n* model, pattern, rule, standard.

aan caadihayn. abnormal *adj* eccentric, exceptional, idiosyncratic, irregular, odd, peculiar, strange, unnatural, unusual, weird.

caadil. equitable *adj* even-handed, impartial, just; adequate, fair, proper, reasonable, right.

caadil. just *adj* equitable, lawful, legitimate, reasonable, right, rightful; good, honest, honourable, straightforward, virtuous.

caado an. traditional *adj* customary, established, historic, old, oral, unwritten.

caado. custom *n* convention, fashion, habit, practice, way.

caado. practice *n* custom, habit; procedure, use; application, drill, exercise, repetition.

caado. practise *vb* apply, do, exercise, follow, perform.

caado. manner *n* custom, habit, practice; degree, extent, measure;

caado. habit *n* addiction, custom, practice, rule, way, wont; apparel, costume, dress, garb.

caadooyin. manners *npl* conduct, habits, morals, behaviour, etiquette.

caafimaad darro. unwholesome *adj* baneful, insalubrious, noisome, unhealthy.

caafimaad qab. wholesome *adj* healthy, healthful, nourishing; fresh, sound, sweet.

caafimaad qaba. sound *adj* entire, intact, unhurt, whole; correct, orthodox, well-founded.

caafimaad qaba. healthy *adj* active, hale, hearty, lusty, sound, vigorous, well.

caafimaad qaba. hale *adj* hardy, healthy, hearty, robust, strong, vigorous, well.

caafimaad-qab. wellbeing *n* comfort, good, happiness, health, prosperity, welfare.

caaganaan. abstinence *n* abstemiousness, avoidance, fast, moderation, restraint, self-denial, sobriety, teetotalism, temperance.

caajib ah. inexplicable *adj* enigmatic, incomprehensible, mysterious, strange, unaccountable.

caajis. indolent *adj* inactive, inert, lazy, listless, lumpish, slothful, sluggish.

caajis. sluggish *adj* drowsy,lazy, listless, slothful, torpid, slow-moving

caajis. lazy *adj* idle, inactive, indolent, inert, slack, slothful, slow, sluggish.

caajis. idle *adj* indolent, inert, lazy, slothful, sluggish.

caalami. international *adj* cosmopolitan, universal.

caan ah. distinguished *adj* celebrated, eminent, famous, illustrious, noted.

caan ah. popular *adj* easy, familiar, admired, approved, favoured, liked.

caan ah. eminent *adj* elevated, high, lofty; celebrated, distinguished, exalted, famous, illustrious, notable, prominent, renowned.

caan ah. renowned *adj* celebrated, distinguished, eminent, famous, honoured, illustrious.

caan ah. celebrated *adj* distinguished, eminent, famed, famous, glorious, illustrious, notable, renowned.

caan ah. noted *adj* celebrated, distinguished, eminent, famous, illustrious, well-known.

ku caan ah. familiar *adj* common, friendly, well-known.

caan ah. famous *adj* celebrated, conspicuous, distinguished, eminent, fabled, illustrious, notable, notorious, remarkable, renowned.

caan ah. illustrious *adj* celebrated, distinguished, eminent, famous.

caan. notable *n* celebrity, dignitary, worthy.

caannimo. publicity *n* limelight, notoriety, spotlight.

caaqil ah. judicious *adj* cautious, considerate, discriminating, prudent, rational, reasonable, sagacious, sensible, sound, wise.

caaqil. chief *n* chieftain, commander; head, leader.

caasi. defiant *adj* recalcitrant, resistant; bold, resistant.

caasiyd. defiance *n* disobedience, disregard, opposition, spite.

caato ah. lank *adj* emaciated, gaunt, lean, scraggy, slender, skinny, slim, thin.

caawimo. help *n* aid, assistance, succour, support; relief, remedy; assistant, helper, servant.

caawin. assist *vb* abet, aid, befriend, further, help, patronize, promote, second, speed, support, sustain; aid, relieve, succour; alternate with, relieve, spell.

caawin. help *vb* relieve, save, succour; abet, aid, assist, back, cooperate, second, serve, support, sustain, wait; alleviate, ameliorate, better, cure, heal, improve, remedy, restore; control, hinder, prevent, repress, resist, withstand; avoid, forbear, control.

caawin. prop *vb* bolster, buttress, support, sustain, uphold.

caawiye. prop *n* brace, support, strut.

caawiye. helper *n* aider, abettor, ally, assistant, auxiliary, colleague, helpmate, partner, supporter.

caay. abuse *n* defamation, insult, rudeness. affront, offence.

caayid. insult *vb* abuse, offend, slander, slight.

caayid. outrage *vb* abuse, insult, maltreat, offend, shock, injure.

cabaadid. howl *vb* bawl, cry, lament, ululate, weep, yell, yowl.

cabasho badan. grumpy *adj* cross, glum, moody, morose, sour, sullen, surly.

cabasho. grievance *n* complaint, injury, wrong.

ka cabasho. grumble *vb* croak, complain, murmur; growl, snarl; roar, rumble.

cabasho. whine *vb* grumble, moan, snivel, wail, whimper.

cabasho. complaint *n* grievance; ailment, disease, disorder, illness, sickness; accusation, charge.

ka cabasho. complain *vb* bemoan, bewail, deplore, grieve, groan, grouch, growl, grumble, lament, moan, murmur, whine.

ka cabasho. sigh *vb* complain, grieve, lament, mourn.

cabbaad. howl *n* cry, yell, ululation.

cabbid. drink *vb* imbibe, sip, swill; swallow, quaff.

cabbitaan. drink *n* beverage, liquid; dram, nip, sip, refreshment.

cabir. gauge *n* indicator, measure, touchstone, yardstick.

cabiraad. utterance *n* articulation, delivery, disclosure, emission, expression, pronouncement, pronunciation, publication, speech.

cabqari. genius *n* flair, gift, talent, turn; brains, ingenuity, intellect; master.

cabsanaaya. fearful *adj* afraid, apprehensive, cowardly, faint-hearted, lily-livered, nervous, timid.

cabsi badan. dreadful *adj* alarming, appalling, awesome, dire, fearful, frightful, horrible, horrid, terrible.

cabsi. fright *n* affright, alarm, consternation, dismay, panic, scare.

ka cabsi. dread *vb* apprehend, fear.

cabsi. fear *n* consternation, dismay, dread, fright, horror, panic, phobia, scare, terror; anxiety, apprehension, concern, misgiving, qualm.

cabudhin. suffocate *vb* asphyxiate, choke, smother, stifle, strangle.

cabudhin. oppressive *adj* close, muggy, stifling, suffocating, sultry.

cabudhin. smother *vb* choke, stifle, suffocate.

cad. pale *adj* ashy, bloodless, pallid, white.

cad. clear *adj* bright, light, limpid, luminous, transparent; free, open, unobstructed; cloudless, fair, undimmed; apparent, evident, indisputable, obvious, undeniable.

cad. obvious *adj* apparent, clear, distinct, evident, visible.

cad. transparent *adj* clear, diaphanous, limpid, lucid; evident, obvious, patent.

cadaadin. persecute *vb* harass, molest, oppress, worry; annoy, beset, importune, pester.

cadaadin. oppress *vb* crush, maltreat, persecute, subdue, suppress, tyrannize, wrong.

cadaadin. overrule *vb* control, govern, supersede, suppress.

cadaadin. suppress *vb* overpower, quash, quell, stifle, subdue.

cadaadin. repress *vb* silence, subdue, suppress, quell; check, curb, restrain.

isku cadaadin. compact *vb* compress, condense, pack, press.

cadaadin. press *vb* compress, crowd, crush, squeeze; flatten, iron, smooth; force, compel, constrain; emphasize, enforce, stress, urge.

cadaadis. oppression *n* abuse, cruelty, injustice, misery, persecution, suffering.

cadaadis. pressure *n* compressing, crushing, squeezing; influence, force; compulsion, exigency, hurry, urgency.

cadaadsan. compact *adj* compressed, condensed, dense, firm, solid; brief, concise, succinct.

cadaawad. antagonism *n* contradiction, discordance, disharmony, dissonant, incompatibility, opposition.

cadaawad. hostile *adj* unfriendly, warlike; adverse, antagonistic, contrary, opposed, opposite.

cadad. issue *n* outcome, result, upshot; outflow, outpouring, stream; copy, edition, number; children, offspring, posterity, progeny .

cadar. perfume *n* aroma, fragrance, incense, scent, smell.

cadar. incense *n* aroma, fragrance, perfume, scent.

cadayn. allege *vb* affirm, assert, declare, maintain, say; adduce, advance, assign, cite, plead, produce, quote.

caddaaan. openly *adv* candidly, frankly, honestly, plainly, publicly.

caddaalad darro. unjust *adj* inequitable, partial, unfair, wrong, wrongful.

caddaalad darro. injustice *n* inequity, unfairness; grievance, iniquity, injury, wrong.

caddaalad. justice *n* fairness, impartiality, right.

caddayn. reveal *vb* disclose, divulge, expose, tell, uncover, unmask, unseal, unveil.

caddayn. testify *vb* affirm, attest, declare, depose, state, swear. *n* certificate, credential, recommendation, voucher.

caddayn. verify *vb* attest, authenticate, confirm, corroborate, prove, substantiate.

aan caddayn. indistinct *adj* ambiguous, doubtful, uncertain; blurred, dim, dull, faint, hazy, misty, shadowy, vague.

caddayn. clarify *vb* cleanse, clear, purify, strain.

caddayn. state *vb* affirm, aver, declare, express, say.

caddayn. prove *vb* ascertain, establish, substantiate, verify.

cadhaysan. angry *adj* chafed, exasperated, furious, galled, incensed, irritated, nettled, piqued, provoked, resentful.

cadhaysan. indignant *adj* angry, incensed, irate, roused, wrathful.

cadhaysan. furious *adj* angry, fierce, frantic, frenzied, fuming, infuriated, mad, raging, violent, wild.

cadhaysan. sullen *adj* glum, morose,sour, sulky.

ka cadhaysiin. incense *vb* anger, enrage, exasperate, inflame, irritate, madden, provoke.

ka cadhaysiin. *n* choler, exasperation, fury, gall, indignation, ire, passion, rage, resentment, spleen, wrath.

ka cadhaysiin. irritate *vb* anger, annoy, enrage, exasperate, incense, nettle, offend, provoke, rasp, rile, ruffle, vex.

ka cadhaysiin. annoy *vb* badger, chafe, disquiet, disturb, fret, hector, irk, irritate, molest, pain, pester, plague, trouble, vex, worry, wound.

ka cadhaysiin. provoke *vb* arouse, excite, incite, inflame, rouse, stimulate; aggravate, anger, annoy, enrage, infuriate, irritate, offend.

cadho dhow. testy *adj* captious, cross, fretful, irascible, irritable, peevish, peppery, petulant.

cadho weji ururin. glower *vb* frown, glare, scowl, stare.

cadho-dhow. touchy *adj* fretful, irascible, irritable, peevish, petulant, quick-tempered.

cadho. irritation *n* anger, exasperation, indignation, ire, provocation, resentment, wrath; (*medical*) inflammation; burn, itch, etc.

cadho. scowl *n* frown, glare, glower.

cadho. fury *n* anger, frenzy, fit, furore, ire, madness, passion, rage; turbulence, vehemence.

cadho. vexation *n* distress, irritation, pique, trouble; affliction, annoyance, curse, nuisance, plague, torment.

cadho. indignation *n* anger, displeasure, exasperation, ire, rage, resentment, wrath.

cadho. exasperation *n* annoyance, irritation, provocation; anger, fury, ire, passion, rage, wrath; aggravation.

cadhodhow. irritable *adj* fiery, hasty, peppery, petulant, snappish, testy, touchy, waspish.

ka cadhysiin. anger *vb* chafe, displease, enrage, gall, infuriate, irritate, madden.

cadow ah. spiteful *adj* ill-natured, malevolent, malicious, rancorous.

cadow ah. malicious *adj* bitter, envious, evil-minded, ill-disposed

cadow. foe *n* adversary, antagonist, enemy, opponent.

cadow. enemy *n* adversary, foe; antagonist, opponent, rival.

cadow. adversary *n* antagonist, enemy, foe, opponent.

cadow. heartless *adj* brutal, cold, cruel, hard, harsh, merciless, pitiless, unfeeling, unsympathetic.

cadownimo. spite *n* grudge, hatred, ill-will, malice, rancour, venom, vindictiveness.

cadownimo. brutal *adj* barbaric, cruel, ferocious, inhuman, ruthless, savage.

cafis. pardon *n* amnesty, excuse, forgiveness.

cagaar. green *n* common, grass plot, lawn, turf, verdure.

cagaaran. green *adj* aquamarine, emerald, olive, verdant; blooming, flourishing, undecayed; fresh, new, recent; immature, unripe; crude, inexperienced, raw, unskilful, young; raw, unseasoned.

cajiib ah. fantastic *adj* imaginary, romantic, unreal; bizarre, odd, strange, wild.

calaamad u ah. symptomatic *adj* characteristic, indicative, symbolic, suggestive.

calaamad. symbol *n* badge, emblem, figure, mark, representation, sign, token.

calaamad. token *n* badge, mark, note, sign, symbol.

calaamad. symptom *n* indication, mark, note, sign, token.

calaamad. mark *n* brand, character, characteristic, impression.

calaamad. badge *n* brand, emblem, mark, sign, symbol.

calaamad. sign *n* indication, mark, proof, signal, symbol.

calaamadsan. marked *adj* conspicuous, distinguished, eminent, notable.

calaamayn. index *vb* alphabetize, catalogue, codify, earmark, file, list, tabulate. *n* catalogue, list, register, tally; contents, table of reference.

calamadin. mark *vb* distinguish, earmark, label, imprint, indicate, print, stamp

calan. banner *n* ensign, flag, standard, streamer.

caleemasaarid. crown *n* coronet, garland, diadem, laurel, wreath; apex, crest, summit, top.

calool u shaqayn. mercenary *adj* hired, paid; avaricious, grasping, mean.

calool u shaqayste. mercenary *n* hireling, soldier.

cambaar ayn. condemn *vb* convict, penalize, sentence; disapprove, blame, censure, upbraid.

cammuud. grit *n* gravel, pebbles, sand; courage, determination, firmness, perseverance, pluck, resolution, spirit.

canaadi. stubborn *adj* headstrong, intractable, obdurate, obstinate, perverse, willful.

canaanasho. scold *vb* berate, chide, reprimand, upbraid.

caniid. wayward *adj* capricious, captious, contrary, headstrong, intractable, unruly, wilful.

caniidi. obstinate *adj* headstrong, inflexible, self-willed, stubborn, unyielding.

canjilid. mock *vb* ape, counterfeit, imitate, mimic, take off; deride, insult, jeer, ridicule. * *n* fake, imitation, phoney, sham.

canjilid. parody *vb* ridicule, imitate, satirize, travesty.

caqiido. dogma *n* belief, creed, doctrine, opinion, precept, principle, tenet.

caqli badan. wise *adj* discerning, intelligent, judicious, philosophical, rational, sensible, sage, sound; informed, learned, scholarly.

caqli badan. discreet *adj* careful, cautious, judicious, prudent, wary, wise.

aan caqli fiicnayn. unwise *adj* foolish, ill-advised, ill-judged, imprudent, indiscreet, injudicious, inexpedient.

caqli gal ah. logical *adj* consistent, rational, reasoned.

caqli gal ah. philosophical *adj* rational, sound, wise, serene, stoical.

caqli gal ah. sensible *adj* intelligent, reasonable, sound, wise.

aan caqli gali karin. illogical *adj* absurd, fallacious, inconsistent, unsound.

caqli xumo. mindless *adj* dull, senseless, stupid, unthinking; careless, forgetful.

caqligal ahayn. irrational *adj* absurd, foolish, preposterous, ridiculous, silly, unwise; unreasonable, unthinking; crazy, demented, idiotic, imbecilic, insane.

caqligal. reasonable *adj* equitable, fair, honest, just, suitable; cheap, inexpensive, low-priced.

caqli gal. rational *adj* equitable, fair, just, proper, reasonable.

caqlileh. knowing *adj* aware, experienced, intelligent, proficient, sensible, thinking, well-informed.

caqlilow. astute *adj* acute, cunning, deep, discerning, ingenious, intelligent, penetrating, perspicacious, quick, sagacious, sharp, shrewd.

ka cararid. flee *vb* abscond, avoid, decamp, depart, escape, fly, leave, run, skedaddle.

carfoon. odorous *adj* aromatic, fragrant, perfumed, scented, sweet-smelling.

carfoon. fragrant *adj* aromatic, odorous, perfumed, redolent, spicy, sweet, sweet-scented, sweet-smelling.

caroqaladayn. handicap *vb* encumber, hamper, hinder, restrict.

caroysiin. plague *n* disease, pestilence.

carqaladayn. hamper *vb* curb, encumber, fetter, hinder, impede, obstruct, prevent, restrain, restrict, shackle.

carruur ah. infantile *adj* babyish, childish, weak; babylike, childlike.

carruurnimo. childish *adj* infantile, juvenile, young; foolish, frivolous, silly.

carruurnimo. infancy *n* babyhood, childhood; beginning, commencement.

carwo. fair *n* bazaar, carnival, exposition, festival, fete, funfair, gala.

cashar. lesson *n* exercise, lecture, task.

cashuur. duty *n* allegiance, obligation, responsibility; custom, excise, tariff, tax, toll.

cashuur. levy *n* duty, tax.

cashuurid. levy *vb* collect, exact, gather, raise, tax.

casri ah. modern *adj* fresh, latest, new, present, recent, up-to-date.

casri ah. contemporary *adj* current, present, simultaneous; modern, progressive, up-to-date.

casuumad weyn. feast *n* banquet, entertainment, repast, treat; celebration, festival, fete, holiday.

casuumid. invite *vb* ask, bid, call, challenge, request, solicit, summon.

cay. insult *n* abuse, affront, cheek, indignity, offence, outrage, sauce, slight.

caydh ah. destitute *adj* distressed, moneyless, needy, penniless, penurious, poor, reduced, wanting.

caydhin. expel *vb* bounce, banish, discharge, exclude, fire, oust, remove.

caymin. insure *vb* assure, guarantee, secure, underwrite.

ceeb. vice *n* depravity, evil, immorality, iniquity, sin, viciousness, vileness, wickedness.

ceebayn. vilify *vb* abuse, backbite, berate, blacken, defame, lampoon, libel, malign, revile, slander, slur, traduce.

ceebayn. libel *vb* defame, lampoon, satirize, slander, vilify.

ceebayn. sully *vb* blemish, contaminate, deface, defame,disgrace, soil, slur, tarnish.

ceeblaawe. spotless *adj* flawless, immaculate, perfect, pure, unblemished.

ceel biyo. fountain *n* fount, reservoir, spring, well; jet.

ceeryaa maysan. cloudy *adj* foggy, hazy, murky, overcast; dark, dim, obscure; dismal, gloomy; blurred, dimmed, muddy.

ceeryaamaysan. nebulous *adj* cloudy, hazy, misty.

ceeryaamaysan. misty *adj* cloudy, clouded, dark, dim, foggy, obscure, overcast.

ceeryaamo leh. foggy *adj* blurred, cloudy, dim, hazy, indistinct, misty, obscure.

ceeryaamo. hazy *adj* foggy, misty; cloudy, dim, obscure; confused, indefinite, indistinct, uncertain, vague.

ceeryaamo. mist *n* cloud, fog, haze; bewilderment, perplexity.

ceeryaan. fog *n* blear, blur, dimness, film, fogginess, haze, haziness, mist, smog, vapour; befuddlement, confusion, fuddle, maze, muddle.

ceeryaansan. fog *vb* blur, cloud, dim, enmist, mist; befuddle, confuse, muddle.

ku celin. repeat *vb* double, duplicate, iterate; echo, renew, reproduce.

dib u celin. replace *vb* refund, repay, restore

ci'. yap *n* bark, cry, yelp.

cidhibtiran. extinction *n* death, extinguishment; annihilation, destruction, extermination.

cidhibtirid. eradicate *vb* uproot; abolish, annihilate, destroy, obliterate.

cidhibtirmay. extinct *adj* dead, ended, lapsed, terminated, vanished.

cifriid. monster *n* brute, demon, fiend, villain, wretch.

cifriid yar. imp *n* demon, devil, elf, flibbertigibbet, hobgoblin, scamp, sprite.

cifriid. demon *n* devil, fiend, kelpie, goblin, troll.

cifriid. ogre *n* demon, devil, goblin, hobgoblin, monster.

ciid. soil *n* earth, ground loam; country, land.

ciidan. army *n* battalions, force, host, legions, troops; host, multitude, throng, vast assemblage.

ciidan. legion *n* army, corps, detachment, detail, division, force, platoon; squad; army, horde, host, multitude, throng.

ciidda masiixiyadda. Xmas *n* Christmas, Christmastide, Noel, Yule, Yuletide.

dinac u ciirid. lean *vb* incline, keel, list, tilt, tip.

cillad. drawback *n* deficiency, disadvantage, fault, flaw, imperfection.

cillad. shortcoming *n* deficiency, drawback, failing, flaw, imperfection.

cillad. defect *n* shortcoming; blemish, flaw, imperfection, mistake.

cilladaysan. defective *adj* deficient, inadequate, incomplete; faulty, imperfect, marred.

cillin ah. stunted *adj* diminutive, dwarfish, little, small, undersized.

cilmi baaris. research *vb* analyse, examine, explore, investigate, probe, study.

cimilo qabo. bleak *adj* bare, exposed, unprotected, unsheltered, windswept; biting, chill, cold, piercing, raw; cheerless, comfortless, dreary.

cimri dheeraan. survive *vb* endure, last, outlast, outlive.

cinwaan. title *n* caption, head, heading, name.

ciqaab. torture *n* agony, anguish, distress, pain, pang, rack, torment.

ciqaabid. chastise *vb* correct, discipline, punish.

ciqaabid. punish *vb* beat, chastise, correct, discipline, flog, lash, scourge, torture, whip.

ciqaabid. torture *vb* distress, pain, rack, torment.

ciriiri. narrow *adj* confined, contracted, cramped, limited, pinched, scanty.

ciriirin. narrow *vb* confine, limit, restrict, straiten.

aad u cirweyn. insatiable *adj* greedy, rapacious, voracious.

cisayn. revere *vb* adore, esteem, venerate, worship.

ciyaalla-suuqnimo. vulgar *adj* common, lowly, plebeian; coarse, flashy, garish, gaudy, ill-bred, loud, showy, tawdry, uncultivated, unrefined.

ciyaar badan. playful *adj* frisky, merry, mirthful, mischievous, roguish.

ciyaar. game *n* amusement, contest, diversion, pastime, sport; prey, quarry, victim.

ciyaarid. play *vb* frisk, frolic, gambol, romp, skip.

ku ciyaarid. scoff *vb* deride, jeer, mock, ridicule, gibe, sneer.

ku ciyaarid. fool *vb* jest, play, toy, trifle; cheat, deceive, delude, dupe, hoodwink, trick.

ku ciyaarid. tamper *vb* alter, damage, interfere, meddle.

ciyar-badan. frisky *adj* frolicsome, lively, playful, sportive.

ciyid. yap *vb* bark, cry, yelp.

cod dhuuban oo dheer. shrill *adj* high-pitched, piercing, sharp.

codbixin. vote *vb* ballot, elect, opt, return.

codcelin. echo *vb* reply, resound, reverberate, ring, repeat.

codsasho. implore *vb* ask, beg, beseech, entreat, petition, supplicate.

codsasho. craving *n* longing, yearning.

codsasho. request *vb* ask, beg, beseech,

codsasho. petition *vb* ask, solicit.

codsi. request *n* invitation, petition, supplication.

colaad. enmity *n* animosity, aversion, bitterness, hatred, hostility, ill-will, malevolence, rancour.

collaad. hatred *n* animosity, enmity, hate, hostility, ill-will, malevolence, malice; abhorrence, antipathy, aversion, detestation, disgust, loathing, repugnance, revulsion.

contrary *adj* adverse, counter, opposite; antagonistic, conflicting, contradictory, repugnant.

crumple *vb* rumple, wrinkle.

cudur daar. justification *n* defence, exoneration, reason, vindication, warrant.

cudur. ailment *n* disease, illness, sickness.

cudur. disease *n* affliction, ailment, complaint, disorder, illness, indisposition, infirmity, malady, sickness.

cudur. infection *n* contagion, contamination, corruption, defilement, pollution, virus.

cudur. plague *vb* annoy, pester, irritate, torment.

cudurdaar. excuse *n* apology, defence, justification, plea.

cufan. dense *adj* close, compact, compressed, condensed, thick; dull, slow, stupid.

culays. load *n* burden, pack, weight; cargo, freight.

culays. weight *n* burden, load, pressure; emphasis, importance, influence, power, significance, value.

culeys. gravity *n* heaviness, weight; importance, moment, momentousness, seriousness, weightiness.

culus. clumsy *adj* heavy, ill-shaped, lumbering; awkward, blundering, bungling, inapt.

culus. cumbersome *adj* burdensome, clumsy, heavy, inconvenient, unmanageable, unwieldy.

culus. onerous *adj* burdensome, difficult, responsible, weighty.

culus. weighty *adj* heavy, massive, onerous, ponderous; forcible, grave, important, influential, serious, significant.

culus. heavy *adj* grave, hard, onerous, ponderous, weighty; burdensome, crushing, cumbersome, oppressive, serious; lifeless, sleepy, slow, sluggish, stupid, torpid; downhearted, gloomy, low-melancholy, sad, sorrowful; cloudy, dark, gloomy, overcast.

culus. encumbrance *n* burden, deadweight, drag, hindrance, impediment, load.

culus. grave *adj* heavy, important, serious, weighty; dignified, serious, solemn, staid, thoughtful.

cunid. eat *vb* chew, consume, devour, ingest, ravage, swallow, dine, feed, lunch, sup.

cunto. feed *n* fodder, food, foodstuff, forage.

cunto. food *n* aliment, bread, diet, fare, meat, nourishment, nutriment, nutrition, provisions, rations, sustenance.

cunug. baby *n* babe, child, infant.

cunug. baby *adj* doll-like, miniature, pocket-sized, small-scale.

cuqdad. prejudice *n* bias, intolerance, partiality, prejudgement, unfairness; harm, hurt, impairment.

cuqdad. prejudice *n* fixation, obsession, preoccupation.

curis. essay *n* composition, dissertation, thesis.

cusboonaysiin. innovation *n* change, introduction; departure, novelty.

cuslayn. burden *vb* encumber, load, oppress, overload, saddle.

cusub. new *adj* fresh, latest, modern, recent, unused.

cusub. fashionable *adj* modish, stylish; current, modern, prevailing, up-to-date; customary, usual.

cusub. recent *adj* fresh, new, modern, young.

cyrin. compose *vb* build, form, make; create, invent, write.

D

da'. age *n* aeon, date, epoch, period, time; decline, old age, senility; antiquity, oldness.

da'id. rain *vb* drizzle, drop, pour, shower, sprinkle.

da'yar. young *adj* green, inexperienced, juvenile, new, recent, youthful.

daa'im ah. eternal *adj* abiding, ceaseless, endless, everlasting, incessant, interminable, never-ending, perpetual; immortal, imperishable, indestructible, undying.

daacad ah. loyal *adj* constant, devoted, faithful, patriotic, true.

daacad ah. faithful *adj* constant, devoted, loyal, staunch, steadfast, true, reliable, trusty.

daacad ah. dutiful *adj* obedient, respectful, reverential.

daacad ah. sincere *adj* genuine, honest, true, unaffected, unfeigned, open, plain.

aan daacad ahayn. dishonest *adj* crafty, crooked, deceitful, false, fraudulent, knavish, slippery, treacherous, unscrupulous.

aan daacad ahayn. disloyal *adj* faithless, false, traitorous, treacherous, unfaithful, unpatriotic, untrue.

aan daacad ahayn. slippery *adj* glib, dishonest, elusive, shifty, treacherous.

aan daacad ahayn. unfaithful *adj* disloyal, false, faithless, perfidious, treacherous.

aan daacad hayn. insincere *adj* deceitful, dishonest, false, hypocritical, two-faced.

daacad la'aan. treacherous *adj* disloyal, false, false-hearted, perfidious, treasonable, unfaithful.

daacad u ah. devoted *adj* affectionate, attached, earnest, loving.

daacad. piety *n* devoutness, holiness, godliness.

daacad. honesty *n* equity, fairness, honour, integrity, justice, probity, trustiness, trustworthiness, uprightness; truth, truthfulness, veracity.

daacadnimo. honest *adj* reliable, sound, square, true, trustworthy, truthful, uncorrupted, upright, virtuous.

daacadnimo. sincerity *n* honesty, truth, unaffectedness, veracity.

daacadnimo. loyalty *n* allegiance, constancy, devotion, faithfulness, fidelity, patriotism.

ka daadanaaya. overflow *vb* brim over, pour out, spill.

daadin. splash *vb* spatter, spray, sprinkle, squirt.

daaficid. defend *vb* fortify, guard, protect, safeguard, shield.

daaficid. vindicate *vb* defend, justify, uphold.

daah. blind *n* curtain, screen, shade, shutter.

daah. curtain *n* blind, partition; protection, shield.

daahid. late *adj* behindhand, delayed, overdue, slow, tardy; deceased, former.

is daahin. loiter *vb* dally, dawdle, delay, dilly-dally, idle, lag, linger, saunter, stroll, tarry.

daahin. dawdle *vb* dally, delay, fiddle, idle, lag, loiter, potter.

daahir ah. chaste *adj* innocent, modest, pure, virtuous, uncorrupt.

daal. weary *adj* drowsy, exhausted, jaded, spent, tired, worn.

daal. fatigue *n* exhaustion, tiredness, weariness.

daal. exhaustion *n* fatigue, weariness.

lagu daalaayo. wearisome *adj* boring, dull, fatiguing, tedious, tiresome, uninteresting, vexatious.

daalid. tire *vb* exhaust, fag, fatigue, harass, jade, weary.

daalid. weary *vb* exhaust, fatigue, harass, jade, tire.

daalid. exhaust *vb* debilitate, deplete, disable, enfeeble, enervate, overtire, weaken.

wax daalinaaya. tedious *adj* dull, irksome, monotonous, uninteresting, wearisome.

daallan. jaded *adj* dull, exhausted, fatigued, satiated, tired, weary.

daaqsiin. graze *vb* brush, glance, scrape, scratch, shave, skim; browse, crop, feed, pasture.

daarad. yard *n* close, compound, court, courtyard, enclosure, garden.

daarid. kindle *vb* ignite, inflame, light; awaken, bestir, excite, provoke, rouse, stimulate, stir.

daash. courtyard *n* courtyard, enclosure, grounds, precinct, yard.

daawade. spectator *n* bystander, looker-on, observer, onlooker, watcher, witness.

daaweyn. treatment *n* care, doctoring, therapy.

daawo siin. drug *vb* dose, medicate.

daawo. drug *n* medicine, remedy; poison.

daayac. neglect *n* carelessness, default, failure, inattention, omission, disregard, indifference, negligence.

daayac. negligent *adj* careless, heedless, inattentive, indifferent, neglectful, regardless, thoughtless.

dab. fire *n* blaze, ardour, fervour, fever, force, heat; passion, spirit, vigour.

daba soocod. trail *vb* follow, hunt, trace, track; drag, draw, haul, pull.

dabaalnimo. daft *adj* absurd, foolish, idiotic, silly, stupid.

dabagal. track *vb* follow, pursue, trail.

dabaq. floor *n* deck, layer, stage, storey, tier.

dabaqad. class *n* grade, rank, status; group, kind, sort; category, division.

dabar. chain *n* fetter, manacle, shackle.

dabasocdo. follow *vb* chase, dog, ensue, hound, pursue, run after, trail; conform, heed, obey, observe; copy, imitate.

dabasocod. tail *vb* dog, follow, shadow, stalk, track.

dabayl leh. gusty *adj* blustering, blustery, puffy, squally, stormy, tempestuous, unsteady, windy.

dabayl leh. windy *adj* breezy, blowy, blustering, boisterous, draughty, gusty, squally, stormy, tempestuous.

dabayl xooga. storm *n* blizzard, gale, hurricane, squall, tempest, tornado, typhoon, whirlwind.

dabayl. blast *n* blow, gust, squall; burst, discharge, explosion.

dabayl. wind *n* breeze, draught, gust, whiff, zephyr; breath, breathing, respiration.

dabbaal degid. celebrate *vb* applaud, praise; commemorate, honour, observe.

dabbaal. brainless *adj* childish, foolish, inept, stupid, unwise.

is dabcin. relax *vb* loosen, slacken.

dabeecad xun. coarse *adj* crude, rough, indelicate, ribald, vulgar; boorish, brutish, gruff, impolite, loutish, rude.

dabeecad. disposition *n* character, nature, temper, temperament, tendency, turn; inclination, willingness.

dabeecad. behaviour *n* conduct, demeanour, manner, manners.

dabid. ensnare *vb* catch, entrap; allure, inveigle, seduce.

dabid. trap *vb* catch, ensnare; ambush, deceive, dupe, trick.

dabid. snag *vb* catch, entangle, hook, snare, tangle.

dabiic ah. natural *adj* indigenous, native, original; normal, regular; simple, spontaneous, unaffected.

aan dabiici ahayn. artificial *adj* counterfeit, sham, spurious; assumed, affected, constrained, fictitious, forced, laboured, strained.

dabin. loosen *vb* liberate, relax, release, separate, slacken, unbind, unloose, untie.

dable. private *n* GI, soldier, tommy.

dabool ka qaadid. unveil *vb* disclose, expose, reveal, show, uncover, unmask.

dabool. veil *n* blind, cloak, disguise, mask, screen.

daboolid. mask *vb* cloak, conceal, cover, disguise, hide, screen, shroud, veil.

daboolid. cover *vb* cloak, conceal, curtain, disguise, hide, mask, screen, shroud, veil; shield; clothe, envelop, sheathe.

daboolid. muffle *vb* cover, wrap; conceal, disguise; deaden, stifle, suppress.

daboolid. screen *vb* cloak, cover, hide, shelter.

daboolid. coat *vb* cover, spread.

dabrid. shackle *vb* chain, fetter, manacle; impede, restrict, trammel.

dacal. border *n* boundary, brink, edge, limit, margin; edge, eve, point, verge.

daciif (tamar daro). feeble *adj* anaemic, debilitated, declining, drooping, exhausted, frail, infirm, sickly.

daciif. weak *adj* debilitated, faint, feeble, frail, infirm, invalid, wasted; defenceless, unprotected, vulnerable; irresolute, pliant, vacillating, wavering, yielding.

daciifin. weaken *vb* debilitate, enfeeble, sap, undermine, unman, unnerve.

daciifnimo. failing *n* defect, deficiency, fault, shortcoming, weakness.

daciifnimo. weakness *n* debility, feebleness, fragility, frailty, infirmity; defect, failing, fault, flaw.

dacwo. indictment *n* (*law*) accusation, arraignment, charge, impeachment.

dad. people *n* folk, humankind, persons, population, public.

dadaal badan. studious *adj* contemplative, meditative, scholarly, reflective, thoughtful, zealous.

dadaal badan. diligent *adj* active, attentive, busy, careful, earnest, hard-working, indefatigable, industriousness, painstaking, persevering, persistent, tireless.

dadaal. pains *npl* care, effort.

dadaal. toil *n* drudgery, effort, exertion, labour, pains, travail, work.

dadajin. speed *vb* hasten, hurry, rush, scurry.

dadjin. precipitate *vb* accelerate, expedite, hasten, hurry, plunge, speed.

aan dadnimo ahayn. inhuman *adj* barbarous, brutal, cruel, fell, ferocious, merciless, pitiless, remorseless, ruthless, savage, unfeeling.

dadweynaha. public *n* citizens, community, everyone, masses, nation, people, population.

dafaac. defence *n* bulwark, fortification, guard, protection, rampart, shield.

dafid. swoop *vb* descend, dive, pounce, rush, sweep.

dagaal. battle *n* action, conflict, contest, engagement, fight, afray.

dagaal. warfare *n* battle, conflict, contest, discord, hostilities, strife, struggle, war.

dagaal. combat *n* battle, contest, encounter, fight, skirmish, war.

dagaal. fight *n* affray, action, battle, brush, combat, conflict, contest, duel, encounter, engagement, melée, quarrel, struggle, war; brawl, broil, riot, row, skirmish.

dagaalan. fight *vb* battle, combat, war; contest, dispute, oppose, struggle, wrestle; engage.

dagaalid. battle *vb* fight, strive, struggle.

dagaalyahan. combative *adj* belligerent, militant, pugnacious, quarrelsome.

daganaansho. equanimity *n* calmness, composure, coolness, peace, regularity, self-possession, serenity, steadiness.

dagen. moderate *adj* temperate; limited, mediocre; mild, reasonable, steady.

dagenaan. moderation *n* abstemiousness, restraint, sobriety; calmness, coolness, equanimity.

daggaandag. incline *n* hill, slope.

daggan. calm *adj* demure, quiet, sedate, serious, unemotional.

daggan. peaceful *adj* quiet, undisturbed, amicable, gentle, mild, calm, composed, placid.

soo daggid dhul. land *vb* disembark.

dahaadh. film *n* coating, membrane, nebula, skin, veil.

dahsoon. incognito, incognita *adj* camouflaged, concealment, disguised, unknown.

dahsoon. unknown *adj* undiscovered, unexplored; anonymous, nameless, obscure, unsung.

dahsoon. mystery *n* enigma, puzzle, riddle, secret.

dajin. soothe *vb* appease, calm, lull, mollify, pacify, quieten.

dajin. mollify *vb* appease, pacify, quiet, soothe, tranquillize.

dajin. tranquillize *vb* allay, calm, lull, pacify, quiet, silence, soothe.

dajin. pacify *vb* appease, conciliate, calm, hush, lull, mollify, quell, quiet, soothe.

dajin. moderate *vb* quell, quiet, soften, still, subdue; control, govern, regulate.

dajin. calm *vb* lull, smooth, tranquillize; appease, mollify, pacify.

wax dajinaysa. sedative *adj* calming, soothing, tranquillizing.

dakhar. bump *n* blow, jolt, knock, shock, thump; lump, protuberance, swelling.

dal. country *n* land, region; countryside; fatherland, home, kingdom, state, territory.

dalaal. attempt *n* effort, endeavour, enterprise, experiment, undertaking.

dalag. crops *n* harvest, produce, yield.

dalcad. uphill *adj* ascending, upward; arduous, difficult, hard, laborious, strenuous, toilsome, wearisome.

dallacaad. promotion *n* advancement, furtherance; elevation, preferment.

dallacsiin. promote *vb* advance, aid, assist, cultivate, encourage, further, help.

dalool. crack *n* chink, hole, fissure, leak.

dalool. opening *n* gap, hole, perforation; chance, opportunity, vacancy.

dalool. vent *n* hole, mouth, opening, orifice; emission, escape, outlet.

daloolin. pierce *vb* gore, prick, stab, transfix, puncture.

daloolin. puncture *vb* bore, penetrate, perforate, pierce, prick.

daloolin. drill *vb* bore, perforate, pierce; discipline, exercise, instruct, teach, train.

daloolin. prick *vb* perforate, pierce, puncture; cut, hurt, pain, sting, wound.

daloolin. bore *vb* drill, perforate, pierce, sink, tunnel.

ugu dambayn. final *adj* eventual, extreme, last. latest, terminal, ultimate; conclusive, decisive, definitive, irrevocable.

xagga dambe. back *adj* hindmost.

dambe. rear *adj* aft, back, following, hind, last.

ka dambe. latter *adj* last, latest, modern, recent.

ka dambeeya. behind *prep* after, following.

ugu dambeeya. last *adj* latest; final, terminal, ultimate; latest, newest; concluding, parting, valedictory.

ka dambeyn. lag *vb* dawdle, delay, idle, linger, loiter, saunter, tarry.

damin. extinguish *vb* choke, douse, put out, quell, smother, stifle, suffocate, suppress; destroy, nullify, subdue.

damin. quench *vb* extinguish, put out, suppress; cool, dampen, extinguish.

dammaanad qaad. guarantee *vb* assure, insure, pledge, secure, warrant.

dammaanad. guarantee *n* assurance, pledge, security, surety, warrant, warranty.

dan ka leh. interested *adj* concerned, involved; biassed, patial, prejudiced; selfish, self-seeking.

danayn. mind *vb* heed, mark, watch; obey, observe; beware, look out, watch out.

danka lahayn. regardless *adj* heedless, indifferent, mindless, neglectful, unconcerned.

danlaawe. slack *adj* careless, lax, negligent; loose, relaxed.

daqiijin. pound *vb* beat, strike, thump; crush, pulverize.

daqiijin. mill *vb* crush, grate, grind, pulverize.

daqiijin. crumble *vb* decay, disintegrate, perish, pulverize.

daqiiqad. second *n* instant, jiffy, minute, moment.

daqiiqad. minute *n* entry, memorandum, note, record; instant, moment, second.

darajo. rank *n* class, division, group, order.

darajo. stage *n* degree, rank.

daray ah. fresh *adj* new, blooming, flourishing, green; sweet; active, energetic, lively, unexhausted, unfatigued, unwearied, vigorous; uncured, undried, unsalted, unsmoked; bracing, invigorating, refreshing; inexperienced, raw, unskilled, untrained.

darbad. knock *n* blow, slap, smack, thump; blame, criticism, rejection, setback.

dareemid. feel *vb* handle, probe, touch; experience, suffer; believe, infer, opine, suppose, think.

dareemis. sense *vb* discern, notice, perceive, suspect.

dareen abuur leh. impressive *adj* moving, powerful, stirring, striking, touching.

dareen kicin. thrill *vb* electrify, inspire, move, rouse, stir, touch. *n* excitement, sensation, shock, tingling, tremor.

dareen leh. sensational *adj* exciting, melodramatic, startling, thrilling.

dareen. instinct *n* natural impulse.

dareen. feeling *n* emotion, impression, notion, notion, opinion, passion, perception, sensation, sense.

dareen. sensation *n* feeling, sense, perception; excitement, impression, thrill.

dareensiin. stimulate *vb* animate, arouse, excite, fire, foment, inflame, provoke, rouse, stir up, urge, whet, work up.

dareere. liquid *adj* fluid, flowing, mellifluous, soft.

ku-darid. include *vb* contain, embrace, incorporate, involve, take in.

ku darid. supplement *vb* add, augment.

isku darid. shuffle *vb* intermix, jumble, mix; dodge, evade, prevaricate.

dariiq. method *n* manner, means, mode, plan, procedure, process, scheme, system.

dariiqo. means *npl* method, mode, way; income, resources, wealth, wherewithal.

dariiqo. way *n* behaviour, habit, manner, means, method, mode, practice, system.

darsid. meditate *vb* contemplate, ruminate, study; cogitate, muse, ponder, think.

darsid. study *vb* analyze, examine, investigate, ponder, reflect, scrutinize, think, weigh. * *n* den, library, office, studio.

daruur. cloud *n* cirrus, cumulus, fog, haze, mist, stratus, vapour.

daryeel. welfare *n* advantage, benefit, happiness, profit, prosperity, success, wellbeing.

daweyn. cure *vb* heal, mend, remedy, restore; pickle, preserve.

dawlad. government *n* administration, cabinet, commonwealth, sovereignty, state.

dawo. remedy *n* cure, medicine, panacea, restorative; aid, assistance, relief.

daxalaysi. blemish *n* blot, spot, stain.

daxallaysi. corrode *vb* erode, consume, rust.

dayaan. echo *n* answer, repetition, reverberation; imitation.

dayac badan. wasteful *adj* extravagant, improvident, lavish, prodigal, profuse, thriftless.

dayac tirid. overhaul *vb* examine, inspect, repair.

dayacid. waste *vb* expend, lavish, lose, misspend, misuse, scatter, spend, squander.

dayactir. repair *vb* mend, patch, refit; correct, restore.

dayactirid. service *vb* check, maintain, overhaul, repair.

ku dayasho. reflect *vb* copy, imitate, mirror, reproduce; consider, contemplate, deliberate, meditate, muse, ponder, ruminate, study, think.

ku dayasho. imitate *vb* ape, copy, counterfeit, duplicate, echo, emulate, forge, impersonate, mimic, mirror, mock, parody, reproduce, simulate.

dayicid. neglect *vb* despise, disregard, forget, ignore, omit, overlook.

isku dayid. tackle *vb* attempt, try, undertake.

isku dayid. endeavour *vb* aim, attempt, strive, struggle, try.

isku dayid. tempt *vb* allure, entice, induce, seduce.

isku dayid. attempt *vb* assail, assault, attack; aim, endeavour, seek, strive, try.

aad isugu dayis. effort *n* exertion, industry, labour, toil, work; childbirth, delivery.

daymaysan. indebted *adj* beholden, obliged, owing.

sii dayn. dismiss *vb* banish, discard, discharge, disperse, reject, remove.

dayow. dizzy *adj* giddy, careless, heedless, thoughtless.

dayr. fence *n* barrier, hedge, hedgerow, limit.

dayr. fence *n* barrier, hedge, stockade, wall; defence, protection, guard, security, shield.

dayrid. hedge *vb* enclose, fence, fortify, guard, protect.

debacsan. lax *adj* loose, relaxed, slow; negligent, remiss.

deddeg ah. premature *adj* hasty, precipitate, unprepared, untimely.

dedejin. hasten *vb* hurry; accelerate, expedite, quicken, urge.

deeq. contribution *n* donation, gift, offering, subscription.

deeq. gift *n* alms, allowance, benefaction, bequest, bonus, boon, bounty, contribution, donation, dowry, endowment, favour, grant, gratuity, honorarium, largesse, legacy, offering, premium, present, prize, subscription, subsidy, tip; faculty, talent.

deeq. donation *n* alms, gift, grant, gratuity, largesse, offering, present, subscription.

deeq. grant *n* allowance, concession, donation, endowment, gift, present.

ku deeqid. grant *vb* bestow, confer, invest.

ku deeqid. volunteer *vb* offer, present, proffer, propose, tender.

ku deeqid. contribute *vb* donate, give, grant, subscribe, supply.

ku deeqid. offer *vb* present, proffer, tender; volunteer;

deeqsi ah. generous *adj* charitable, liberal, openhanded; abundant, ample, plentiful.

deeqsi. unselfish *adj* generous, lavish, liberal, profuse; altruistic, disinterested, generous, high-minded, selfless, self-sacrificing, unsparing.

deeqsinimo. magnanimity *n* chivalry, disinterestedness, high-mindedness, generosity,

deformity *n* abnormality, defect, disfigurement, distortion, irregularity, misshapenness.

deg deg ah. express *adj* fast, nonstop, quick, rapid, speedy, swift.

deg deg ah. urgency *n* drive, exigency, haste, pressure, stress.

deg deg. urgent *adj* critical, crucial, immediate, imperative, important, insistent, instant, pressing, serious.

degan. calm *adj* peaceful, placid, quiet, serene, still, tranquil, unruffled; composed, controlled, untroubled.

degan. cool *adj* calm, collected, composed, dispassionate, placid, sedate, self-possessed, quiet, staid, unexcited, unruffled; cold-blooded, indifferent, unconcerned; apathetic, frigid.

deganaansho. dwell *vb* abide, inhabit, live, lodge, reside, stay, stop.

aan deganayn. restless *adj* disturbed, sleepless, unsettled; agitated, fidgety, fretful, turbulent.

degdeg. rash *adj* careless, foolhardy, hasty, impetuous, impulsive, reckless.

xalad degdega. emergency *n* crisis, difficulty, dilemma, exigency, necessity, strait, urgency.

degdega. fast *adj* intensive, rushed, speed-up.

degdegid. hurry *vb* hasten, quicken, speed, scurry.

degdegid. bustle *vb* fuss, hurry, scurry.

degdegsan. hurried *adj* cursory, hasty, slight, superficial.

degdegsan. impetuous *adj* hasty, impulsive, overzealous.

degene. inhabitant *n* citizen, denizen, dweller, inhabiter, resident.

deggan. domicile *vb* dwell, inhabit, live, lodge, remain, reside, stay.

deggan. serene *adj* peaceful, tranquil, undisturbed, unclouded.

deggan. tranquil *adj* calm, peaceful, quiet, serene, undisturbed, untroubled.

deggan. untroubled *adj* calm, composed, peaceful, serene, smooth, tranquil, undisturbed.

degganaan. composure *n* calmness, coolness, equanimity, self-possession, serenity, tranquillity.

deggen. peace *n* calm, quiet, silence, stillness, tranquillity.

deggen. placid *adj* calm, equable, gentle, serene, tranquil.

ka soo degid. descend *vb* drop, fall, plunge, sink.

degmo. district *n* circuit, department, neighbourhood, province, quarter, region, section, territory, ward.

degmo. precinct *n* boundary, confine, limit, neighbourhood, area, district.

dekad. harbour *n* asylum, refuge, resting place, retreat, sanctuary, shelter; anchorage, destination, haven, port.

dekad. port *n* anchorage, harbour, haven, shelter.

deldelid. hang *vb* execute, truss; dangle, swing, suspend.

dembi ah. sinful *adj* bad, immoral, unholy, wicked, wrong.

dembi ah. criminal *adj* illegal, immoral, unlawful, wicked, wrong.

dembi dhaaf doonid. penitent *adj* conscious-stricken, contrite, remorseful, repentant.

dembi falid. sin *vb* do wrong, err, transgress.

dembi ku waaysis. clear *vb* absolve, acquit, discharge, exonerate, vindicate; rid; clean up, scour, sweep.

dembi la'aan. innocent *adj* blameless, clean, clear, faultless, guiltless, immaculate, pure, spotless, upright; harmless, innocuous, inoffensive.

dembi lahayn. irreproachable *adj* blameless, faultless, innocent.

dembi. offence *n* crime, fault, misdeed, misdemeanour, sin.

dembi. sin *n* misdeed, offence, transgression, wickedness, wrong.

dembi. guilt *n* blame, culpability.

dembi. crime *n* felony, misdeed, misdemeanour, offence, violation, sin, transgression, wickedness, wrong.

dembiile. criminal *n* convict, culprit, delinquent, felon, offender, sinner, transgressor.

dembiile. delinquent *n* criminal, defaulter, malefactor, offender, transgressor, wrong-doer.

dembiile. culprit *n* delinquent, criminal, felon, offender.

demdiile. offender *n* convict, criminal, culprit, delinquent, felon.

deris ku nool. sponger *n* scrounger, hanger-on, parasite.

deris ku-nool. parasite *n* bloodsucker, hanger-on, leech.

derisnimo. neighbourhood *n* district, locality, vicinage, vicinity.

deyn. debt *n* arrears, debit, liability, obligation.

sii deyn. release *vb* free, liberate, relinquish. * *n* discharge, freedom, liberation.

la soo dhaafay. back *adv* ago, gone, since; behind, astern, backwards.

dhaafid. abstain *vb* avoid, cease, deny oneself, desist, forbear, refrain, refuse, stop, withhold.

iska dhaafid. drop *vb* shed; leave, omit, relinquish, quit; cease, discontinue.

dhaar. oath *n* curse, expletive; affirmation, pledge, promise, vow.

dhaarasho. swear *vb* affirm, attest, declare, depose, state, testify, vow; blaspheme, curse.

dhaawac. damage *n* injury, loss, mischief.

dhaawac. hurt *n* damage, injury, ache, bruise, pain, suffering, wound.

dhaawac. wound *n* hurt, injury.

dhaawac. injury *n* damage, harm, hurt, impairment, loss.

dhaawicid. injure *vb* damage, disfigure, harm, hurt, impair, mar, spoil, sully, wound; abuse, aggrieve, wrong; affront, dishonour, insult.

dhaawicid. wound *vb* damage, harm, hurt, injure; cut, lacerate, prick, stab; annoy, mortify, offend.

dhaawicid. hurt *vb* damage, disable, harm, impair, injure, mar, pain, wound.

dhab ah. orthodox *adj* conventional, correct, sound, true.

dhab ah. positive *adj* definite, direct, explicit, precise, unequivocal, unmistakable; assured, confident, convinced, sure.

dhabcaal. stingy *adj* grudging, mean, miserly, niggardly.

dhabcaal. miser *n* money-grabber, niggard, skinflint.

dhabcaalnimo. miserly *adj* grasping, mean, stingy, tight-fisted.

dhac. plunder *n* loot, robbery, sack; booty, spoils.

dhac. loot *n* booty, plunder, spoil.

isku dhac. collision *n* clash, crash, encounter, impact, shock.

dhacdo. occurrence *n* event, happening, incident, proceeding, transaction.

dhacdo. event *n* circumstance, episode, fact, happening, incident, occurrence.

dhacdo. incident *n* circumstance, episode, event, fact, happening, occurrence.

dhacid. plunder *vb* loot, maraud, pillage, ransack, ravage, rob.

dhadhamin. taste *vb* relish, savour, sip.

dhadhan. taste *n* flavour, relish, savour; morsel, mouthful, sample.

dhadhan. flavour *n* seasoning, taste; aroma, essence, soul, spirit.

dhadhan. tang *n* aftertaste, flavour, relish, savour, smack, taste.

dhadhaqaaqayn. stable *adj* abiding, established, fixed, lasting, permanent, firm, durable.

wax ku dhagaaya. sticky *adj* adhesive, clinging, gluey, glutinous, gummy, tenacious, viscose.

dhagax ah. stony *adj* gritty, rocky; hard, inflexible, obdurate; cruel, hard-hearted, unfeeling.

dhagax. rock *n* boulder, cliff, crag, reef, stone; granite, marble, slate, etc.

dhagax. stone *n* boulder, pebble, rock; gem, jewel, precious stone; nut, pit; agate, flint, granite, marble, slate, etc.

dhagaystayaal. audience *n* assemblage, congregation; hearing, interview, reception.

ku dhagid. cling *vb* adhere, stick; embrace, entwine.

dhago fudeyo. obedience *n* agreement, compliance, duty, respect, submission.

dhahabi. golden *adj* brilliant, bright, gilded, resplendent, shining, splendid.

ku dhajin. stick *vb* adhere, affix, attach, cement, glue, paste; (*with* by) adhere to, be faithful, support.

isku dhajin. cement *vb* attach, bind, join, combine, connect, stick, unite, weldk. * *n* glue, paste, mortar.

dhaka-faarid. bewilder *vb* confound, confuse, daze, distract, embarrass, muddle, mystify, perplex, puzzle.

dhakali. proceeds *npl* earnings, effects, income, profits, receipts, returns, yield.

dhakhali. revenue *n* income, proceeds, receipts, wealth.

dhakhli. rent *n* income, rental, revenue.

dhakhsi ah. hasty *adj* brisk, fast, quick, rapid, speedy, swift; ill-advised, precipitous, rash, reckless; headlong, helter-skelter, pell-mell, precipitate; excitable, hot-headed.

dhakhsi. swift *adj* expeditious, fast, quick, prompt, rapid, speedy.

dhakhsi. rapid *adj* fast, fleet, quick, swift.

dhakhsi. instant *adj* immediate, prompt, quick, urgent; fast, ready cooked.

dhakhsi. soon *adv* before long, by and by, in a short time, presently, shortly.

dhakhsi. haste *n* rapidity, speed, *with* despatch.

dhakhsi. quick *adj* agile, alert, brisk, fast, hasty, lively, nimble, prompt, ready; clever, skilful.

dhakhso. immediate *adj* direct, instant, instantaneous, present, pressing, prompt.

dhakli. income *n* earnings, pay, perquisite, proceeds, profits, receipts, revenue, salary, wages.

dhakli. earnings *npl* allowance, emoluments, income, pay, proceeds, profits, remuneration, reward, salary, stipend.

dhalaal. sheen *n* gloss, glossiness, shine, spendour.

dhalaal. lustre *n* brightness, brilliance, splendour.

dhalaalaaya. starry *adj* bright, brilliant, lustrous, shining, sparkling, twinkling.

dhalaalaya. bright *adj* blazing, brilliant, dazzling, gleaming, glowing, light, luminous, radiant, shining, sparkling, sunny; clear, cloudless; intelligent, keen; cheerful, genial, happy, lively, merry, pleasant, smiling, vivacious.

dhalaalid. shimmer *vb* glimmer, glisten, shine.

dhalanteel. unreal *adj* dreamlike, fanciful, ghostly, illusory, insubstantial, shadowy.

dhalid. reproduce *vb* copy, duplicate, imitate, repeat; breed, procreate, propagate.

dhaliya. effect *vb* cause, create, produce; do, execute, perform, realize. *n* consequence, outcome, result.

dhallin yaro. youth *n* adolescence, childhood, immaturity; boy, lad, schoolboy, stripling, youngster.

dhallin yarro. youthful *adj* boyish, childish, girlish, immature, juvenile, young.

dhallinyar. juvenile *n* boy, child, girl, youth.

dhallinyaro. juvenile *adj* childish, immature, puerile, young, youthful.

dhamaad ah. interminable *adj* long-drawn-out, tedious, wearisome.

dhamaad. end *n* close, finale, finish, last; completion, conclusion; consequence, result, upshot; aim, design, goal, intent, intention, object, objective, purpose.

dhamaanaaya. terminal *adj* final, terminating, ultimate.

aan dhamaanayn. endless *adj* boundless, immeasurable, infinite, limitless; eternal, everlasting, never-ending, perpetual, unending, undying.

dhamayn. terminate *vb* end, finish, close, complete, conclude.

dhammaad lahayn. infinity *n* absoluteness, boundlessness, endlessness, eternity, vastness.

aan dhammaad lahayn. infinite *adj* boundless, endless, limitless, unbounded; absolute, eternal.

dhammaad. finale *n* conclusion, end, termination.

dhammaad. close *n* conclusion, end, termination.

dhammaad. termination *n* end, completion, conclusion.

dhammaad. finish *n* end, death, termination, wind-up; close.

dhammaad. terminal *n* end, extremity, termination.

dhammaan. absolutely *adv* completely, definitely, unconditionally; actually, downright, indeed, indubitably, infallibly, positively, really, truly, unquestionably.

dhammaan. universal *adj* general, ubiquitous, unlimited; all, complete, entire, total, whole.

aan dhammaanayn. unending *adj* endless, eternal, everlasting, interminable, never-ending, perpetual, unceasing.

dhammayn. settle *vb* adjust, order, regulate; decide, agree, fix.

dhammayn. end *vb* abolish, cease, close, conclude, discontinue, dissolve, drop, finish, stop, terminate.

dhammays tiran. absolute *adj* complete, ideal, independent, perfect, supreme, unqualified, unrestricted; arbitrary, authoritative, autocratic, despotic, dictatorial; genuine, positive, real, unequivocal, unquestionable, veritable.

dhammaystir. perfect *vb* complete, finish.

dhammaystiran. complete *adj* entire, total, whole.

dhammaystiran. unmitigated *adj* absolute, complete, sheer, stark, thorough, unqualified, utter.

dhammaystirid. finish *vb* accomplish, achieve, complete, fulfil, perform; close, conclude, end, terminate.

dhammeystir. complete *vb* do, end, execute, finish, fulfil.

dhan. full *adv* completely, fully; directly, exactly, precisely.

dhan. integral *adj* complete, entire, total, whole.

dhan. whole *adj* all, complete, entire, intact, total, undivided; faultless, firm, perfect, unbroken, undivided, uninjured.

dhanaan. sour *adj* acid, sharp, tart, vinegary; bitter, glum, ill-natured, ill-tempered, morose, surly.

dhanbaal. message *n* communication, letter, missive, notice, telegram.

aan la dhaqaajin karin. unshaken *adj* constant, firm, resolute, steadfast, steady, unmoved.

dhaqaalayn. economize *vb* manage, save; retrench.

dhaqaale. economy *n* saving, skimping, stinginess, thrift, thriftiness; administration, management.

aan dhaqdhaqaaq lahayn. calm *adj* hushed, inert, motionless, mum, mute, noiseless, quiet, serene, silent stagnant, stationary. tranquil, unruffled.

dhaqiiqi karo. mobile *adj* changeable, variable, volatile.

dhar. fabric *n* cloth, material, stuff, textile, tissue, web.

dhar. garment *n* clothes, clothing, dress, habit, vestment.

dhar. clothes *n* apparel, attire, clothing, costume, dress, garb, garments, gear, raiment, vestments.

dharag. surfeit *n* excess, glut, overindulgence, satiety, superabundance, superfluity.

dhargashi. clothe *vb* dress, rig; cover, swathe.

isku-dharid. mingle *vb* blend, combine, intermix, join, mix, unite.

aad ugu dhaw. approximate *adj* approaching, proximate; almost exact, inexact, rough.

dhawaan. near *adj* adjacent, close, neighbouring, nigh.

ku dhawaansho. approach *vb* advance, approximate, come close; broach; resemble. ku haboon. appropriate *adj* adapted, apt, befitting, fit, opportune, seemly, suitable.

dhawaaq dheer. loud *adj* boisterous, clamorous, deafening, noisy, resounding, vociferous; ostentatious, showy, vulgar.

dhawaaq. beat *n* accent, metre, rhythm; course, round.

dhawaaq. statement *n* account, announcement, assertion, declaration, report, specification.

dhawaaq. sound *n* noise, note, tone, voice, whisper.

dhawaaqid. exclaim *vb* call, cry, declare, ejaculate, shout, utter, vociferate.

ku dhawaaqid. pronounce *vb* articulate, enunciate, say, speak, utter, state.

ku dhawaaqid. announce *vb* advertise, communicate, declare, disclose, proclaim, promulgate, publish, report, reveal, trumpet.

dhawaaqid. ring *vb* chime, clang, jingle, peal, resound, reverberate, toll; call, phone, telephone.

dhawac. mischief *n* damage, harm, misfortune, trouble; devilry, wrong-doing.

dhawr. several *adj* some, many, sundry, various.

dhaxaltooyo. inheritance *n* heritage, legacy, patrimony.

dhaxlid. inherit *vb* get, receive.

dheddigood ah. feminine *adj* graceful, modest, soft, tender, womanly; softness, weakness.

dheecaan leh. juicy *adj* lush, moist, succulent, watery.

dheecaan. smear *n* blur, blot, smudge, smut.

ku dheeldheelid. gibe, jibe *vb* deride, jeer, mock, ridicule, scoff, sneer, taunt.

isu dheelitir. balance *vb* compensate, counteract, adjust, equalize, square.

dheelitiran. firm *adj* firm, fixed, stable, steady; constant, persevering, resolute, stable, staunch, steadfast, unchangeable, unwavering.

dheelitirid. stabilize *vb* balance, stabilize, steady, support.

dheeliyid. overbalance *vb* capsize, overset, overturn, tumble, upset.

hoose u dheer. deep *adj* profound, penetrating, unfathomable.

dheer. long *adj* drawn-out, extended, extensive, far-reaching, lengthy, prolonged, protracted, stretched.

dheeraad ah. surplus *adj* additional, leftover, remaining, spare.

dheeraad ah. extra *adj* accessory, additional, another, further, more, other, plus; spare, supplementary, surplus. *adv* additionally, also, beyond, furthermore, more, moreover, plus. *n* accessory, appendage, nonessential; bonus, leftover, remainder, spare, surplus.

dheeraad. supplement *n* addition, appendix, complement, extra, postscript.

dheeraad. surplus *n* balance, excess, residue.

dheeraad. glut *n* excess, saturation, surfeit, surplus.

si dheerayn. prolong *vb* extend, lengthen, protract, sustain; defer, postpone.

dheerayn. lengthen *vb* elongate, extend, prolong, stretch.

dheerayn. scurry *vb* bustle, dash, hurry, scamper.

ka dheereen. lap *vb* distance, pass, outdistance, overlap.

dheereynaaya. speedy *adj* fast, fleet, hurried, hurrying, nimble, quick, rapid, swift.

dheeri. redundant *adj* excessive, needless, superfluous, unnecessary, useless.

dhegeysi. listen *vb* eavesdrop, harken, hear, heed, obey, observe.

dhego fudud. obedient *adj* compliant, dutiful, respectful, submissive, yielding.

dherer hoose. depth *n* extent, measure; profoundness.

dherer. altitude *n* elevation, height, loftiness.

dherer. height *n* altitude, elevation, tallness; climax, pinnacle, summit, top.

dhex ka qabasho. intercept *vb* cut off, interrupt, obstruct, seize.

dhexaad. medium *adj* average, mean, mediocre, middle.

dhexda. middle *n* centre, halfway, mean.

dhexdhexaad. neutral *adj* impartial, indifferent; colourless.

dhexdhexaad. impartial *adj* equitable, even-handed, fair, just, unbiased, unprejudiced.

dhexdhexaadiye. intermediary *n* go-between, mediator.

dhexdhexadin. mediation *n* arbitration, intercession, intervention.

dhexdhexadiye. mediator *n* advocate, arbitrator, propitiator, umpire.

dhexe. intermediate *adj* in between, intervening, middle, transitional.

dhexe. mean *adj* average, medium, middle. *n* measure, medium, average;

dhexe. interim *n* intermediate time, interval, meantime.

dhexe. middle *adj* central, halfway, mid; intermediate, intervening.

dhexgelid. intervene *vb* come between, interfere, mediate; befall, happen, occur.

dhibaato lahayn. harmless *adj* innocent, innocuous, inoffensive, safe, unoffending.

dhibaato leh. mischievous *adj* destructive, harmful, hurtful; annoying, impish, naughty, troublesome, vexatious.

dhibaato. distress *n* affliction, misery, misfortune, adversity, hardship, tribulation.

dhibic roob. drop *n* droplet, globule.

dhici kara. probable *adj* apparent, likely, presumable, reasonable.

dhicid. fall *vb* collapse, descend, drop, sink, topple, tumble, stumble, trip. *n* comedown, flop, tumble; cascade, cataract, waterfall.

dhicid. rob *vb* fleece, pilfer, pillage, plunder; appropriate, deprive, embezzle, plagiarize.

dhicid. loot *vb* pillage, plunder, ransack, rifle, rob, sack.

dhicid. fail *vb* fall, miscarry, miss.

hoos u dhicid. slump *vb* droop, fall, sag, sink.

ku dhicid. jostle *vb* collide, elbow, hustle, shake, shove.

wax loo dhigaa jirin. incomparable *adj* matchless, peerless, surpassing, unequalled, unparalleled, unrivalled.

dhigid. put *vb* deposit, lay, place, set; offer, present, propose, state.

dhigid. arrange *vb* arrange, lay, place, position, plant, posit, put, set, settle.

dhigid. place *vb* arrange, fix, install, pose, put, classify, identify.

dhigid. position *vb* fix, locate, place, put, set.

meel dhigid. station *vb* establish, fix, locate, place, post, set. *n* footing, grade, rank, standing, state, status.

kala dhigid. analysis *n* decomposition, dissection, resolution, separation.

iska dhigid. copy *vb* duplicate, reproduce, trace; follow, imitate.

dhigid. settle *vb* place, put, fix.

u dhigma. equivalent *adj* commensurate, equal; interchangeable, synonymous. *n* counterpart, double, equal, match, parallel, quid pro quo.

dhihid. say *vb* declare, express, pronounce, speak, tell, utter.

dhihid. word *vb* express, phrase, put, say, state, term, utter.

dhihid. imply *vb* insinuate, involve, mean, presuppose, signify.

ku dhiidid. disagree *vb* argue, bicker, clash, debate, dispute, quarrel, wrangle.

dhiiragelin. incentive *n* encouragement, inducement, motive, spur, stimulus.

dhiiran. courage *n* boldness, bravery, daring, fearlessness, gallantry, heroism, nerve, pluck, prowess, resolution, spirit, spunk, valour.

dhiiran. fearless *adj* bold, brave, courageous, daring, heroic, intrepid, valiant.

dhiiran. daring *n* adventurousness, boldness, bravery, courage, valour.

dhiiran. intrepid *adj* bold, brave, courageous, daring, dauntless, fearless, heroic.

dhiiran. resolution *n* boldness, backbone, courage, determination, earnestness, firmness, fortitude, grit, pluck, perseverance, steadfastness, tenacity.

dhiiranaan. fortitude *n* braveness, bravery, courage, determination, endurance, firmness, hardiness, patience, pluck, resolution, strength, valour.

dhiiranaan. enterprising *adj* adventurous, bold, daring, resourceful.

dhiiranaan. bold *adj* adventurous, audacious, courageous; brave, daring, fearless, gallant, heroic, intrepid, spirited, undaunted; assured, confident, self-reliant; forward, impertinent, impudent, pushing, rude; prominent, striking.

dhiiranaan. daring *adj* bold, brave, fearless, gallant, heroic, intrepid.

ku dhiirasho. dare *vb* challenge, defy, provoke, risk.

dhiiri galin. spur *n* incentive, inducement, stimulus.

dhiiri galin. stimulus *n* encouragement, incentive, motivation, spur.

dhiirin. spur *vb* animate, arouse, drive, goad, incite, prod, stimulate, urge.

dhiirin. pluck *n* courage, daring, grit, nerve, resolution, spirit, valour.

dhiman. sketchy *adj* cursory, slight, superficial, incomplete, vague.

dhimanaaya. dying *adj* expiring; mortal, perishable.

dhimasho. perish *vb* die, expire, vanish.

dhimasho. pass away die, fade, expire, vanish.

dhimasho. die *vb* decease, demise, depart, expire, pass on; perish, wither; cease.

dhimasho. mortality *n* death, fatality.

dhinac kaliya. one-sided *adj* partial, prejudiced, unfair, unilateral, unjust.

dhinac. border *n* edge, flank, margin, verge; cause, faction, party, team.

dhinaca isku haya. juxtaposition *n* adjacency, contiguity, contact, proximity.

dhinacqaad. along *adv* lengthways, lengthwise; forward, onward; beside, together, simultaneously.

dhinbiil bixin. sparkle *vb* coruscate, flash, gleam, glisten, glitter, scintillate, twinkle.

dhinbiil. spark *n* spark.

dhintay. lifeless *adj* dead, deceased, defunct, extinct, inanimate; frigid, inert, lethargic, passive, slow, sluggish, torpid.

dhintay. dead *adj* b deceased, departed, gone, inanimate, lifeless.

dhira-gelin. encourage *vb* assure, cheer, comfort, console, embolden, fortify, hearten, reassure, stimulate, strengthen, support.

dhirbaaxid. slap *vb* clap, pat, smack, spank, strike.

dhirbaaxid. smack *vb* hit, slap, strike.

dhirbaaxo. smack *n* blow, clap, slap.

dhirbaaxo. smack *n* blow, hit, slap.

dhisan. muscular *adj* athletic, brawny, powerful, sinewy, strong, sturdy, vigorous.

dhisid. institute *vb* begin, commence, establish, found, install, originate, start.

dhisid. build *vb* construct, erect, fabricate, fashion, model, raise, rear.

dhisisd. construct *vb* build, fabricate, erect, make, raise, set up.

dhismo. constitution *n* establishment, organization, structure; character, disposition, physique.

ku dhofosho. jolt *vb* jar, jolt, shake, shock.

dhoolatus ciidan. manoeuvre *n* evolution, exercise, movement, operation

dhoolatus. parade *n* ceremony, display, spectacle.

u dhow. close *adj* adjacent, adjoining, near, neighbouring; attached, devoted, intimate.

dhow. imminent *adj* close, impending, near, threatening.

dhowaansho. vicinity *n* nearness, proximity; locality, neighbourhood.

ka dhufosho. grab *vb* capture, clutch, seize, snatch.

dhul gariir. earthquake *n* quake, shudder.

dhul. land *n* earth, ground, soil; country, territory, tract, weald.

dhulka. ground *n* area, clod, earth,, sod, soil, turf; acres, estate, field, land, property.

wax dhumay. abandoned *adj* lost.

dhum. smash *n* crash, disaster, ruin.

dhumid. stray *vb* deviate, digress, err, meander, ramble, range, roam, rove, straggle, stroll, swerve, transgress, wander.

dhumid. ramble *vb* digress, roam, stray, wander.

dhumuc-weyn. thick *adj* bulky, chunky, solid, stubby, thickset; dense, dim, dull; compact, crowded.

dhutin. lame *vb* cripple, disable, hobble.

dhuuban. thin *adj* bony, flimsy, lean, narrow, poor, scanty, slender, slim, sparse.

dhuuban. slender *adj* lean, lithe, narrow, skinny, slim, slight, thin.

dhuuban. meagre *adj* lean, poor, skinny, starved, spare, thin; barren, poor, sterile.

dhuuban. slim *adj* lean, narrow, skinny, slender, spare.

dhuubasho. slim *vb* lose weight, reduce, slenderize.

uga dhuumasho. lurk *vb* hide, prowl, skulk, slink, sneak, snoop.

ka dhuumasho. dodge *vb* evade, prevaricate.

dhuuqid. infiltrate *vb* absorb, pervade, soak.

kala dhuwan. different *adj* distinct, nonidentical, unlike; dissimilar, various.

dib u dhacsan. tardy *adj* behindhand, dilatory, late, loitering, overdue.

dib u dhig. delay *n* postponement, stoppage.

dib u dhig. procrastinate *vb* adjourn, defer, delay, postpone, retard; neglect, omit; lag, loiter.

dib u dhigid. adjourn *vb* defer, delay, postpone, procrastinate; close, dissolve, end, interrupt, prorogue, suspend.

dib u dhigid. postpone *vb* adjourn, defer, delay, procrastinate, prorogue.

dib u dhigid. delay *vb* defer, postpone, procrastinate; dawdle, linger, loiter, tarry.

dib u dhigid. defer1 *vb* adjourn, delay, procrastinate, postpone, shelve, table.

dib u egid. review *vb* reconsider, re-examine; analyse, scrutinize, study.

dib u helo. reclaim *vb* recover, regain, restore.

dib-u-dhac. setback *n* hitch, disappointment, reverse.

dib-u-socosho. reverse *vb* overturn, quash, rescind, revoke; back, back up, retreat.

dibad. exterior *adj* external, outer, outside, surface.

dibedda. foreign *adj* alien, distant, exotic, external, outlandish, remote, strange; extraneous, inappropriate, irrelevant, outside, unrelated.

dibu-helid. retrieve *vb* recover, recoup, regain.

difaac. defence *n* defence, protection, security.

difaacid. defend *vb* defend, excuse, exonerate, justify, maintain, vindicate, support, warrant.

difaacid. shield *vb* cover, defend, guard, protect.

difaacid. protect *vb* cover, defend, guard, shield.

u digid. caution *vb* admonish, forewarn, warn.

digniin siin. warn *vb* alarm, arouse, caution, forewarn, signal.

digniin. warning *n* admonition, advice, caution; indication, intimation, omen, portent, sign, symptom.

digniin. alert *n* alarm, signal, warning.

digniin. portent *n* omen, sign, warning.

digniin. omen *n* foreboding, sign, warning.

digniin. alarm *n* alarm-bell, warning; apprehension, fear, fright, terror.

digtoon. alert *adj* awake, circumspect, vigilant, watchful, wary; active, brisk, lively, nimble, quick, prompt, ready, sprightly, spry.

digtoon. vigilant *adj* alert, attentive, careful, cautious, observant, unsleeping, wakeful, watchful.

digtoon. attentive *adj* alive, awake, careful, civil, considerate, courteous, heedful, mindful, observant, watchful.

digtooni. attention *n* care, mindfulness, observation, regard, watch, watchfulness; application, reflection, study; civility, courtesy, deference, politeness, regard, respect; devotion.

diidan. reluctant *adj* disinclined, hesitant, unwilling.

diidid. protest *vb* complain, object, remonstrate, repudiate.

is diidid. clash *n* collision; disagreement.

diidid. object *vb* disapprove of, except to, oppose, protest, refuse.

diidid. mind *vb* grudge, object, resent.

diidid. decline *vb* refuse, reject.

diidid. negation *n* denial, disclaimer, rejection, renunciation.

diidid. refuse *vb* decline, deny, withhold; decline, disallow, exclude, reject, veto.

diidid. reject *vb* discard, dismiss, decline, deny, disallow, despise, disapprove, disbelieve, rebuff, refuse, renounce, spurn, veto.

diidmada qayaxan. veto *n* ban, embargo, interdict, prohibition, refusal.

diidmo. denial *n* contradiction, negation; refusal, rejection.

diidmo. dissidence *n* disagreement, dissent, nonconformity, sectarianism.

diiqadayn. vex *vb* annoy, badger, distress, harass, irritate, provoke, torment, trouble, worry.

diirin. stew *vb* boil, seethe, simmer.

diirin. warm *vb* animate, chafe, excite, heat, rouse.

dil. carnage *n* killing, massacre, murder.

dilaac. breach *n* break, crack, fracture, opening, rift, rupture; split.

dilaac. tear *n* fissure, laceration, rent, rip.

dilaanimo, axmaqnimo. murderous *adj* barbarous, bloodthirsty, bloody, cruel, savage.

dilid. assassinate *vb* dispatch, despatch, kill, murder, slaughter, slay; accelerate, expedite, finish, hasten, hurry, quicken, speed.

dilid. assassinate *vb* dispatch, kill, murder, slay.

dilid. assassinate *vb* butcher, destroy, kill, massacre, murder, slaughter, slay.

dilid. murder *vb* assassinate, butcher, destroy, kill, massacre, slaughter, slay;

dilid. slay *vb* assassinate,dispatch, kill, massacre, murder, slaughter.

dillaac. outbreak *n* eruption, explosion, outburst; affray, broil, conflict, commotion, riot, row; flare-up.

dillaaca. crack *n* breach, break, chink, cleft, fissure, fracture, opening, rift, split.

dillacin. hatch *vb* breed, incubate.

dinikh. dim *adj* cloudy, dark, dusky, faint, ill-defined, indefinite, indistinct, mysterious, obscure, shadowy.

dirid. post *vb* dispatch, mail.

dirid. send *vb* convey, dispatch, forward, transmit.

dirqin. persuasion *n* inducement, influence.

diwaanin. record *vb* chronicle, note, register.

diyaar ah. ready *adj* alert, prepared, prompt.

diyaargarow. preliminary *adj* introductory, preparatory, previous, prior.

diyaarin. prepare *vb* adapt, adjust, fit, qualify; arrange, concoct, fabricate, make, order, plan, procure, provide.

diyaarin. schedule *vb* line up, list, plan, programme.

dood. debate *n* controversy, discussion, disputation.

ka doodid. discuss *vb* argue, debate, deliberate.

doodid. haggle *vb* argue, bargain, dispute.

doodid. debate *vb* argue, discuss, dispute.

ku doodid. urge *vb* beg, entreat, implore, press, solicit; egg on, encourage, goad, incite, spur, stimulate.

doodid. reason *vb* argue, debate, infer, think.

doonanaan. engage *vb* employ, enlist, hire, retain; interlock.

doonid. offer *n* proposal, proposition, tender, bid.

doonid. need *vb* demand, lack, require, want.

doonid. urge *n* compulsion, desire, drive, impulse, longing, wish, yearning.

doonid. want *vb* crave, desire, need, require, wish.

doonid. yearn *vb* crave, desire, hanker after, long for.

doonid. desire *vb* covet, crave, fancy, hanker after, long for, lust after, want, wish, yearn for.

doonid. sue *vb* beg, demand, entreat, petition, plead.

doonid. intent, intention *n* aim, design, drift, end, intent, meaning, object, plan, purpose, view.

doonis. entice *vb* allure, attract, bait, cajole, coax, decoy, inveigle, lure, persuade, prevail on, seduce, tempt, wheedle, wile.

ka doorasho. select *vb* choose, cull, pick, prefer.

doorasho. choice *n* alternative, option, preference.

doorasho. option *n* choice, discretion, preference, selection.

doorasho. election *n* appointment, choice, preference, selection.

dooratid. choose *vb* elect, pick, prefer, select.

doorbidid. prefer *vb* choose, elect, fancy, pick, select.

doorid. elect *vb* appoint, choose, designate, pick, prefer, select.

dooxid. stab *vb* gore, jab, pierce, puncture.

doqon. halfwitted *adj* doltish, dull, feeble-minded, foolish, silly, simple, soft, stupid, thick.

doqon. stupid *adj* brainless, dim, dull, foolish, idiotic, inane, inept, senseless.

doqon. inane *adj* empty, fatuous, vacuous, void; foolish, senseless, silly, stupid.

doqon. silly *adj* brainless, childish, foolish, inept, stupid; absurd, frivolous, imprudent, unwise.

dorasho. preference *n* choice, election, estimation, selection.

dudomo. mount *n* hill, mountain, peak.

dufaan. gale *n* blast, hurricane, squall, storm, tempest, tornado, typhoon.

dul qaad la'aan. intolerant *adj* bigoted, narrow, proscriptive; dictatorial, impatient, imperious, overbearing.

dul qaad leh. understanding *adj* forgiving, patient, sympathetic, tolerant.

loo dul qaadan karo. tolerable *adj* bearable, endurable; middling, ordinary, passable, so-so.

dul-saarid. impose *vb* (*with* on, upon) abuse, deceive, exploit.

dullayn. humiliate *vb* debase, degrade, humble, mortify, shame.

dulli ah. humble *adj* meek, modest, lowly, simple, submissive, unambitious, unassuming; low, meek, obscure, plain, poor, small, undistinguished.

dullinimo. humility *n* diffidence, humbleness, lowliness, meekness, modesty, self-abasement, submissiveness.

dulmar. cursory *adj* brief, desultory, hasty, passing.

dulqaad leh. uncomplaining *adj* long-suffering, meek, patient, resigned, tolerant.

dulqaad. tolerance *n* endurance, receptivity, sufferance, toleration.

u dulqaadasho. tolerate *vb* admit, allow, indulge, let, permit..

dulqaadsho. patience *n* endurance, fortitude, composure, quietness, forbearance.

dumid. ruin *n* demolition, downfall, loss, shipwreck.

dumid. collapse *vb* break down, fail, fall.

dumid. smash *vb* break, crush, shatter.

dumin. ruin *vb* destroy, devastate, shatter, smash, wreck.

dun. thread *n* cord, fibre, filament, hair, line, twist.

duq ah. decrepit *adj* feeble, wasted, weak; aged.

duqad. mince *n* hash, mash, mincemeat.

is duqayn. impact *vb* collide, crash, strike.

is duqayn. clash *vb* collide, crash; contend, disagree, interfere.

durid. insert *vb* introduce, force in, inject.

duriyad. offspring *n* brood, children, descendants, issue, child.

duriyad. descendants *npl* offspring, issue, posterity, progeny; ancestry, derivation, extraction, genealogy, lineage, parentage, pedigree

duruuf adag. hardship *n* affliction, burden, misfortune, privation, suffering, trial, trouble.

dusha. top *n* crest, crown, head, summit.

duub. band *n* bandage, belt, binding, tourniquet.

ku duubid. coil *vb* curl, twirl, twist, wind.

duubid. bundle *vb* bale, pack, package, parcel, truss, wrap.

duubid. wind *vb* coil, encircle, reel, turn, twine, twist; bend, curve, meander, zigzag.

duubid. curl *vb* twist, wind; bend buckle, ripple, wave.

duudoobid. wrinkle *vb* crease, pucker, rumple.

duuduub. wrinkle *n* corrugation, crease, crinkle, crumple, furrow, ridge, rumple.

duufaan. whirlwind *n* blizzard, gale, hurricane, squall, tempest, tornado, typhoon.

duufaan. hurricane *n* cyclone, gale, storm, tempest, tornado, typhoon.

duufsasho. influence *vb* affect, direct, sway; move, persuade, prevail upon.

wax duug ah. threadbare *adj* old, frayed, shabby, worn; commonplace, hackneyed, stale, trite.

duug ah. shabby *adj* faded, ragged, threadbare, worn-out.

duulid. fly *vb* aviate, glide, hover, mount, soar; abscond, decamp, depart, flee, vanish.

duulin. pilot *vb* conduct, navigate, steer.

duuliye. pilot *n* helmsman, navigator, steersman; airman, aviator.

duurjoog. wild *adj* feral, undomesticated, untamed; desolate, rough, uncultivated; disorderly, frenzied, turbulent, uncontrolled, violent; crazy, extravagant, fanciful, grotesque. madax adag. wilful; capricious, headstrong, perverse, self-willed, unruly; deliberate, intentional, premeditated.

kala duwan. manifold *adj* complex, diverse, many, various.

kala duwanaan. discrepancy *n* difference, divergence, incongruity, inconsistency, variance, variation.

duwid. divert *vb* deflect, distract, digress; amuse, entertain, exhilarate, refresh, solace.

E

eber. zero *n* cipher, naught, nadir, nil, nothing, nought.

edbin. ine *vb* control, regulate; chastise, punish.

edeb leh. polite *adj* attentive, affable, civil, courteous, obliging, well-bred, well-mannered.

edeb-daran. rude *adj* boorish, ignorant, uncivilized, uncouth, undisciplined; impertinent, impolite, insulting, rough, uncivil.

edeb-darro. misconduct *n* bad conduct, misbehaviour, misdemeanour, rudeness, transgression;

edeble. courteous *adj* affable, attentive, civil, gracious, obliging, polite, refined, well-bred, well-mannered.

edeyn. accuse *vb* arraign, charge, censure, impeach, indict, tax.

edeyn. incriminate *vb* accuse, blame, charge, impeach.

edeyn. indict *vb* (*law*) accuse, charge, present.

ee guurka, ama arooska. nuptial *adj* bridal, conjugal, matrimonial.

eedayn. blame *vb* accuse, censure, condemn, reprehend, upbraid.

eedeyn. charge *vb* accuse, blame; require, tax; assault, attack, bear down.

eedeyn. prosecute *vb* indict, sue, summon.

eegid. see *vb* behold, look, discern, observe, know, notice, understand.

eegid. eye *vb* inspect, ogle, scrutinize, survey, view, watch.

aad u eegid. scan *vb* examine, investigate, scrutinize, search, sift.

eegid. look *vb* behold, examine, gaze, inspect, investigate, notice, observe, see, search, study, survey, view.

eegid. glimpse *vb* espy, look, spot, view.

isku eegid. compare *vb* liken, resemble.

eegid. observe *vb* notice, remark, watch; comply, follow, fulfil, obey; celebrate, keep.

eegid. regard *vb* gaze, look, notice, observe, see, view, watch; esteem, honour, reverence, value;

eegid. view *vb* behold, contemplate, eye, inspect, scan, survey.

isu eekaan. likeness *n* resemblance, similarity; copy, effigy, facsimile, image, picture, portrait, representation.

ehel. kin *n* kindred, kinsfolk, relations, relatives, siblings.

ehel. relation *n* kin, kindred, kinsman, kinswoman, relative.

ehel. folk *n* kindred, nation, people.

ehel. relations *n* folks, kin, kindred, kinsfolk, kinsmen, relatives.

ergay. envoy *n* ambassador, minister; courier, messenger.

ergo. delegate *n* ambassador, commissioner, deputy, envoy, representative.

ergo. mission *n* duty, errand.

u ergeyn ergo. delegate *vb* authorize, deputize, transfer, entrust.

eryasho. pursue *vb* chase, follow, hunt, shadow, track; seek, strive.

eryasho. chase *vb* follow, hunt, pursue, track.

eryid. pursuit *n* chase, hunt, race; hobby, pastime, occupation, vocation.

eryid. dislodge *vb* dismount, displace, eject, expel, oust, remove.

eryid. discharge *vb* dismiss, sack; execute, perform, fulfil, observe.

eryid. oust *vb* dislodge, dispossess, eject, evict, expel.

— F —

faa'ido lahayn. needless *adj* superfluous, unnecessary, useless.

faa'iido darro. disadvantage *n* drawback, hindrance.

faa'iido lahayn. useless *adj* futile, ineffectual, unavailing, unproductive, unserviceable, valueless, worthless.

faa'iido leh. futile *adj* fruitless, idle, ineffectual, useless, vain, valueless, worthless.

faa'iido leh. beneficial *adj* advantageous, favourable, helpful, profitable, useful.

faa'iido leh. fruitless *adj* futile, ineffectual, unprofitable, useless, vain.

faa'iido leh. useful *adj* advantageous, beneficial, convenient, effective, helpful, practical, profitable, serviceable.

faa'iido leh. productive *adj* fertile, fruitful, prolific.

faa'iido leh. profitable *adj* advantageous, beneficial, desirable, gainful, productive, useful; lucrative, remunerative.

faa'iido leh. advantageous *adj* beneficial, favourable, profitable.

faa'iido. advantage *n* benefit, blessing, gain, profit, return; interest; convenience, prerogative, privilege.

faa'iido. benefit * *n* kindness, service; advantage, gain, profit.

faa'iido. utility *n* avail, benefit, profit, service, use, usefulness.

faa'iido. advantage *n* benefit, good, profit, share, stale; attention, concern, regard, sympathy.

faa'iido. profit *n* advantage, benefit, interest.

faafid. rash *n* breaking-out, eruption, epidemic, outbreak, plague.

faafreebid. censor *vb* cut, edit, expurgate; classify, suppress.

faafsan. epidemic *n* outbreak, pestilence, plague, spread, wave.

ka faalayn. comment *vb* criticize, explain, remark.

faallo. review *n* commentary, critique, notice.

faallo. comment *n* explanation, observation, remark.

faanin. coax *vb* cajole, entice, flatter, persuade, soothe.

ka faaruqin. drain *vb* empty, evacuate, exhaust; dry.

faaruqin. evacuate *vb* empty; discharge, clean out, clear out, eject, excrete, expel, purge, void; abandon, desert, forsake, leave, quit, relinquish.

faaruqin. void *vb* clear, eject, emit, empty, evacuate.

faaruqin. vacate *vb* abandon, evacuate, relinquish, surrender.

fadeexad ah. scandalous *adj* disgraceful, disreputable, infamous, odious, shameful.

fadhiisin. still *vb* calm, check, immobilize, pacify, quiet, restrain, silence, stop, subdue, tranquilize.

fadooli. inquisitive *adj* curious, inquiring, scrutinizing; curious, meddlesome, peeping, peering, prying.

fadooli. curious *adj* interested, inquisitive, prying; extraordinary, rare, strange, unique, unusual.

fadooli. officious *adj* dictatorial, impertinent, meddlesome, pushy.

fadooli. meddlesome *adj* interfering, intrusive, officious, prying.

fadoolin. interfere *vb* meddle; clash, collide, conflict.

faham. insight *n* discernment, intuition, perception, understanding.

la fahmi karo. conceivable *adj* imaginable, picturable; comprehensible, intelligible, rational, thinkable.

fahmid. comprehend *vb* grasp, know, perceive, understand.

fahmid. understand *vb* catch, comprehend, grasp, know, perceive, see.

fahmo daran. dull *adj* stupid, unintelligent; lifeless, slow, sluggish; dismal, dreary, gloomy, sad, sombre; dim, matt; tedious, uninteresting.

fakar badin. meditative *adj* contemplative, pensive, reflective, thoughtful.

aan fakarayn. thoughtless *adj* casual, heedless, inconsiderate, negligent, rash, reckless.

fakarid. think *vb* contemplate, meditate, reflect; believe, consider, imagine, judge, suppose.

ka fakarid. consider *vb* contemplate, examine, ponder, reflect, study, weigh; cogitate, deliberate, muse, ponder, ruminate, think.

fakarsan. pensive *adj* contemplative, dreamy, meditative, thoughtful.

fakarsan. wistful *adj* contemplative, meditative, musing, pensive, thoughtful; eager, earnest, longing.

fakarsan. thoughtful *adj* absorbed, pensive, reflective; attentive, considerate, helpful, kind-hearted.

fal. deed *n* achievement, act, exploit, feat, performance; charter, contract, document.

fal. do *n* event, feast, function, party.

fal. action *n* achievement, activity, agency, deed, exertion, exploit, feat; battle, combat, conflict, contest, encounter, engagement, operation; lawsuit, prosecution.

falanqayn. criticism *n* analysis, appreciation, comment, critique, evaluation, judgement, review.

falid. do *vb* accomplish, achieve, act, commit, effect, execute, perform; complete, conclude, end, finish, settle, terminate.

fallaag. outlaw *n* bandit, crook, highwayman, lawbreaker, robber, thief.

fallaar-eeg. X-ray *n* roentgen ray, röntgen ray.

fallid. act *vb* do, execute, function, make, operate, work; enact, feign, perform, play.

fantasiye. festival *n* anniversary, carnival, feast, fete, gala, holiday, jubilee.

faragalin. meddle *vb* interfere, interpose, intrude.

faragelin. intervention *n* interference, mediation.

faras. nag *n* bronco, crock, hack, horse, pony.

farax. rapture *n* delight, enthusiasm, bliss, happiness, joy.

farax. happiness *n* delight, gaiety, joy, light-heartedness, pleasure; bliss, felicity, enjoyment, well-being.

faraxsan. cheerful *adj* gay, glad, gleeful, happy, joyful, jolly, joyous, light-hearted, lively, merry, sunny.

ka faraxsan. delight *vb* charm, enchant, enrapture, please, satisfy.

faraxsan. hilarious *adj* boisterous, cheerful, convivial, happy, jolly, jovial, joyful, merry, mirthful, noisy.

faraxsan. merry *adj* agreeable, cheerful, jolly, lively, pleasant, vivacious.

ku faraxsan. thankful *adj* appreciative, beholden, grateful, indebted, obliged.

faraxsan. delightful *adj* agreeable, captivating, charming, enchanting, enjoyable, rapturous, ravishing.

faraxsan. jaunty *adj* airy, cheery, gay, showy, sprightly, unconcerned.

faraxsan. jovial *adj* convivial, festive, jolly, joyous, merry, mirthful

faraxsan. happy *adj* blissful, cheerful, contented, glad, joyful, joyous, light-hearted, merry, pleased.

faraxsan. glad *adj* delighted, happy, pleased; animated, blithe, cheerful, cheery, elated, joyful, joyous, light-hearted, merry.

aad u faraxsan. joyful *adj* delighted, elated, glad, happy, jolly, joyous, merry, rejoicing.

farqi. difference *n* disparity, dissimilarity, variation; controversy, disagreement, dispute, falling out.

farxad leh. pleasant *adj* delightful, enjoyable, nice, cheerful, good-humoured, gracious, likable.

farxad. mirth *n* cheerfulness, jollity, laughter, merriment, merry-making, rejoicing.

farxad. zest *n* appetite, enjoyment, exhilaration, gusto, relish; flavour, salt, savour, tang, taste.

farxad. joy *n* delight, gladness, glee, pleasure, rapture; bliss, felicity, happiness.

farxid. content *vb* delight, gladden, gratify, please, satisfy.

ka farxin. amuse *vb* charm, cheer, divert, enliven, entertain, gladden, relax, solace; beguile, cheat, deceive, delude, mislead.

ka farxin. cheer *vb* encourage, applaud, clap.

ka farxin. please *vb* charm, delight, oblige, satisfy.

ka farxin. entrance2 *vb* bewitch, captivate, charm, delight, enchant, enrapture, fascinate.

ka farxin. charm *vb* allure, attract, captivate, delight, fascinate.

fasaadin. subvert *vb* confound, corrupt, injure, pervert.

fasahaadin. taint *vb* contaminate, corrupt, defile, pollute, spoil.

fasax. leave *n* permission, licence; adieu, farewell, goodbye.

fasax. permit *n* licence, passport, permission, warrant.

fasax. holiday *n* feast, festival, vacation.

fasax. pass *n* route, way; authorization, licence, passport, permission, permit, ticket.

u fasaxid. allow *vb* authorize, grant, permit, warrant.

fashil. failure *n* breakdown, collapse, fiasco; bankruptcy, crash, downfall, insolvency, ruin.

fasiix. fluent *adj* flowing, gliding, smooth; easy, talkative, voluble.

fasixid. permit *vb* allow, let, tolerate; authorize, consent.

fatahid. swamp *vb* engulf, flood, overwhelm, sink, submerge.

fatahid. teem *vb* abound, bear, produce, swarm; discharge, empty, overflow.

fatahid. flood *n* deluge, overflow, tide; downpour, flow, outburst, spate, rush; abundance, excess.

feedh. blow *n* blow, box, fight, hit, spar.

feedhtan. box *vb* fight, hit, mill, spar.

feejigan. wary *adj* careful, cautious, chary, circumspect, guarded, vigilant, watchful; alert, attentive, awake, heedful, observant, vigilant, wakeful.

feejigan. agile *adj* active, alert, brisk, lively, nimble, prompt, smart, ready.

feejigan. painstaking *adj* careful, conscientious.

feejignaan la'aan. careless *adj* heedless, inattentive, inconsiderate, neglectful, negligent, remiss, thoughtless, unconcerned, unthinking.

feejignaan. care *n* concern, worry; attention, caution, regard, vigilance, watchfulness.

u feejignaan. careful *adj* attentive, heedful, mindful, thoughtful; cautious, discreet, watchful.

feejignaan. mindful *adj* attentive, careful, observant, thoughtful.

feejignaan. prudent *adj* cautious, careful, discreet, judicious, wise.

aan feejignayn. unwary *adj* heedless, imprudent, incautious, indiscreet, unguarded.

aan feejignayn. inattentive *adj* absent-minded, careless, heedless, neglectful, remiss, unobservant.

aan fekerin. unthinking *adj* careless, heedless, inconsiderate, thoughtless, unreasoning, unreflecting.

aad u fican. outstanding *adj* due, owing, unpaid; conspicuous, eminent, prominent, striking.

aad u fican. matchless *adj* excellent, exquisite, incomparable, perfect,

fiddid. branch *vb* diverge, fork, spread.

fidid. expand *vb* develop, spread, unfold, enlarge, extend, stretch.

fidin. extend *vb* reach, stretch; continue, elongate, lengthen, prolong, protract; enlarge, expand, increase; spread.

fidin. disseminate *vb* circulate, diffuse, disperse, proclaim, promulgate, propagate, publish, scatter, spread.

fidin. spread *vb* expand, extend, open, stretch, unfold; disperse, distribute.

fidnayn. agitate *vb* disturb, jar, rock, shake, trouble; disquiet, excite, ferment, rouse, trouble; confuse, fluster; canvass, debate, discuss, dispute, investigate.

fidsan. extensive *adj* broad, comprehensive, far-reaching, large, wide, widespread.

figta (halka ug dheer). summit *n* apex, crest, crown, pinnacle, top, zenith.

aad u fiicaan. excellence *n* goodness, perfection, purity, quality, superiority.

ka fiican. better *vb* exceed, improve. *adj* bigger, fitter, greater, larger, preferable.

fiican. nice *adj*; neat, tidy, trim; refined, dainty, delicate, delightful, good, pleasant.

ugu fiican. prize *adj* best, champion, first-rate, outstanding.

fiican. well *adj* hale, healthy, hearty, sound; profitable, satisfactory, useful.

ugu fiican. best *adj* chief, first, foremost, highest, leading. *adv* extremely, greatly.

aad u fiicnaan. excellent *adj* admirable, choice, crack, eminent, first-rate, prime, sterling, superior, tiptop; estimable, praiseworthy.

fiid. evening *n* dusk, eve, even, eventide, nightfall, sunset, twilight.

fiidsan. sweeping *adj* broad, comprehensive, exaggerated, extensive, general.

fiijigan. observant *adj* attentive, mindful, vigilant, watchful.

fiiq. tip *n* apex, cap, end, extremity, peak, pinnacle, point, top.

fiiqa. point *n* apex, spike, tip; cape, headland, promontory; instant, moment; place, site, spot; aim, object, purpose, theme;

fiiqa. zenith *n* acme, apex, climax, culmination, prime, summit, top, utmost, height.

fiiqan. sharp *adj* acute, cutting, keen, needle-shaped, pointed; astute, canny, cunning, shrewd; caustic, sarcastic, severe, tart; intense, painful.

fiiqan. precipitous *adj* abrupt, perpendicular, uphill, sheer, steep.

fiiqan. tart *adj* acid, pungent, sharp, sour; caustic, curt, harsh, ill-humoured, ill-tempered, sarcastic, sharp.

fiiqid. sweep *vb* clean, brush, rake, scour.

fiirfiircoon. strenuous *adj* active, ardent, eager, earnest, energetic, resolute, vigorous, zealous. stress *n* accent, emphasis; strain, tension, pressure, urgency.

fiirin. stare *vb* gape, gaze, look intently, watch.

fiirin. peer *vb* gaze, look, peek, peep, pry.

fiirin. notice *vb* mark, observe, perceive, regard, see.

fiirsi la'aan. offhand *adv* carelessly, casually, clumsily, haphazardly.

fikrad. thought *n* meditation, reflection; concept, consciousness, deliberation, idea, intellect, understanding; theory, conjecture, hypothesis, idea, postulation, speculation.

fikrad. idea *n* belief, fancy, illusion, impression, judgement, notion, opinion, sentiment, supposition, thought.

ku filan. adequate *adj* competent, fit, satisfactory, sufficient, suitable.

ku filan. enough *adj* abundant, adequate, ample, plenty, sufficient. *adv* satisfactorily, sufficiently. *n* abundance, plenty, sufficiency.

filid. expect *vb* anticipate, await, forecast, foresee, hope, rely.

aan ku filnayn. insufficient *adj* deficient, inadequate, incommensurate, scanty.

fiqqa. peak *n* apex, pinnacle, summit, top, zenith.

firdhad. stampede *vb* charge, flee, panic. *n* charge, flight, panic, rout, rush.

firfircoon. energetic *adj* active, enterprising, forceful, strenuous, strong, vigorous.

firfircoon. vivacious *adj* animated, frolicsome, lively, merry, spirited, sprightly.

firfircooni. active *adj* assiduous, bustling, busy, diligent, industrious, restless; agile, alert, brisk, energetic, lively, nimble, prompt, quick, smart, spirited, sprightly, supple; animated, ebullient, fervent, vigorous.

firfircooni. mercurial *adj* active, lively, quick, sprightly; cheerful, light-hearted, lively; changeable, fickle, flighty, inconstant.

kala firidhsan. sparse *adj* dispersed, infrequent, scanty, scattered, sporadic, thin.

fog. distant *adj* far, far-away, remote; aloof, cool, haughty, stiff, uncordial.

ka fog. farther *adj* further, remoter. *adv* beyond, further; besides, furthermore, moreover.

fog. remote *adj* distant, far, out-of-the-way; isolated, removed, secluded.

fog. far *adj* at a distance; elsewhere; out of the way.

fog. far *adj* distant, long, protracted, remote. *adv* considerably, extremely, greatly, very much; afar, far away, remotely.

aad u fool xun. hideous *adj* abominable, appalling, awful, dreadful, frightful, ghastly, ghoulish, grim, grisly, horrible, horrid, repulsive, revolting, shocking, terrible, terrifying.

fool xun. unsightly *adj* disagreeable, hideous, repellent, repulsive, ugly.

fool xun. clumsy *adj* heavy, ill-shaped, lumbering; awkward, blundering, bungling, inapt.

fool xun. inept *adj* awkward, unfit, unsuitable; useless.

fool xun. ugly *adj* ill-favoured, plain, unprepossessing, unsightly; hideous, monstrous, repellent, repulsive.

fool xun. ungainly *adj* awkward, gawky, inelegant, lumbering, slouching, ungraceful.

foorarsi. stoop *vb* bend forward, bend down, bow, lean, sag, slouch, slump.

fudud. brisk *adj* active, alert, agile, lively, nimble, perky, quick, smart, spirited, spry.

fudud. simple *adj* bare, elementary, unmixed; plain, natural, unadorned; straightforward, true, unaffected, unsophisticated.

fudud. easy *adj* manageable, informal, natural, lenient, comfortable, loose.

fudud. nimble *adj* active, agile, alert, brisk, lively, quick, spry, swift, tripping.

fudud. flimsy *adj* slight, thin, insubstantial, weak.

fudud. delementary *adj* simple, uncomplicated, rudimental, rudimentary.

fudud. flimsy *adj* feathery, light, insubstantial, weightless; airy, buoyant, carefree, light-hearted.

fulay. cowardly *adj* chicken-hearted, faint-hearted, fearful, timid, yellow.

fulay. timid *adj* faint-hearted, fearful, irresolute, nervous, timorous, unadventurous.

fulin. execute *vb* accomplish, achieve, carry out, complete. do, effect, finish, perform; behead, electrocute, guillotine, hang.

fulin. perpetrate *vb* commit, do, execute, perform.

fulin. fulfil *vb* accomplish, complete, consummate, effect, execute, realize; discharge, do, perform; answer, meet, satisfy.

fulin. transact *vb* conduct, enact, execute, do, manage, negotiate, perform, treat.

fulin. implement *vb* effect, execute, fulfil.

furan. open *adj* aboveboard, candid, honest, sincere; ajar, unclosed, uncovered; accessible, public, unenclosed, unrestricted.

ka furdaamin. exorcise *vb* cast out, drive away, expel.

fure. key *n* lock-opener, opener; clue, explanation, guide, solution, translation.

kala furfuran. disjointed *adj* disconnected, incoherent, loose.

furfurid. resolve *vb* disentangle, solve, unravel; conclude.

furfurid. undo *vb* annul, cancel, neutralize,offset, reverse; unfasten, untie.

furid. untie *vb* free, loosen, unfasten, unknot, unloose; clear, resolve, solve, unfold.

furid. open *vb* begin, commence; uncover, unlock, unseal, untie.

furid. preface *vb* begin, introduce, launch, open, precede. * *n* foreword, introduction, preamble, prelude, premise, prologue.

furid. divorce *vb* dissolve, disunite, part, separate, sever, split up.

furiin. divorce *n* dissolution, parting, separation, severance.

furitaan. opening *adj* commencing, first, inaugural, introductory.

fursad. scope *n* capacity; extent, latitude, opportunity, range, space, sphere.

fursad. chance *adj* casual, incidental, unexpected, unforeseen.

fursad. opportunity *n* chance, convenience, moment, occasion.

G

gaabin. shorten *vb* abbreviate, abridge, curtail, cut short, reduce.

soo gaabin. abbreviate *vb* abridge, compress, condense, contract, cut, curtail, reduce, retrench, shorten.

gaabin. backward *adj* dull, slow, stupid.

soo gaabis. abbreviation *n* abridgment, compression, condensation, contraction, curtailment, cutting, reduction, shortening

gun ka gaadhid. achieve *vb* accomplish, acquire, attain, complete, consummate, do, effect, execute, finish, fulfil, perform, realize; acquire, gain, get, obtain, win.

gaadhid. reach *vb* extend, stretch; arrive at, attain, get.

gaadhsiin. transfer *vb* convey, consign, move, transmit.

gaajo. famine *n* hunger, scarcity, starvation.

gaal. infidel *n* agnostic, atheist, disbeliever, heathen, heretic, sceptic, unbeliever.

gaar ah. individual *adj* one, particular, personal, separate, single, special, unique.

gaar ah. special *adj* especial, particular, peculiar; exceptional, extraordinary, memorable.

wax gaar ah. specific *adj* characteristic, especial, particular, peculiar; definite, limited, precise, specified.

gaar ah. personal *adj* individual, private, special.

gaar ah. particular *adj* especial, special, specific; distinct, characteristic, individual, personal, careful, fastidious, scrupulous.

u gaar ah. characteristic *adj* peculiarity, quality, trait.

gaar ah. private *adj* secluded, sequestrated, solitary; confidential, hidden, secret.

gaar. own *adj* personal, private.

gaardin. march *vb* go, pace, parade, step, tramp, walk.

gaardis. march *n* hike, walk; parade, procession.

gaashangaad. adult *adj* grownup, mature, ripe, ripened. * *n* grownup person.

gabadh. girl *n* damsel, lass, lassie, maiden, miss, virgin.

gabadh. miss *n* damsel, girl, lass, maid, maiden.

gabagbayn. conclude *vb* close, end, finish, terminate; deduce, gather, infer, judge.

gabagbo. conclusion *n* deduction, inference; decision, judgement; completion, end, finale, termination, settlement.

gabi ahaan. altogether *adv* completely, entirely, totally, utterly.

gaboobay. stale *adj* flat, fusty, insipid, mouldy, musty, old, sour, tasteless.

gabow. old *adj* aged, ancient, elderly, obsolete, olden, old-fashioned, worn-out.

kal gacaltinimo. harmonious *adj* comfortable, consistent, orderly, symmetrical; agreeable, amicable, cordial, friendly.

gacan (ka biyuhu maraan). ditch *n* channel, drain, moat, trench.

gadaal. back *n* end, hind part, posterior, rear.

gadaal. rear *n* posterior, rear end, rump, tail.

gadaal. stern *n* behind, butt, buttocks, hind part, posterior, rear, tail, rump.

gadaal. behind *n* rear, stern, tail; bottom, buttocks, posterior, rump.

gadiid. transport *n* carriage, conveyance, transportation.

gadoodid. rebel *vb* mutiny, resist, revolt, strike.

gadoodid. mutiny *vb* rebel, revolt, rise, resist

gaf. error *n* error, fault, mistake.

gafid. blunder *vb* err, flounder, stumble.

gafid. mistake *vb* misjudge, misunderstand, err.

gal. file *n* dossier, folder, portfolio; column, line, row, queue.

galayn. envelop *vb* enfold, enwrap, pack, wrap; cover, encircle, encompass, enfold, enshroud, surround.

galayn. wrap *vb* cover, encase, envelop, muffle, swathe.

galid. penetrate *vb* bore, cut, enter, invade, perforate, pierce, stab.

galid. access *vb* broach, enter, open, open up.

ganaax. fine *n* forfeit, forfeiture, penalty, punishment.

ganaax. penalty *n* fine, forfeiture, punishment, retribution.

ganaaxid. fine *vb* penalize, punish.

ganaay. forfeit *n* fine, penalty.

ganacsade. merchant *n* dealer, retailer, shopkeeper, trader, tradesman.

ganacsi gal. mercantile *adj* commercial, marketable, trading.

ganacsi. trade *n* barter, business, commerce, dealing, exchange; craft, occupation.

ganacsi. commerce *n* business, trade.

garaac. tap *n* pat, tip, rap, touch.

garaacid xoog ah. batter *vb* beat, break, bruise, demolish, destroy, smash; disfigure* *n* batsman, striker.

garaacid. beat *vb* bang, cudgel, hammer, hit, knock, pound, punch, strike, thrash, thump, whack, whip; conquer, defeat, overcome, rout, subdue, vanquish; pulsate, throb.

garaacid. ring *vb* announce, knell, peal, toll.

garaacid. thump *vb* bang, batter, beat, belabour, punch, strike. garaac. thump *n* blow, punch, strike, stroke.

garaacid. tap *vb* knock, pat, rap, strike, tip, touch.

garaacid. bang *vb* beat, knock, thump; slam; clatter, rattle.

garac. bastard *adj* baseborn, counterfeit, false, illegitimate.

garac. love child *n*

garasho. judgment, judgement *n* understanding, wisdom, wit; decision, estimation, opinion, thought; adjudication, award, censure, condemnation, decree, sentence.

garasho. know *vb* comprehend, discern, distinguish, perceive, recognize, see, understand.

kala garasho. distinguish *vb* differentiate, discriminate, single out, demarcate, separate.

garasho. discretion *n* carefulness, caution, consideration, heedfulness, judgement, maturity, responsibility.

garasho. recognize *vb* identify, remember.

gardaro badan. aggressive *adj* assailing, assailant, assaulting, attacking, invading, offensive; pushing, self-assertive.

gariir. flutter *n* tremor, quiver. tremble; agitation, commotion, confusion, excitement, flurry, fluster, hurry-scurry, perturbation.

gariir. tremble *n* quake, quiver, shake, tremor, vibration; agitation, quaking, quivering, shaking, trembling.

gariirid. quake *vb* shake, shiver, shudder, move, vibrate.

gariirid. tremble *vb* quake, quaver, quiver, shake, shiver.

gariirid. shudder *vb* quake, quiver, shake, shiver, tremble. * n quiver, spasm, tremor.

gariirid. shiver *vb* quake, quiver, shake, shudder, tremble.

garriirid. flutter *vb* beat, palpitate, quiver, tremble.

garriirid. palpitate *vb* flutter, throb; quiver, shiver, tremble.

garsiin. convey *vb* bear, bring, carry, deliver, fetch, transmit, transport.

garsoore. referee *n* arbiter, arbitrator, judge, umpire.

garsoore. judge *n* adjudicator, arbiter, arbitrator, justice, magistrate, moderator, referee, umpire; connoisseur, critic.

garsoorid. judge *vb* decide, determine, pronounce; arbitrate, condemn, sentence, try, umpire; appreciate, estimate.

gashanti. miss *n* damsel, girl, lass, maid, maiden.

gawracid. slaughter *vb* butcher, kill, massacre, murder, slay.

gax. emigration *n* departure, exodus, migration.

gebi-ahaan. thorough *adj* absolute, complete, entire, exhaustive, radical, sweeping; accurate, correct, reliable.

gebiahaan. entire *adj* complete, unimpaired, whole; full, thorough, unmitigated.

gees. corner *n* angle, bend, joint; niche, nook, recess.

geesi ah. gallant *adj* bold, brave, chivalrous, courageous, daring, fearless, heroic, high-spirited, magnanimous, noble.

geesi. courageous *adj* audacious, brave, bold, chivalrous, daring, dauntless, fearless, gallant, hardy, heroic, intrepid, lion-hearted, plucky.

geesi. valiant *adj* bold, brave, courageous, daring, doughty, fearless, heroic, intrepid, lion-hearted, undaunted.

geesi. game *adj* ready, eager, willing.

geesi. bravery *n* courage, daring, fearlessness, gallantry, valour.

geesinimo. brave *adj* bold, courageous, fearless, heroic, intrepid, stalwart.

geesinimo. heroism *n* boldness, bravery, courage, daring, endurance, fearlessness, fortitude, gallantry, intrepidity, prowess, valour.

geesinimo. gallantry *n* boldness, bravery, chivalry, courage, courageousness, courteousness, fearlessness, politeness.

geesnimo. valour *n* boldness, bravery, courage, daring, gallantry, heroism, prowess, spirit.

giftin. edge *n* border, brim, brink, fringe, hem, lip, margin, rim, verge.

giftin. fringe *n* border, edge, edging, tassel, trimming.

giigsan. taut *adj* strained, stretched, tense, tight.

giigsan. tight *adj* close, fast, firm; taut, tense, stretched.

giijin. tense *vb* flex, strain, tauten, tighten.

giijin. fasten *vb* attach, bind, bolt, catch, chain, fix, lace, lock, pin, secure, strap, tether, tie.

giraangirin. wheel *vb* gyrate, revolve, roll, rotate, spin, swing, turn, twist, whirl, wind.

giriingirin. roll *vb* revolve, rotate, turn, wheel.

go' yar. piece *n* bit, fragment, part, quantity, scrap, shred, slice, portion.

go'. robe *n* attire, costume, dress, garment, gown.

go'. bit *n* fragment, piece, rag, scrap, shred.

go'. cut *n* cut, gash, slit.

go'aamin. decide *vb* conclude, determine, end, settle, terminate; resolve.

aan go'aan lahayn. irresolute *adj* changeable, faltering, hesitant, inconstant, spineless, uncertain, unstable, unsteady, vacillating, wavering.

go'aan leh. decided *adj* determined, firm, resolute, unwavering.

go'aan leh. unshrinking *adj* firm, determined, resolute, unblenching, unflinching.

go'aan qaadashu la'aan. indecision *n* fickleness, hesitation, inconstancy, irresolution, vacillation.

gobol. region *n* country, district, division, locality, province, quarter, territory; area, neighbourhood, vicinity.

gobol. province *n* district, region, territory, colony, dependency; sphere; department, division, jurisdiction.

god. pit *n* crater, excavation, well; abyss, chasm, gulf.

god. poke *n* dig, punch, thrust.

god. hole *n* aperture, opening, perforation; abyss, cave, cavern, cavity, chasm, depression, excavation, hollow, pit, pore, void; burrow, cover, den, lair, retreat; hovel, kennel.

goglid. furnish *vb* decorate, equip, fit; contribute, give, offer, present, produce.

gole. assembly *n* company, collection, concourse, congregation, gathering, meeting, rout, throng; caucus, congress, conclave, convention, convocation, diet, legislature, meeting, parliament, synod.

gole. council *n* assembly, congress, convention, meeting, parliament, synod.

goobaabin. circle *vb* encompass, gird, ring.

goobo. circle *n* corona, hoop, ring, circumference, cordon, ball, globe, orb, sphere; enclosure.

gooni ah. reclusive *adj* secluded, solitary.

gooni ah. secluded *adj* isolated, private, retired, screened,

gooni. hermit *n* ascetic, monk, recluse, solitary.

gooni. isolation *n* loneliness, solitariness, solitude.

gooni. seclusion *n* privacy, retirement, secrecy, solitude, withdrawal.

gooniyeen. isolate *vb* detach, quarantine, segregate, separate, set apart.

goor hore. early *adv* beforehand, shortly, soon.

dalag gooyn. harvest *vb* gather, glean, reap.

goslid. chuckle *vb* giggle, laugh, snigger, titter.

guban kara. inflammable *adj* combustible, ignitible; excitable.

gubid. scorch *vb* burn, char, sear, singe.

gubid. burn *vb* blaze, conflagrate, fire, flame, ignite, kindle, light, smoulder; cremate, incinerate; scald, scorch, singe, sunburn.

gudaha ah. internal *adj* inner, inside, interior, inward; mental, secret, spiritual; domestic, home, inland, inside, interior.

gudaha. inner *adj* interior, internal.

gudaha. inward *adj* inner, interior, internal; hidden, mental, private, secret, spiritual.

gudaha. interior *adj* inmost, inner, internal, inward; inland, remote; domestic, home.

gudaha. inside *adj* inner, interior, internal, intimate. *prep* in, in the interior of, within. *n* inner part, interior.

gudbin. transmit *vb* forward, remit, send; conduct, radiate.

guddoomiye. governor *n* commander, comptroller, director, head, headmaster, manager, overseer, ruler, superintendent, supervisor.

gudo. inner part *n* inland, inside.

guntid. knot *vb* entangle, tie, weave.

guntin. knot *n* complication, entanglement; connection, tie.

gunuus. murmur *n* complaint, grumble, whisper.

gunuusid. murmur *vb* hum, mumble, mutter, whisper.

guri. home *n* abode, dwelling, quarters, residence.

guri. flat *n* apartment.

guri. domicile *n* abode, dwelling, habitation, home, house, residence.

guri. house * *n* abode, domicile, dwelling, habitation, home, mansion, residence; building, edifice; hotel, inn, public house, tavern.

guri. residence *n* home, house, lodging, mansion.

gurracnaan. perverse *adj* contrary, wayward, wilful, wrong-headed.

guud ah. superficial *adj* external, shallow, skin-deep, slight, surface.

guud ahaan. total *n* aggregate, bulk, gross, whole.

guud. general *adj* broad, generic, popular, universal, widespread; common, ordinary, usual; inexact, vague.

guud. public *adj* civil, common, general, national; open, popular, well-known.

guud. comprehensive *adj* all-embracing, full, inclusive, sweeping, wide.

guudka. outside *n* exterior, surface; appearance.

guul. triumph *n* celebration, joy, jubilation; achievement, victory.

guul. win *n* conquest, success, triumph, victory.

guul. success *n* attainment, fortune, happiness, hit, luck, prosperity, triumph.

guul. victory *n* achievement, conquest, mastery, triumph.

ka guulaysi. defeat *vb* beat, conquer, overcome, repulse, rout, vanquish.

ku guuleys. accomplished *adj* achieved, completed, done, effected, executed, finished, fulfilled, realized; able, educated, experienced, expert, finished, instructed, practised, proficient, qualified, skilful, versed; elegant, fashionable, fine, polished, polite, refined.

aan lagu guuleysan. unsuccessful *adj* ineffectual, profitless, unavailing, unfortunate.

ku guuleysi. realize *vb* accomplish, achieve; comprehend, experience, recognize, understand.

ka guuleysi. overcome *vb* conquer, crush, defeat, overpower, overthrow, overturn, overwhelm, rout, subdue, subjugate, vanquish; conquer, prevail.

guuleysi. win *vb* achieve, acquire, earn, gain, get, obtain, succeed, triumph; convince, influence, persuade.

guuleysi. triumph *vb* exult, rejoice; prevail, succeed, win.

ku guuleysi. attain *vb* accomplish, achieve, acquire, get, obtain, secure; arrive at, come to, reach.

guuleysi. succeed *vb* flourish, gain, hit, prevail, prosper, thrive, win.

guuleystay. triumphant *adj* boastful, exultant, jubilant, successful, victorious.

ka guuleystay. victorious *adj* conquering, successful, triumphant, winning.

guuleystay. successful *adj* booming, flourishing, fortunate, prosperous, victorious, wealthy.

guur la xiriira. matrimonial *adj* conjugal, marital, nuptial.

guur. marriage *n* wedding, matrimony, wedlock; union, alliance, association.

guurka. nuptials *npl* marriage, wedding.

guursasho. mate *vb* marry, match, wed;

guuxid. growl *vb* complain, croak, find fault, gnarl, groan, grumble, lament, murmur.

H

hab isasin. clasp *vb* clutch, grasp, grip, seize; embrace, hug. *n* buckle, catch, hasp, hook; embrace, hug.

hab. style *n* fashion, form, genre, manner, method, way.

hab. pattern *n* model, plan, sample, specimen.

hab. method *n* manner, means, mode, plan, procedure, process, scheme, system.

hab. system *n* method, order, plan.

hab. procedure *n* method, policy, practice, process.

habaar. curse *n* affliction, annoyance, plague, scourge, torment, trouble.

habaarid. curse *vb* damn, denounce; blaspheme.

habayn. file *vb* order, pigeonhole, tidy.

habaysan. methodical *adj* exact, orderly, regular, systematic.

aan habaysnayn. inarticulate *adj* blurred, indistinct, thick; dumb, mute.

habbon. proper *adj* appropriate, becoming, befitting, convenient, fitting, pertinent, right, suitable; correct, exact, precise, real.

aan habbonayn. inconvenient *adj* annoying, awkward, cumbersome, troublesome, untimely, vexatious.

ku habboon. fit *adj* competent; adequate, appropriate, apt, pertinent, proper, seemly, suitable.

ku habboon. eligible *adj* desirable, preferable, suitable, worthy.

ku habboon. favourable *adj* auspicious, propitious, well-disposed, helpful, suitable.

habboon. relevant *adj* applicable, appropriate, apt, fit, germane, pertinent, proper, suitable.

ku habboon. suitable *adj* appropriate, apt, convenient, eligible, fitting, pertinent, relevant, worthy.

ku habboon. timely *adj* appropriate, opportune, seasonable, well-timed.

ku habboonaan. suit *vb* adapt, adjust, fit, harmonize, please, satisfy.

aan habboonayn. improper *adj* immodest, inappropriate, indecent, incorrect, wrong.

aan ku habboonayn. unsuitable *adj* ill-adapted, inappropriate, unfit; inapplicable, inapt, unbecoming, unfitting.

ku habboonayn. infelicitous *adj* ill-chosen, inappropriate, unfitting, unfortunate, unhappy.

aan ku habboonayn. unseasonable *adj* ill-timed, inappropriate, inopportune, untimely.

aan habboonayn. unbecoming *adj* inappropriate, indecorous, improper, unbefitting, unseemly.

haboon. opportune *adj* convenient, fitting, fortunate, lucky, timely, well-timed.

ku haboon. convenient *adj* appropriate, fit, proper, suitable, suited, useful.

ku haboonayn. awkward *adj* bungling, clumsy, inept, maladroit, unskilful; lumbering, unfit, ungainly, unmanageable; boorish; inconvenient, unsuitable.

habsiin. snuggle *vb* cuddle, nestle, nuzzle.

had iyo jeer. always *adv* continually, eternally, ever, evermore, perpetually, unceasingly.

hadal badan. talkative *adj* chatty, communicative, garrulous, loquacious, voluble.

aan hadal lag sheegi karin. unutterable *adj* indescribable, ineffable, inexpressible, unspeakable.

haddidaad. intimidate *vb* browbeat, bully, cow, daunt, frighten, overawe, scare, terrify, terrorize.

hadh. shadow *n* shade, dimness, gloom, obscurity.

hadhaa. sediment *n* dregs, grounds, residue.

hadhaa. remainder *n* balance, excess, leavings, remains, remnant, residue, rest, surplus.

hadhayn. overcast *vb* cloud, darken, overshadow.

hadiyad. present *n* donation, favour, gift, grant, gratuity.

aan hadli karin. dumb *adj* inarticulate, mute, silent, soundless, speechless, voiceless.

hadlid. talk *vb* communicate, converse, discuss, gossip, speak. hadal. talk *n* communication, conversation, gossip, speech.

hadlid. speak *vb* articulate, communicate, express, say, talk, tell, utter.

hadrid. jabber *vb* chatter, gabble, prate, prattle.

hafto. instalment *n* payment, portion.

aan hagaagsanayn. imperfect *adj* defective, faulty, impaired.

hagaajin. adjust *vb* adapt, arrange, dispose, rectify; regulate, set right, settle, suit; compose, harmonize, pacify, reconcile, settle; accommodate, adapt, fit, suit.

hagaajin. piece *vb* mend, patch, repair

hagaajin. amend *vb* better, correct, improve, mend, redress, reform.

hagaajin. reform *vb* amend, better, correct, improve, rectify, repair, restore;

hagaamin. captain *vb* command, direct, head, lead, manage, preside. saddex xiddigle. captain *n* chief, chieftain, commander, leader, master, officer.

hagardaamayn. harass *vb* annoy, badger, distress, disturb, molest, pester, plague, tantalize, tease, torment, trouble, vex.

hagardaamayn. torment *vb* distress, badger, harass, irritate, plague, trouble, vex.

haghagid. stammer *vb* falter, hesitate, stutter.

haghago. stammer *n* faltering, hesitation, stutter.

hagid. navigate *vb* cruise, direct, guide, pilot, plan, sail, steer.

hagid. steer *vb* direct, conduct, govern, guide, pilot, point.

hagid. pilot *vb* conduct, navigate, steer.

hagid. guide *vb* conduct, direct, escort, lead, manage, pilot, preside, regulate, rule, steer, superintend, supervise. *n*counsellor, instructor, mentor; guidebook, itinerary, landmark.

hakad. bar *n* grating, rail, rod; barricade, hindrance, impediment, obstacle, obstruction.

hakad. barrier *n* bar, barricade, hindrance, impediment, obstacle, obstruction, stop.

hakad. impediment *n* barrier, block, check, curb, difficulty, hindrance, obstacle, obstruction, stumbling block.

hakad. hindrance *n* check, deterrent, impediment, obstacle, obstruction, restraint, stop, stoppage.

hakad. obstacle *n* barrier, difficulty, hindrance, obstruction, snag, stumbling block.

hakad. barrier *n* block, brake, check, hindrance, impediment, obstacle, obstruction.

hakad. obstruction *n* barrier, hindrance, impediment, obstacle, stoppage.

hakin. stall *vb* block, delay, equivocate, filibuster, hinder,procrastinate, temporize.

hakin. hinder *vb* bar, impede, obstruct, prevent, restrain, retard, stop, thwart.

hakin. obstruct *vb* bar, barricade, block, close, jam, hinder, impede, oppose, prevent, stop; arrest.

hal-abuur leh. imaginative *adj* creative, fanciful, inventive, visionary.

u halgamid. strife *n* battle, combat, conflict, discord, quarrel.

halgamid. struggle *vb* endeavour, strive, toil, try; battle, contend, contest, fight, wrestle.

halgan. battle *n* battle, conflict, contest, fight.

halis aa. critical *adj* crucial, decisive, important.

halis ah. hazardous *adj* dangerous, insecure, perilous, precarious, risky, uncertain, unsafe.

halis ah. poisonous *adj* deadly, fatal, noxious, toxic, venomous.

halis ah. dangerous *adj* hazardous, insecure, perilous, risky, unsafe.

halis ah. deadly *adj* fatal, lethal, mortal, murderous, poisonous, venomous.

halis-gelin. imperil *vb* endanger, expose, hazard, jeopardize, risk.

halis. risk *n* chance, danger, hazard, jeopardy, peril, venture.

halis. danger *n* jeopardy, insecurity, hazard, peril, risk.

halis. menace *n* danger, hazard, peril, nuisance, pest, troublemaker.

halis. peril *n* danger, insecurity, risk.

halis. insecurity *n* danger, hazard, peril; instability, shakiness, weakness, wobbliness.

halis. malignant *adj* dangerous, fatal, virulent.

halkay. instead *adv* in lieu, in place, rather.

halxiraale. puzzle *n* conundrum, labyrinth, maze, problem, riddle.

halxiraale. riddle *n* conundrum, enigma, mystery, puzzle.

hamaansi. yawn *vb* gape, open wide.

hambalyeen. congratulate *vb* compliment, felicitate, gratulate, greet, hail, salute.

hambalyen. compliment *vb* commend, congratulate, flatter, praise.

hambalyo. compliment *n* commendation, honour, tribute.

hammo badan. ambitious *adj* aspiring, avid, eager, intent.

handaraab. handle *n* hilt.

hanjebaad. threat *n* intimidation, menace..

u hanjebid. threaten *vb* endanger, intimidate, menace; forebode, foreshadow, presage, warn.

hanti. property *n* assets, belongings, effects, estate, goods, possessions, resources, wealth.

hardan. skirmish *n* affray, fight, scuffle, tussle.

harddan. combat *vb* contest, fight, struggle; oppose, resist, withstand.

hareeraha. around *prep* about, encircling, encompassing, round, surrounding.

hargoodka. bond *n* link, tie, union, yoke; servitude, subjection.

harraad. thirst *n* aridity, dryness; craving, desire, longing, yearning. *adj* arid, dry, parched; eager, longing, yearning.

hawl kar. active *adj* busy, diligent, industrious.

hawl kar. industrious *adj* diligent, hard-working, busy.

hawl kar. efficient *adj* capable, competent, effective; able, skilful.

hawl-gal. operation *n* manipulation, procedure, process.

hawo siin. ventilate *vb* aerate, air, freshen, purify; comment, discuss, publish, review.

hawo-raacid. waft *vb* carry, convey, drift, float, transmit, transport.

hawo. waft *n* breath, breeze, draught, puff.

hawo. air *n* atmosphere, breeze; appearance, aspect, manner; melody, tune.

haybad leh. imperial *adj* kingly, regal, royal, sovereign.

haybad leh. sublime *adj* exalted, glorious, grand, great, lofty, majestic, noble.

haybadle. majestic *adj* august, dignified, imperial, imposing.

hayn. keep *vb* confine, hold, preserve, restrain, retain, withhold; guard, protect; care for, maintain, support, sustain.

haysasho. withhold *vb* repress, restrain, retain, suppress.

ku dul heehaaw. hover *vb* flutter; hang; vacillate, waver.

heer sare ah. superb *adj* fine, gorgeous, grand, magnificent, majestic, noble, splendid, sumptuous.

heer. rank *n* position, reputation, standard, status.

heer. degree *n* class, grade, rank, standing, station.

heerka ugu sarreeya. extreme *adj* drastic, excessive, extravagant, immoderate, outrageous, radical.

heesid. warble *vb* sing, trill, yodel.

heesid. chant *vb* sing, warble; intone, recite.

la heli karo. available *adj* accessible, advantageous, applicable, beneficial, profitable, serviceable, useful.

ka helid. like *vb* cherish, desire, fancy, enjoy, love, please, prefer.

helid. gain *vba* attain, earn, get, net, obtain, procure, profit, reach, win.

helid. recover *vb* restore, revive; rescue, salvage, save; convalesce, recuperate.

helid. get *vb* achieve, acquire, attain, earn, gain, obtain, procure, receive, secure, win.

helid. procure *vb* acquire, gain, get, obtain.

helid. obtain *vb* acquire, attain, bring, earn, gain, get.

ka helid. wonder *vb* admire, gape, marvel; conjecture, ponder, query, question, speculate.

soo helid. discover *vb* ascertain, discern, see.

ka helid. admire *vb* approve, esteem, respect; adore, prize, cherish, revere, treasure. allowance, assent, avowal, concession.

ka helid. fond *adj* affectionate, amorous, doting, loving, tender.

helid. incur *vb* acquire, bring, contract.

helid. find *vb* discover, fall upon; gain, get, obtain, procure. *n* acquisition, catch, discovery.

helid. acquire *vb* achieve, attain, earn, gain, gather, get, have, obtain, procure, realize, secure, win; accomplish, learn thoroughly, master.

ku heshiin. coincide *vb* agree, harmonize, concur.

heshiis. correspondence *n* communication, letters, writing.

heshiis. unison *n* accord, accordance, agreement, concord, harmony.

heshiis. unanimity *n* accord, agreement, concord, union, unity.

heshiis. treaty *n* agreement, alliance, concordat, convention, league, pact.

heshiis. agreement *n* accordance, compliance, concord, harmony, union; bargain, compact, contract, pact, treaty.

heshiis. tune *n* air, aria, melody, strain; agreement, concord, harmony.

heshiis. pact *n* agreement, alliance, bargain, bond, covenant.

heshiis la'aan. disagreement *n* argument, clashing, conflict, dispute, misunderstanding, quarrel, wrangle.

u hibayn. dedicate *vb* devote, hallow, sanctify.

hibo leh. gifted *adj* able, capable, clever, ingenious, intelligent, inventive, sagacious, talented.

hibo. endowment *n* bequest, gift, grant, largesse, present; foundation, fund; qualification, quality, talent.

hilmaam badan. forgetful *adj* careless, heedless, inattentive, mindless, neglectful, negligent, oblivious, unmindful.

himilo. aspiration *n* aim, ambition, craving, desire, hankering, hope, longing.

hindise. design *n* drawing, outline, plan, sketch; invention.

hindisid. model *vb* design, mould, plan, shape.

hindisid. design *vb* draw, outline, sketch, trace.

hinraag. pant *n* gasp.

hlimaam. omission *n* failure, forgetfulness, neglect, oversight.

aan hobboonayn. inappropriate *adj* inapposite, unbecoming, unfit, unsuitable.

hog. hole *n* aperture, opening, perforation; abyss, cave, cavern, cavity, chasm, depression, excavation, hollow, pit, pore, void; burrow, cover, den, lair, retreat; hovel, kennel.

hoggaamin. rule *vb* command, control, govern, reign; prevail, predominate.

hoggaamin. head *vb* command, control, direct, govern, guide, lead, rule.

hoggaamin. lead *vb* conduct, deliver, direct, draw, escort, guide; front, head, precede.

hoggaaminaaya. leading *adj* capital, chief, first, foremost, highest, principal, superior.

hoggaamiye. leader *n* conductor, director, guide; captain, chief, chieftain, commander, head.

hoggaamiye. ruler *n* chief, governor, king, lord, master, monarch; controller, guide, rule.

hoggaan. leadership *n* direction, guidance.

holac. flame *n* blaze, brightness, fire, flare.

holcin. flare *vb* blaze, flicker, flutter, waver; dazzle, flame, glare; splay, spread, widen. *n* blaze, dazzle, flame, glare.

hollac. blaze *n* flame, flare, flash, glow, light.

homarid. precede *vb* antedate, head, herald, introduce, lead.

hoo u dagid. ebb *vb* recede, subside, wane.

ka hoorjeesi. oppose *vb* combat, dispute, obstruct, resist, thwart, withstand.

hoos. bottom *adj* base, basic, ground, lowest.

hoos u dhicid. wane *vb* abate, decrease, ebb, subside; decline, fail, sink. *n* decrease, diminution, lessening.

hoos u dhicid. subside *vb* settle, sink; abate, decrease, diminish, drop, fall, lessen, wane.

hoos u gedis. upside down *adj* confused, head over heels, inverted, topsy-turvy.

hoos u hadal. mutter *vb* grumble, muffle, mumble, murmur.

hoos. under *prep* below, beneath, subordinate to, underneath. *adv* below, beneath, down, lower.

ka hooseeya. subordinate *adj* ancillary, inferior, junior, minor, subsidiary.

ka hooseeya. beneath *prep* below, under, underneath; unbecoming, unbefitting, unworthy. hoos. beneath *adv* below, underneath.

hooseeya. inferior *adj* junior, minor, secondary, subordinate; deficient, imperfect, mediocre, second-rate, shabby.

hooseya. menial *adj* base, low, mean, servile, vile.

hooy siin. accommodate *vb* contain, furnish, hold, oblige, serve, supply; adapt, fit, suit; adjust, compose, harmonize, reconcile, settle.

hooy. sanctuary, shelter *n* asylum, protection, refuge.

hooyonimo. maternal *adj* motherlike, motherly.

hooysiin. harbour *vb* protect, lodge, shelter.

hor u kac. improvement *n* advancement, amendment, betterment, progress.

hordhac. prologue *n* foreword, introduction, preamble, preface, preliminary, prelude.

hordhac. introduction *n* preface, prelude; presentation.

hore u socod. proceed *vb* advance, continue, go, pass, progress.

hore. previous *adj* earlier, foregoing, former, preceding, prior.

hore. forward *adj* front, fore, head; eager, earnest, hasty, impulsive, quick; bold, brazen, confident, impertinent, presumptuous, presuming. *adv* ahead, onward.

hore. former *adj* antecedent, earlier, foregoing, preceding, previous, prior; late, old-time; bygone, foregone, gone, past, previous.

iska horimaad. encounter *n* clash, collision, meeting; brush, combat, conflict, contest, dispute, engagement, skirmish.

horjooge. mentor *n* adviser, counsellor, guide, instructor, monitor.

horjooge. monitor *n* adviser, counsellor, instructor, mentor, overseer.

ugu horreeya. foremost *adj* first, front, highest, leading, main, principal.

is hortaagid. avoid *vb* dodge, elude, escape, eschew, shun; forebear, refrain from.

ka hortag. prevention *n* obstruction, preclusion, prohibition, restriction, stoppage.

ka hortagid. prevent *vb* bar, check, debar, deter, forestall, hinder, impede, prohibit, restrain, save, stop, thwart.

horumar. advance *adj* beforehand, forward, leading.

horumar. advance *n* march, progress; advancement, enhancement, growth, promotion, rise; offer, overture, proffering, proposal, proposition, tender; appreciation, rise.

horumarid. progress *vb* advance, better, gain, improve.

horumarin. advance *vb* propel, push, send forward; aggrandize, dignify, elevate, exalt, promote; benefit, forward, further, improve, promote

horyaal. champion *n* hero, victor, warrior, winner.

horyaal. victor *n* champion, conqueror, vanquisher, winner.

hoy-siin. house *vb* harbour, lodge, protect, shelter.

hoy. refuge *n* asylum, harbour, haven, protection, retreat, safety, sanctuary, security, shelter.

hoy. shelter *n* asylum, cover, harbour, haven, refuge, safety.

hoysiin. shelter *vb* harbour, hide, protect, screen.

hubaal. definite *adj* certain, exact, positive, precise, specific.

hubaal. assurance *n* certainty, conviction, persuasion, pledge, promise; arrogance, brass, boldness, effrontery, face, front, impudence.

hubaal. certain *adj* absolute, incontestable, indisputable, indubitable, positive, undeniable, unquestionable; assured, confident, sure.

hubin. check *vb* block, control, counteract, curb, hinder, obstruct, restrain; chide, rebuke, reprimand, reprove.

la hubo. really *adv* absolutely, certainly, indeed, positively, truly.

la hubo. infallible *adj* certain, indubitable, oracular, sure, unerring.

hunguri weyn. avid *adj* eager, greedy, voracious.

hunguri weyn. greed, greediness *n* gluttony, hunger, ravenousness, voracity; averice, covetousness, desire, selfishness.

hunguri weyn. predatory *adj* greedy, rapacious, ravaging, ravenous, voracious.

hunguri weyni. greedy *adj* desirous, eager; avaricious, grasping, rapacious, selfish.

hurda. drowsy *adj* dozy, sleepy; comatose, lethargic, stupid, soporific.

hurdaysan. sleepy *adj* comatose, dozy, drowsy, heavy, somnolent.

hurdo keenaaya. soporific *adj* hypnotic, narcotic, opiate, sleep-inducing.

hurdo. snooze *n* catnap, nap, sleep, slumber.

huruuf. scowl *n* frown, glower.

huruufid. scowl *vb* frown, glower.

I

ibir. nothing *n* nonentity, nonexistence, nothingness; bagatelle, trifle.

ifaaya. luminous *adj* incandescent, radiant, resplendent, shining; bright, brilliant, clear, lucid.

ifaaya. brilliant *adj* beaming, bright, dazzling, gleaming, glistening, glittering, lustrous, radiant, shining, sparkling, splendid; admirable, glorious, illustrious, renowned.

ifaaya. shiny *adj* bright, brilliant, burnished, glossy, polished.

ifaaya. radiant *adj* beaming, brilliant, glittering, lustrous, shining, happy.

ifid. twinkle *vb* flash, glimmer, scintillate, sparkle.

ifid. glow *vb* radiate, shine; blush, burn, flush, redden.

ifid. shine *vb* beam, give light, gleam, glisten, glitter, glow, sparkle.

ifid. radiate *vb* beam, gleam, glitter, shine; spread.

iftiimid. gleam *vb* glimmer, glitter, shine, sparkle.

iftiin. beam *n* flash, glimmer, gleam, glow, ray; brightness, lustre, splendour.

iftiin. twinkle *n* gleam, glimmer, sparkle.

iftiin. brightness *n* gloss, polish, sheen, shine.

iftin. bright *adj* clear, fair, light, luminous, pale, whitish.

iibin. trade *vb* bargain, barter, deal, exchange, sell.

iibin. vend *vb* dispose, hawk, retail, sell.

iibsasho. purchase *vb* buy, get, obtain, pay for, procure.

iin. handicap *n* disadvantage, encumbrance, hindrance, restriction.

iin. blemish *n* blot, defect, disfigurement, fault, flaw, imperfection, spot, stain.

ijaarid. rent *vb* hire, lease, let.

ijaarid. hire *vb* rent; charter, employ, engage, lease, let.

ikhtiraacid. invent *vb* concoct, contrive, design, devise, discover, fabricate, find out, frame, originate.

il-dhuuf. oversight *n* blunder, error, fault, lapse, miss, mistake, omission, slip.

ilaa. except *conj* unless.

ilaalin. monitor *vb* check, observe, oversee, supervise, watch.

ilaalin. secure *vb* protect, safeguard; fasten.

ilaalin. guard *vb* defend, keep, patrol, protect, safeguard, shield, watch.

ilaalin. watch *vb* attend, guard, oversee, protect, superintend; eye, mark, observe.

ilaalin. safeguard *vb* guard, protect.

ilaalin. custody *n* care, charge, guardianship, safe-keeping, protection; confinement, imprisonment.

ilaalin. preserve *vb* defend, guard, keep, protect, rescue, save, secure, shield; maintain, uphold, sustain, support.

ilaaliye. guard *n* protection, rampart, safeguard, shield; keeper, guardian, patrol, sentinel, sentry, warden, watchman.

ilaaliye. guardian *n* custodian, defender, guard, keeper, preserver, protector, trustee, warden.

ilaaliye. keeper *n* caretaker, curator, custodian, defender, gaolkeeper, governor, guardian, jailer, superintendent, warden, warder, watchman.

ilaaliye. protector *n* champion, custodian, defender, guardian, patron, warden.

ilays. ray *n* beam, moonbeam, shaft, streak, sunbeam.

ilbax ah. refined *adj* courtly, cultured, genteel, polite.

ilbaxnimo la'aan. barbaric *adj* rude, savage, uncivilized, uncouth, untamed, wild.

ilbixin. civilize *vb* cultivate, educate, enlighten, humanize, improve, polish, refine.

ilbixin. humanize *vb* civilize, cultivate, educate, enlighten, improve, polish, reclaim, refine, soften.

ilka caddayn. smile *vb* grin, laugh, simper, smirk.

illaalin. attend *vb* accompany, escort, follow; guard, protect, watch; minister to, serve, wait on; give heed, hear, harken, listen; be attendant, serve, tend, wait.

ilma-aragto (wax aad iyo aad u yar). microscopic *adj* infinitesimal, minute, tiny.

ilmo. babe *n* child, ingénue.

ilmo. infant *n* babe, baby, bairn, brat, minor, tot.

ilmo. child *n* babe, baby, bairn, infant, offspring, progeny.

isu imaatin. coalesce *vb* amalgamate, blend, combine, mix, unite; concur, fraternize.

imaatin. arrive *vb* attain, come, get to, reach.

imow. come *vb* advance, approach.

imtixaan. test *n* examination, experiment, ordeal, trial.

imtixaanid. test *vb* examine, prove, try.

indho tirid. blind *vb* deprive of sight; blindfold, hoodwink.

indho-cawarid. dazzle *vb* blind, daze; astonish, confound, overpower, surprise.

indhoole. blind *adj* eyeless, sightless, unseeing; ignorant; concealed, dark, dim, obscure; careless, headlong, heedless, thoughtless.

inkastoo. although *conj* albeit, even if, for all that, notwithstanding, though.

inqilaab. revolution *n* coup, insurrection, mutiny, rebellion, uprising.

inqilaabid. overthrow *vb* overturn, upset, subvert; demolish, destroy, subjugate, vanquish.

inyar. bit *n* crumb, fragment, morsel, piece, scrap; grain, jot, mite, particle; instant, minute, moment, second.

irid. entrance *n* access, approach, avenue, aperture, door, doorway, entry, gate, hallway, lobby, mouth, passage, portal, vestibule; beginning, commencement, introduction.

is dhex gelid. intermingle *vb* blend, commingle, commix, intermix, mingle, mix.

is gedgeddiyaya. variable *adj* changeable, mutable, alterable; capricious, fickle, fluctuating, shifting, vacillating.

is le'eg. equal *adj* alike, equivalent, like; even, level, uniform; even-handed, fair, impartial, just, unbiased; corresponding, parallel. *n* match, peer.

is qorid. embark *vb* engage, enlist.

is-afgarad waa. variance *n* disagreement, difference, discord, dissension, incompatibility, jarring, strife.

is-bedel weyn oo degdega. upheaval *n* cataclysm, convulsion, disorder, eruption, explosion, outburst, overthrow.

is-casilid. abdicate *vb* abandon, cede, forgo, forsake, give up, quit, relinquish, renounce, resign, retire, surrender.

is-dhiib. surrender *n* capitulation, cession, delivery, relinquishment, resignation, yielding.

is-dhiibid. surrender *vb* capitulate, cede, forgo, relinquish, resign, yield.

is-faanin. pride *vb* boast, brag, crow, preen, revel in.

is-hortaagid. confront *vb* face, challenge, encounter, oppose, threaten.

is-qorid. enrol *vb* engage, enlist, register.

isbahaysi. alliance *n* affinity, intermarriage, relation; coalition, combination, confederacy, league, treaty, union; affiliation, connection, relationship, similarity.

isbahaysi. ally *vb* combine, connect, join, league, marry, unite.

isbarbardhig. contrast *vb* compare, differentiate, distinguish, oppose.

isbarid. present *vb* introduce, nominate; exhibit, offer; give, grant; express, prefer, proffer, tender.

aan isbedelin. invariable *adj* changeless, constant, unchanging, uniform, unvarying.

isburin. contradict *vb* challenge, dispute; counteract, oppose, thwart.

isdabajoog. perpetual *adj* ceaseless, continual, constant, incessant, interminable, uninterrupted.

wax isdhaafsi. barter *vb* bargain, exchange, sell, trade.

isdhiib. submission *n* capitulation, cession, surrender; acquiescence, compliance, obedience, resignation. submissive adj compliant, docile, obedient, passive, tame, uncomplaining.

isdiidsin. ignore *vb* disregard, neglect, overlook, reject, skip.

isha. eye *n* aperture, eyelet, peephole, perforation.

isha. source *n* beginning, fountainhead, origin, root, wellspring.

isir. parentage *n* ancestry, family, lineage, origin.

isir. ancestor *n* father, forebear, forefather, progenitor.

iska dhigid. impersonate *vb* ape, imitate, mimic, mock, personify, typify.

iska dhigid. pretend *vb* dissemble, falsify, feign, sham, simulate, imagine, lie, claim.

iska indho tirid. overlook *vb* disregard, miss, neglect; excuse, forgive, pardon.

iska jirid. beware *vb* avoid, heed, look out, mind.

iska-tuurid. scrap *vb* discard, drop, junk, trash.

iskaashi. cooperation *n* assistance, concurrence, collaboration.

iskaashi. cooperate *vb* abet, collaborate, combine, concur, conspire, help.

isku beddelid. interchange *vb* alternate, change, exchange, vary.

isku dar. blend *vb* amalgamate, combine, fuse, mix, unite.

isku dayid. venture *vb* dare, hazard, risk, speculate, try, undertake.

isku duwid. group *vb* arrange, assemble, dispose, order.

isku kalsoon. self-possessed *adj* calm, collected, composed, cool, unruffled.

isku mid ah. same *adj* ditto, identical, selfsame; corresponding, like.

isku mid. sameness *n* monotony, resemblance, selfsameness, uniformity.

isku xidh. bunch *vb* assemble, collect, crowd, group, pack.

isku xidhid. yoke *vb* connect, couple, harness, join, link, unite.

isku xirid. brace *vb* make tight, tighten; reinforce, strengthen, support, truss.

isku xirid. lace *vb* bind, fasten, intertwine, tie, twine.

isku xirid. muster *vb* assemble, collect, congregate, gather, marshal, meet, rally, summon. * *n* assembly, collection, gathering, meeting, rally.

isku-day. try *n* attempt, effort, trial.

isku-dayid. try *vb* examine, test; attempt, endeavour, strain, strive.

isku-mid ah. identical *adj* equivalent, same, selfsame.

isku-tag. union *n* combination, incorporation, joining, unification, uniting.

iskudarid. combine *vb* cooperate, merge, pool, unite; amalgamate, blend, incorporate, mix.

iskudarid. mix *vb* combine, incorporate, mingle, unite; associate, join, unite.

iskuday. attempt *n* aim. effort, endeavour, exertion, struggle, trial.

iskuduwid. coordinate *vb* harmonize, integrate, synchronize.

iskujir *n* compound, mixture; hotchpotch, jumble, medley; variety.

isla markii ba. immediately *adv* closely, directly, forthwith, instantly, presently, presto, pronto.

isla weyni. conceited *adj* egotistical, opinionated, overweening, self-conceited, vain,

islaweyne. haughty *adj* arrogant, imperious, lofty, proud, scornful, snobbish.

islaweyni. self-important *adj* conceited, pompous, overbearing.

islaweyni. proud *adj* conceited, egotistical, overweening, self-conscious, self-satisfied, vain; arrogant, boastful, haughty, uppish.

islaweyni. overbearing *adj* overpowering; arrogant, dictatorial, dogmatic, domineering, haughty, imperious, overweening, proud.

islaweyni. pride *n* conceit, egotism, self-importance, vanity; arrogance, disdain, haughtiness, insolence, pomposity.

islaweyni. egotistic, egotistical *adj* conceited, opinionated, self-asserting, self-admiring, self-centred, self-important, vain.

isleeg. symmetry *n* balance, evenness, harmony, order, parallelism, proportion.

aan isleekayn. unequal *adj* disproportionate, disproportioned, ill-matched, uneven.

ismoogaysiin. slight *vb* cold-shoulder, disdain, neglect, snub.

ismuujin. parade *vb* display, vaunt.

isqaab geddiyin. disguise *n* mask, veil; masquerade, pretence, veneer.

isqaadhsin. communication *n* conversation, correspondence, intercourse; announcement, dispatch, information, message, news.

istagid. pose *n* attitude, posture, affectation, mannerism, pretence.

istic maalid. treat *vb* handle, manage, use.

isticmaal. usage *n* custom, habit, method, mode, practice, tradition, use.

wax la isticmaalay. spent *adj* exhausted, fatigued, played out, used up, wearied, worn out.

isticmaalid. wield *vb* brandish, flourish, handle, manipulate, ply, work; control, manage, sway, use.

isticmaalid. apply *vb* bestow, lay upon; appropriate, convert, employ, exercise, use; addict, address, dedicate, devote, direct, engage.

isticmaalid. exploit *vb* use, utilize.

isticmaalid. use *vb* apply, avail oneself of, employ, handle, operate, utilize, work.

isticmaalid. consume *vb* destroy, devour, exhaust, expend, spend.

isticmaalid. utilize *vb* employ, exploit, make use of, put to use, turn to account, use.

istus ah. showy *adj* dressy, flashy, garish, gaudy.

istusid. ostentatious *adj* flaunting, pompous, pretentious, showy, vain; gaudy.

istusid. pretentious *adj* affected, conceited, ostentatious, showy, tawdry, unnatural, vain.

isu bogid. smug *adj* complacent, self-satisfied.

isu dhiibid. submit *vb* accede, capitulate, comply, surrender, yield.

isu eekaan. similarity *n* analogy, likeness, resemblance, sameness, similitude.

isu eg. alike *adj* akin, analogous, duplicate, identical, resembling, similar.

aan isu ekayn. dissimilar *adj* different, divergent, diverse, heterogeneous, unlike, various.

isugeyn. incorporate *vb* affiliate, amalgamate, blend, combine, consolidate, include, merge, mix, unite.

isu tagid. unite *vb* amalgamate, coalesce, combine, confederate, incorporate, merge, link, join.

isugeyn. fuse *vb* amalgamate, blend, coalesce, combine, commingle, intermingle, intermix, merge, unite.

isugeyne. consolidate *vb* condense, combine, fuse, unite.

isururin. marshal *vb* arrange, array, gather, muster;

wax isweydarsi. traffic *vb* deal, exchange, trade.

ixtiraam weyn. veneration *n* adoration, devotion, esteem, respect, reverence, worship.

ixtiraamid. respect *vb* admire, esteem, honour, regard, revere, value, venerate.

ixtraam darr. disrespect *n* discourteousness, impertinence, impolite, rudeness.

J

jaahil. illiterate *adj* ignorant, uneducated.

jaahil. ignorant *adj* illiterate, unaware, uneducated, uninformed, unlearned, unread, untaught.

jaajaalayn. jest *vb* banter, joke, quiz.

jaajaale. zany *adj* comic, comical, crazy, droll, eccentric, scatterbrained. khudhuuc. zeal *n* alacrity, ardour, devotion, eagerness, energy, enthusiasm, fervour, warmth.

jaalle. comrade *n* accomplice, ally, associate, chum, companion, compatriot, crony, mate, pal.

jaamici. graduate *n* alumna, alumnus, degree-holder, laureate, postgraduate.

jaariyad. domestic *n* charwoman, help, home help, maid, servant.

jab. fragment *n* bit, chip, fraction, morsel, part, piece, remnant, scrap.

jab. downfall *n* defeat, overthrow.

jaban. broken *adj* fractured, rent, ruptured, separated, severed, shattered; defective, imperfect.

jaban. cheap *adj* inexpensive, low-priced; common, inferior, mean.

jabi kara. fragile *adj* breakable, brittle, delicate, frangible; feeble, frail, infirm, weak.

jabid. fracture *vb* break, crack, split.

jabin. snap *vb* break, crack, fracture.

jabin. crack *vb* break, cleave, split; snap.

jabin. reverse *n* calamity, defeat.

jabin. violate *vb* break, disobey, infringe, invade; desecrate, pollute, profane; abuse, debauch, deflower, outrage, ravish.

jadwal. plan *n* catalogue, inventory, record, register, timetable.

jadwal. table *n* chart, list, schedule, syllabus, tabulation.

jahli ka saarid. enlighten *vb* illuminate, illumine; educate, civilize, inform, instruct, teach.

jajabin. break *vb* crack, fracture, sever; shatter, smash; infringe, transgress, violate; disclose, open, unfold.

jalaafayn. undermine *vb* demoralize, foil, frustrate, thwart, weaken.

jalleecid. glance *vb* gaze, glimpse, look, view.

u janjeedh. tendency *n* bent, bias, course, disposition, direction, drift, inclination, leaning, proneness.

janjeedhin. tilt *vb* incline, slant, slope.

janjeedhin. incline *vb* lean, slant, slope; gradient, rise.

janjeerdhin. tip *vb* cant, incline, overturn, tilt, upset.

janno. heaven *n* firmament, sky; bliss, ecstasy, happiness, paradise, rapture, transport

jarid. slit *vb* cut, gash, slash, split.

ka jarid. subtract *vb* deduct, detract, diminish, remove, take, withdraw.

jarid. cut *vb* carve, chop, cleave, divide, incise, lance, sever, slice, slit, wound.

jarid. chop *vb* cut, hack, hew.

jarid. slash *vb* cut, gash, slit.

jarid. fell *vb* cut, demolish, hew.

jarjarid. carve *vb* cut, divide, engrave, incise, sculptur, shape.

jarjarid. mince *vb* chop, cut.

jarrid. knife *vb* cut, slash, stab.

jawaab. reply *n* acknowledgement, answer, response, retort.

jawaab. answer *n* rejoinder, reply, response, retort; confutation, rebuttal, refutation.

ka jawaabid. respond *vb* answer, reply, rejoin; correspond.

ka jawaabid. reply *vb* answer, echo, respond.

jawaabid. answer *vb* fulfil, rejoin, reply, respond, satisfy.

jecayl. love *n* affection, courtship, fondness, friendship, tenderness, warmth.

jecel aargoosiga. vindictive *adj* avenging, malicious, spiteful, unforgiving, unrelenting, vengeful.

jecel. love *vb* adore, like, worship.

loogu jecelyahay. favourite *adj* beloved, choice, fancied, pet, preferred.

la jecelyahay. darling *adj* beloved, cherished, dear, loved, precious, treasured.

la jeclaan karo. desirable *adj* agreeable, beneficial, eligible, enviable, good, pleasing, preferable.

jeclaan. affection *n* bent, bias, feeling, inclination, passion, proclivity, propensity; accident, attribute, character, mark, modification, mode, note, property; attachment, endearment, fondness, goodwill, kindness, partiality, love.

jeclaysi. itching *n* craving, longing, teasing desire.

jecleysi. admiration *n* affection, approbation, approval, astonishment, delight, esteem, pleasure, regard.

ku soo jeedanaaya. irresistible *adj* overpowering, overwhelming.

soo jeedin. suggest *vb* advise, advocate, hint, indicate, prompt, propose, recommend.

jeermi ka diliíd. disinfect *vb* cleanse, deodorize, fumigate, purify, sterilize.

jeexid. shred *vb* tear.

jeexid. tear *vb* burst, slit, rend, rip.

jiditaan. tug *n* drag, haul, pull, tow, wrench.

soo jiidasho. attract *vb* draw, pull; allure, captivate, charm, decoy, enamour, endear, entice, engage, fascinate, invite, win.

soo jiidasho. lure *vb* allure, attract, decoy, entice, inveigle, seduce, tempt.

jiidid. tow *vb* drag, draw, haul, pull, tug.

jiidid. tug *vb* drag, draw, haul, pull, tow, wrench.

ka soo jiidid. pluck *vb* cull, gather, pick; jerk, pull, snatch, tear, tug, twitch.

jiidis. haul *vb* drag, draw, lug, pull, tow, tug.

kala jiidis. tense *adj* rigid, stiff, stretched, taut; excited, intent, nervous.

jiidis. drag *vb* draw, haul, pull, tow, tug. *n* brake, check, curb, resistance, retardation, slackening, slack-off, slowing.

jiidmiya. elastic *adj* rebounding, recoiling, springy.

jiifsad. lie *vb* recline, repose, rest.

jiil. generation *n* age, epoch, era, period, time.

jilicsan. soft *adj* pliable, yielding; delicate, gentle, lenient, mild, tender.

jilicsan. vulnerable *adj* assailable, defenceless, exposed, weak.

jilicsan. tender *adj* delicate, fragile, soft; compassionate, gentle, loving, sensitive, sympathetic.

jilicsan. dainty *adj* delicate, nice, charming, neat.

jilicsan. delicate *adj* fine, nice; dainty, fragile, frail, refined, slight, tender.

jilicsan. yielding *adj* compliant, passive, submissive, unresisting; bending, flexible, pliant, soft, supple, tractable.

jilicsan. brittle *adj* breakable, crumbling, fragile, frail.

jilicsan. venerable *adj* respected, revered, sage, wise; aged, old, patriarchal.

jilid. stage *vb* dramatize, perform, present, produce, put on.

jilid. performance *n* execution, fulfilment; acting, entertainment, play.

jilid. acting *n* enacting, impersonation, performance, portrayal; imitation, pretence.

jilid. mimic *vb* ape, imitate, impersonate, mime, mock, parody. *n* imitator, impersonator, mime, parrot.

jimicsi. exercise *vb* exert, practise.

jiran. ill *adj* ailing, indisposed, sick, unwell. *adv* badly, poorly, unfortunately.

jirid. last *vb* abide, continue, endure, persist, prevail, survive.

jirid. exist *vb* be, breathe, live; endure, last, remain.

jirjiroole. volatile *adj* capricious, changeable, fickle, flighty, light-headed, mercurial, unsteady, wild.

jirran. morbid *adj* ailing, corrupted, diseased, sick, sickly, tainted, unhealthy, unsound, vitiated; depressed, downcast, gloomy, pessimistic, sensitive.

jirrid. stem *n* axis, branch, shoot, stalk, trunk.

jirro. illness *n* ailment, complaint, disease, disorder, indisposition, malady, sickness.

jirro. malady *n* affliction, ail, ailment, complaint

jooga. present *adj* actual, current, existing, immediate; available, quick, ready. hadda. now *n* present, time being, today.

joogga qofka. stature *n* height, physique, size, tallness; altitude, consequence, eminence, prominence.

joogid. stay *vb* abide, dwell, lodge, rest, sojourn, tarry; arrest, check, curb, hold, keep in, prevent, rein in, restrain, withhold; hold up, prop, shore up, support.

joogid. remain *vb* endure, last, stay; continue, halt, rest, sojourn, stay, stop, tarry, wait.

joogid. linger *vb* dally, dawdle, delay, idle, lag, loiter, remain, saunter, stay, tarry, wait.

joogsi. hindrance *n* block, obstruction, impediment, obstacle.

joogsi. standstill *n* cessation, interruption, stand, stop; deadlock.

joogsi. halt *n* end, impasse, pause, standstill, stop.

joogta ah. ceaseless *adj* continual, continuous, incessant, uninterrupted; endless, eternal, everlasting, perpetual.

joogta ah. routine *adj* conventional, familiar, habitual, ordinary, standard, typical, usual; boring, dull, humdrum, predictable, tiresome.

joogta ah. incessant *adj* ceaseless, constant, continual, continuous, never-ending, perpetual, uninterrupted, unremitting.

joogta ah. persistent *adj* constant, continuing, steady, tenacious; dogged, indefatigable, pertinacious. personable *adj* comely, good-looking, graceful, seemly, well-turned-out.

joogta ah. constant *adj* abiding, enduring, fixed, invariable, permanent, perpetual, stable, unchanging, unvaried; devoted, faithful, loyal, true, trusty.

aan joogta ahayn. temporary *adj* brief, fleeting, impermanent, momentary, short-lived, transient.

aan joogta ahayn. spasmodic *adj* convulsive, erratic, fitful, intermittent, irregular, sporadic.

joogto ah. permanent *adj* constant, durable, fixed, immutable, stable, unchanging.

joogto. perennial *adj* constant, enduring, lasting, permanent, perpetual.

joojin. inhibit *vb* bar, check, debar, hinder, obstruct, prevent, repress, restrain, stop; forbid, prohibit.

joojin. embargo *n* ban, bar, blockade, exclusion, hindrance, impediment, prohibition, stoppage.

ka joojin. disqualify *vb* disenable, incapacitate, preclude, prohibit.

joojin. cease *vb* desist, refrain, stop; discontinue, end, quit, terminate.

joojin. halt *vb* cease, desist, rest, stand, stop.

ka joojin. bar *vb* exclude, hinder, obstruct, prevent, prohibit, restrain, stop.

joojin. stop *vb* block, obstruct, halt, hold, pause, stall, stay; bar, hinder, impede, intercept, interrupt, obstruct.

joojin. stagnate *vb* idle, languish, rot, stand still, vegetate.

ka joojin. deter *vb* debar, discourage, frighten, hinder, prevent, restrain, stop, withhold.

joojin. impede *vb* bar, block, check, clog, hinder, interrupt, obstruct.

jornaal. periodical *n* magazine, paper, review, serial, weekly.

jujuub. coercion *n* compulsion, force.

K

ka dib. after *prep* later than, subsequent to; behind, following; about, according to; because of, in imitation of. *adj* behind, consecutive, ensuing, following, later, succeeding, successive, subsequent; aft, back, hind, rear, rearmost, tail. *adv* afterwards, later, next, since, subsequently, then, thereafter.

ka kooban. comprise *vb* contain, include, involve.

ka xun. dismal *adj* cheerless, dark, dreary, dull, gloomy; blue, doleful, dolorous, melancholy, mournful, sad, sombre, sorrowful.

ka yar. minor *adj* less, smaller; inferior, junior, younger; petty, unimportant, small.

ka-hor-jeedid. rival *vb* emulate, match, oppose.

ka-sii-badan. further *adj* additional. *adv* also, besides, farther, furthermore, moreover.

kaafirnimo. infidelity *n* adultery, disloyality, faithlessness, treachery, unfaithfulness.

kaaliso. nurse *n* auxiliary, orderly, sister; amah, *au pair*, babysitter, nanny, nursemaid, nurserymaid,

kaaliye. subordinate *n* assistant, inferior, junior, underling.

kaaliye. assastant *n* aider, ally, associate, coadjutor, colleague, friend, partner.

kaaliye. assistant *n* backer, supporter.

kaalmayn. aid *vb* assist, help, serve, support; relieve, succour; advance, facilitate, further, promote.

kaalmo. relief *n* aid, assistance, comfort, deliverance, help, respite, rest, succour.

kaalmo. maintenance *n* defence, preservation, support, sustenance, bread, food, provisions.

kaalmo. aid *n* assistance, cooperation, help, patronage; alms, subsidy, succour, relief.

kaamil ah. utter *adj* complete, entire, perfect, total; absolute, downright, unconditional, unqualified, total.

kacaan. rebellion *n* revolution, uprising.

kacaanyahan. radical *n* fanatic, revolutionary.

kacdoomid. mutinous *adj* insubordinate, insurgent, rebellious, riotous, seditious, turbulent, unruly.

kacdoon. rebellion *n* anarchy, insurrection, mutiny, resistance, revolt, revolution, uprising.

kacsan. hectic *adj* animated, excited, feverish.

kacsan. raving *adj* delirious, deranged, frenzied, mad.

kacsan. stormy *adj* furious, passionate, squally, tempestuous, riotous, rough, turbulent, violent, wild.

kacsan. frantic *adj* distraught, frenzied, furious, mad. phrenetic, raging, raving, wild.

kacsan. turbulent *adj* agitated, restless, stormy, tumultuous, wild; boisterous, disorderly, rebellious, violent.

kafiil. sponsor *n* backer, guarantor, patron, promoter.

kafiilasho. sponsor *vb* back, finance, guarantee, promote, support.

kaftamid. joke *vb* banter, jest, frolic.

kaftamid. chat *vb* babble, chatter, gossip.

kaftan qosol leh. joke *n* jest, pleasantry, prank, quip, riddle, witticism.

kaftan. chat *n* chit-chat, conversation, gossip.

ku kajamid. ridicule *vb* deride, disparage, jeer, mock, lampoon, satirize, taunt.

kakarin. boil *vb* aggitate, bubble, foam, froth, rage, seethe, simmer.

kal furid. detach *vb* disengage, disconnect, disjoin, disunite, part, separate, sever.

kala bixin. unfold *vb* expand, open, separate, unfurl, unroll.

kala duduwid. vary *vb* alter, transform; alternate, exchange, rotate; diversify, modify, variegate; depart, deviate, swerve.

kala duwan. miscellaneous *adj* diverse, jumbled, many, mixed, various.

kala goo go'an. intermittent *adj* broken, discontinuous, fitful, flickering, periodic, recurrent, spasmodic.

kala nooc nooc ah. various *adj* different, diverse, manifold, many, numerous, several, sundry.

la kala qaadi karo. infectious *adj* catching, communicable, contagious, contaminating, polluting.

kala sooc. discrimination *n* difference, distinction; in-sight, judgement.

kala sooc. separate *vb* detach, divide, divorce, part.

kala soocan. separate *adj* detached, distinct, unconnected.

kalago'is. junction *n* conjunction, connection, hook-up, joining, joint, juncture, linking, seam, union.

kale. else *adv* besides, differently, otherwise.

oo kale. beside, besides *adv* additionally, also, further, furthermore, in addition, more, moreover, over and above, too, yet.

kali ah. single *adj* alone, sole, solitary; particular, separate.

kali-tal'ye. dictator *n* autocrat, despot, tyrant.

kali-talis. dictatorship *n* authoritarianism, autocracy, despotism, iron rule, totalitarianism, tyranny.

kali. lonely *adj* alone, companionless, desolate, forlorn, forsaken, friendless, solitary, unaccompanied.

kali. only *adj* alone, single, sole, solitary.

kaliya. sole *adj* one, only, single, solitary, unique.

kaljarid. intersect *vb* cross, cut, divide, interrupt.

kalkaalle. accomplice *n* abettor, accessory, ally, assistant, associate, confederate, partner.

kallifisa. necessitate *vb* compel, demand, force, oblige.

kalmayn. subsidize *vb* aid, finance, fund, sponsor, support, underwrite.

kalmo. subsidy *n* aid, bounty, grant, support.

lagu kalsoon yahay. reliable *adj* authentic, dependable, sure, trustworthy, unfailing.

aan lagu kalsoonayn. untrustworthy *adj* deceitful, dishonest, slippery, unreliable.

isku kalsooni. unabashed *adj* bold, brazen, confident, unblushing, undaunted, undismayed.

isku kalsooni. composed *adj* calm, collected, cool, imperturbable, placid, self-possessed, tranquil, unruffled.

ku kalsooni. confident *adj* assured, certain, cocksure, positive, sure.

kalsoono. confidence *n* assurance, boldness, courage, self-reliance; secrecy.

kama-danbays. decisive *adj* conclusive, final.

kamas'uul ah. liable *adj* accountable, answerable, bound, responsible

kanaal. duct *n* canal, channel, conduit, pipe, tube; blood-vessel.

kanal. channel *n* canal, duct, passage; aqueduct, canal, drain, furrow, groove, gutter.

kanal. canal *n* channel, duct, pipe, tube.

karaahiyo. detestable *adj* abominable, damnable, hateful, odious; disgusting, loathsome, vile.

karaahiyo. abhorrent *adj* hateful, horrifying, horrible, loathsome, nauseating, odious, offensive, repellent, repugnant, repulsive.

karaahiyo. repulsive *adj* abhorrent, disagreeable, disgusting, hateful, loathsome, nauseating, odious, offensive, repellent, repugnant, revolting, sickening, ugly, unpleasant.

karaahiyyo. hateful *adj* abhorrent, disgusting, loathsome, obnoxious, repugnant, repulsive, revolting, vile.

karaarsiin. accelerate *vb* dispatch, expedite, forward, hasten, hurry, pick up, precipitate, press on, quicken, speed, step up, urge on.

karah. hate *n* animosity, antipathy, dislike, enmity, hostility, loathing.

karbaashid. lash *vb* beat, flagellate, flail, flay, flog, thrash, whip.

karbaashid. flog *vb* beat, flagellate, lash, scourge, thrash, whip.

karbaashid. thrash *vb* beat, bruise, conquer, defeat, flog, lash, trounce, whip.

karbaashid. whip *vb* beat, flog, horsewhip, lash, scourge, slash; jerk, snap, snatch, whisk.

la karhay. damnable *adj* abominable, cursed, hateful, odious.

karhid. hate *vb* abhor, detest, dislike, loathe.

karhid. loathe *vb* abhor, abominate, detest, dislike, hate, recoil.

karhid. detest *vb* abhor, despise, hate, loathe.

kari kara. able *adj* accomplished, adroit, clever, expert, ingenious, practical, proficient, qualified, quick, skilful, talented, versed; competent, effective, efficient, fitted, quick; capable, talented.

kari kara. capable *adj* able, clever, competent, skilful.

karin. cook *vb* bake, boil, broil, fry, grill, microwave, roast, spit-roast, steam, stir-fry; falsify, garble.

karkarin. bubble *vb* boil, effervesce, foam. * *n* blob, globule.

karti daro. disability *n* inability, incapacity, incompetence, unfitness, weakness.

karti u leh. competent *adj* able, capable, clever, equal, qualified; adequate, fit, sufficient, suitable.

karti. ability *n* ableness, adroitness, aptitude, aptness, cleverness, dexterity, efficacy, efficiency, facility, ingenuity, knack, power, readiness, skill, strength, talent, vigour; competency, qualification; calibre, capability, capacity, faculty.

karti. talent *n* ability, aptitude, capacity, cleverness, gift.

karti. competence *n* ability, fitness, qualification, suitableness; adequacy, sufficiency.

kas. knowingly *adv* consciously, intentionally, purposely, wittingly.

kasbid. earn *vb* acquire, gain, get, obtain, procure, win; deserve, merit.

kawyadeen. mangle2 *vb* calender, polish, press, smooth.

kaydin. conserve *vb* keep, maintain, preserve, protect, save.

kediso. sudden *adj* abrupt, hasty, impulsive, rash, unexpected, unforeseen.

keenid. fetch *vb* bring, get.

keenid. bring *vb* convey, fetch; accompany, guide, lead.

keli ah. solitary *adj* alone, lone, lonely, only, single, unaccompanied.

keli-talis. tyrannical *adj* absolute, arbitrary, autocratic, despotic, dictatorial, domineering, oppressive, severe.

keli-taliye. tyranny *n* autocrat, despot, dictator, oppressor; autocracy, despotism, dictatorship, harshness, oppression.

keli. alone *adj* companionless, deserted, forsaken, isolated, lonely, only, single, sole, solitary.

keli. unique *adj* matchless, only, single, sole, singular, unexampled, unmatched.

keydin. stock *vb* accumulate, hoard, save, store, treasure up.

keydin. deposit *vb* drop, dump; bank, put, save, store; commit, entrust.

keydin. store *vb* accumulate, amass, hoard, put by, save, stow away, treasure up.

khaa'in ah. treasonable *adj* disloyal, traitorous, treacherous.

khaa'in. traitor *n* apostate, betrayer, deceiver, renegade, turncoat.

khaayin ah. deceptive *adj* deceiving, false, illusive, illusory, misleading.

khaayin ah. devious *adj* confusing, crooked, misleading, treacherous.

khaayin. cheat *n* charlatan, impostor, knave, mountebank, trickster, rogue, swindler.

khaayin. fraudulent *adj* crafty, deceitful, deceptive, dishonest, false, knavish, treacherous, trickish, tricky, wily.

khabiir. expert *n* authority, connoisseur, crack, master, specialist. *adj* able, adroit, apt, clever, dextrous, proficient, skilful.

khabiir. versed *adj* accomplished, acquainted, clever, practised, proficient, qualified, skilled, trained.

khafif. frail *adj* breakable, brittle, delicate, fragile, frangible, slight; feeble, fragile, infirm, weak.

khafiifin. mitigate *vb* diminish, lessen.

khajilid. squirm *vb* fidget, twist, wriggle, writhe.

khajilsan. sheepish *adj* bashful, embarrassed, shamefaced, timid..

khalaawe. trance *n* dream, ecstasy, hypnosis, rapture

khalad ah. inaccurate *adj* defective, erroneous, faulty, incorrect, inexact, mistaken, wrong.

khalad u faham. misunderstanding *n* error, mistake; disagreement, quarrel.

khalad. mistake *n* blunder, error, failure, fault, inaccuracy, oversight.

khalad. error *n* blunder, fallacy, inaccuracy, mistake, oversight; fault, misdeed, offence, shortcoming, sin, transgression, wrongdoing.

khalad. wrong *adj* bad, immoral, improper; inappropriate, unfit, unsuitable; erroneous, false, incorrect, mistaken, untrue.

khalad. blunder *n* error, lapse, mistake, oversight, slip.

khaladan. mistaken *adj* erroneous, inaccurate, incorrect, misinformed, wrong.

khaldamid. err *vb* deviate, stray, wander; offend, sin, trespass.

khamaar. gamble *n* chance, risk, speculation; bet, punt, wager.

khamaarid. gamble *vb* bet, hazard, speculate, wager.

sharad khammaar. bet *n* gamble, stake, wager.

khammaarid. wager *vb* back, bet, gamble, lay, pledge, risk, stake. khammaar. wager *n* bet, gamble, pledge, risk, stake.

khamri cab. drunkard *n* alcoholic, boozer, drunk.

nooc khamri. liquor *n*.

qof kharash badan. spendthrift *n* prodigal, spender, squanderer, waster.

kharash-garayn. spend *vb* disburse, dispose of, expend, lay out, part with.

kharash. expenditure *n* disbursement, outlay, spending; cost.

kharasil badan. extravagant *adj* excessive, lavish, prodigal, profuse, spendthrift.

kharibaad. vandalism *n* barbarism, barbarity, savagery.

kharibid. spoil *vb* damage, disfigure, harm, impair, mar.

khariirad. map *n* chart, outline, plot, sketch.

khasaare. loss *n* casualty, damage, defeat, deprivation, failure, injury, privation, ruin, waste.

khasab. obligatory *adj* binding, compulsory, necessary, unavoidable.

khasabid. oblige *vb* bind, compel, force, require; accommodate, please.

khasbid. force *vb* coerce, compel, oblige.

khatar ah. virulent *adj* deadly, malignant, poisonous, toxic, venomous.

khatar ah. fatal *adj* deadly, lethal, mortal; ruinous, doomed, predestined.

khatar ah. lethal *adj* deadly, destructive, fatal, mortal.

khatar ah. serious *adj* earnest, grave, solemn, important, weighty.

khatar ah. hazardous *adj* hazardous, insecure, perilous, risky, uncertain, unsettled, unstable, unsteady.

khatar ah. unsafe *adj* dangerous, hazardous, insecure, perilous, precarious, risky.

khatar badan. perilous *adj* dangerous, hazardous, risky, unsafe.

khatar leh. insecure *adj* risky, uncertain, unsure; exposed, ill-protected, unprotected, unsafe; dangerous, hazardous, perilous;0 shaking, shaky, tottering, unstable, weak, wobbly.

khatar-gelin. endanger *vb* compromise, hazard, imperil, jeopardize, risk.

khatar. risk *n* speculation, stake, venture.

khatar. menace *n* danger, hazard, peril, nuisance, pest, troublemaker.

khatar. jeopardy *n* danger, hazard, peril, risk.

khatar-gelin. jeopardize *vb* endanger, hazard, imperil, risk.

khatarl. mortal *adj* deadly, fatal, final, human.

khilaaf. odds *npl* difference, disparity; advantage, superiority.

khilaaf. conflict *n* battle, collision, contest, encounter, fight, struggle.

khilaafid. infringe *vb* break, contravene, disobey, intrude, invade, transgress, violate.

khiyaal. ideal *adj* fancied, imaginary, visionary, shadowy; complete, perfect, utopian.

khiyaal. illusion *n* false appearance, fantasy, hallucination, phantasm.

khiyaali. fanciful *adj* capricious, imaginary, whimsical.

khiyaali. hallucination *n* aberration, delusion, illusion, phantasy, self-deception, vision.

khiyaali. visionary *adj* dreamy, fanced, fanciful, fantastic, illusory, imaginary.

khiyaali. fiction *n* fancy, fantasy, imagination, invention; novel, romance; fable, fabrication, falsehood, figment, invention, lie.

khiyaalian. fictitious *adj* assumed, fanciful, imaginary, invented, mythical; counterfeit, false.

khiyaamayn. fiddle *vb* cheat, swindle, tamper.

khiyaamayn. dupe *vb* cheat, deceive, hoodwink, swindle, trick.

khiyaamayn. outwit *vb* cheat, deceive, defraud, diddle, dupe, outmanoeuvre, swindle.

khiyaamayn. victimize *vb* cheat, deceive, defraud, diddle, dupe, fool, hoax, hoodwink, swindle, trick.

khiyaamayn. defraud *vb* cheat, deceive, delude, diddle, dupe, embezzle, outwit, pilfer, rob, swindle, trick.

khiyaamayn. cheat *vb* deceive, defraud, dupe, fool, hoodwink, inveigle, mislead, outwit, swindle, trick.

khiyaamayn. hoodwink *vb* deceive, dupe, fool, trick.

khiyaamayn. trick *vb* cheat, deceive, defraud, dupe.

khiyaamayn. swindle *vb* cheat, con, defraud, dupe, trick, victimize.

khiyaamayn. hoax *vb* deceive, dupe, fool, hoodwink, swindle, trick.

khiyaamayn. deceive *vb* cheat, double-cross, fool, hoodwink, mislead, trick.

la khiyaami karo. gullible *adj* confiding, credulous, naive, overtrustful, unsophisticated, unsuspicious.

khiyaamo badan. tricky *adj* artful, cunning, deceitful, deceptive.

khiyaamo badan. deceitful *adj* deceptive, misleading; cunning, false, fraudulent, insincere, underhanded, wily.

khiyaamo. fraud *n* deceit, duplicity, hoax, humbug, imposture, sham, trick, trickery.

khiyaamo. crooked *adj* bent, bowed, curved, winding, zigzag; askew, aslant, awry, deformed, disfigured, distorted, twisted; crafty, deceitful, devious, dishonest, knavish, tricky, unscrupulous.

khiyaamo. swindle *n* con, deception, fraud, trickery.

khiyaamo. trick *n* artifice, deception, dodge, fraud, manoeuvre.

khiyaamo. collusion *n* connivance, conspiracy, deceit.

khiyaamo. fiddle *n* fraud, swindle; fiddler, violin, violinist .

khiyaamu badan. sly *adj* artful, crafty, cunning, wily, stealthy, underhand.

khiyaamu. hoax *n* deception, fraud, joke, trick, swindle.

khiyaano. treason *n* betrayal, disloyalty, sedition, treachery.

khiyaari. voluntary *adj* free, spontaneous, unasked, unforced; discretionary, optional.

khiyaari. optional *adj* discretionary, elective, voluntary.

khiyaari. spontaneous *adj* impulsive, impromptu, instinctive, voluntary, willing.

khraafaad ah. fabulous *adj* amazing, imaginary, marvellous, unbelievable, unreal.

khudbad. speech *n* articulation, language, words; conversation, talk; address, discourse, oration.

khudbad. oration *n* address, discourse, harangue, speech.

khudbad. lecture *n* address, discourse, lesson; reprimand, reproof, scolding.

khudbeyn. lecture *vb* reprimand, reprove, scold, sermonize; address, harangue, teach.

khuraafaad ah. legendary *adj* fabulous, fictitious, mythical, romantic.

khuraafaad. legend *n* fable, fiction, myth, narrative, romance, story, tale.

khuraafad. fable *n* allegory, legend, myth, parable, story, tale.

kor u kicid. soar *vb* ascend, fly aloft, glide, mount, rise.

kicid. insolvent *adj* bankrupt, broken, failed, ruined.

kicid. mutiny *n* insurrection, rebellion, revolt, revolution, riot, uprising.

kicin. rouse *vb* arouse, awaken, raise, shake, wake, waken; excite, inspire, rally, stimulate, stir.

kicin. arouse *vb* animate, awaken, excite, incite, kindle, provoke, rouse, stimulate, warm, whet.

kicin. electrify *vb* charge, galvanize, excite, rouse, stir, thrill.

kicin. inflame *vb* animate, arouse, enrage, exasperate, excite, incite, infuriate, madden, provile, rouse, stimulate.

kooban. brief *adj* concise, curt, pithy, short, succinct, terse; fleeting, momentary, short, temporary.

kooban. concise *adj* brief, compact, compressed, condensed, short, succinct, terse.

kooban. succinct *adj* compact, concise, condensed, pithy, short, summary, terse.

kooban. short *adj* brief, curtailed, concise, condensed, terse.

soo koobid. summary *adj* brief, concise, pithy, short, succinct, terse.

koobid. condense *vb* compress, consolidate; abbreviate, abridge, reduce, shorten, summarize.

koodh. coat *n* frock, jacket; covering,layer.

koofiyad. cap *n* beret, head-cover, head-dress; peak, summit, top.

koonjayn. monopolize *vb* control, dominate.

koooban. fleeting *adj* brief, passing, short-lived, temporary, transient, transitory.

koormeerid. supervise *vb* control, direct, manage, oversee, superintend.

koox buuqsan. crowd *n* assembly, company, flock, herd, horde, host, multitude, throng.

koox ciidan. corps *n* band, company, division, platoon, regiment, squad, squadron, troop.

koox. group *n* assembly, body, combination, cluster, collection.

koox. band *n* gang, horde, ensemble, group, orchestra.

koox. troop *n* band, body, company, party, squad.

kor. above *adj* above-mentioned, aforementioned, aforesaid, foregoing, preceding, previous, prior. *adv* aloft, overhead; before, previously; of a higher rank. *prep* higher than, on top of; exceeding, greater than, more than, over; beyond, superior to.

kordhin. increase *vb* enhance, heighten, extend, prolongg.

kore. outward *adj* exterior, external, outer, outside.

korid. wax *vb* become, grow, increase, mount, rise.

korid. grow *vb* enlarge, expand, extend, increase, swell; arise, burgeon, develop, germinate, shoot, sprout, vegetate; advance, extend, improve, progress, swell, thrive, wax; cultivate, produce, raise.

korid. flourish *vb* grow, thrive.

korid. develop *vb* cultivate, grow, mature, progress.

kormeere. inspector *n* boss, examiner, overseer, superintendent, supervisor.

kormeerid. inspect *vb* examine, investigate, look into, pry into, scrutinize.

kormeerid. superintend *vb* control, direct, inspect, manage, oversee, supervise.

koror. increase *n* addition, crescendo, development, enlargement, expansion, extension, growth, heightening, increment, multiplication, swelling.

korriin. growth *n* development, expansion, extension, growing, increase; cultivation, germination, produce, sprouting, vegetation; improvement, progress; adulthood, maturity

kowaad. first *adj* capital, chief, foremost, highest, leading, prime, principal; earliest, eldest, original; elementary, primary, rudimentary; aboriginal, primal, primitive. * *adv* chiefly, firstly, initially, mainly, primarily, principally; before, foremost rather, rather than, sooner, sooner than.

kowaad. prime *adj* first, initial, original, primary, chief, foremost, principal; dambeeya. primitive *adj* aboriginal, first, original, primal, primary, prime, primitive, primordial, pristine; antiquated, crude, old-fashioned, quaint, simple, unsophisticated.

ku dhawaaqid. declare *vb* affirm, assert, proclaim, pronounce, publish, state, utter.

ku doodis. claim *vb* ask, assert, demand, require.

ku dufasho. bump *vb* collide, knock, strike, thump.

ku khasbid. enforce *vb* compel, constrain, exact, force, oblige, require, urge.

ku noolaasho. inhabit *vb* abide, dwell, live, occupy, people, reside, sojourn.

ku tiirsasho. recline *vb* lean, lie, lounge, repose, rest.

ku-dhag. tenacious *adj* clinging, dogged, firm, persistent, retentive, unyielding

ku-filan. sufficient *adj* adequate, ample, enough, plenteous, satisfactory.

aan ku-filnayn. inadequate *adj* incapable, insufficient, unequal.

kubbad. sphere *n* ball, globe, orb; ambit, compass, domain, function, office, range, scope.

kufid. slip *vb* trip, fall.

kulan. meeting *n* encounter, interview; assembly, audience, company, conference; intersection, junction.

kulayl. heat *n* excitement, fever, flush, passion; ardour, earnestness, fervency, fervour, glow, intensity, zeal.

kulaylin. simmer *vb* boil, bubble, seethe, stew.

la kulmid. encounter *vb* confront, face, meet; attack, combat, strive, struggle.

kulmid. meet *vb* cross, intersect; confront, encounter, engage; comply, fulfil.

kulul oo cabudhan (hawo). sultry *adj* close, damp, hot, humid, muggy, sweltering.

kulul. hot *adj* burning, fiery, scalding; boiling, flaming, heated, roasting; oppressive, sweltering, warm; angry, animated, furious, passionate, vehement; highly seasoned, peppery, piquant, pungent, sharp, stinging.

kululayn. steam *vb* coddle, cook, poach; navigate, sail; be hot, sweat.

kuraafaad ah. mythical *adj* allegorical, fabled, fanciful, fictitious, imaginary, legendary.

kuraafaad. myth *n* fable, legend, tradition; parable, story; falsehood, fancy, lie, untruth.

kusime. acting *adj* interim, provisional, substitute, temporary.

kusmid. deputy *adj* acting, assistant, vice, subordinate.

kuus. knob *n* lump, protuberance, stud.

kuusan. stocky *adj* chubby, chunky, dumpy, plump, short, stout, stubby, thickset.

kuxirid. bind *vb* confine, fetter, restrain, restrict; bandage, tie up, wrap; fasten, secure, truss.

L

la fahmi karo. intelligible *adj* clear, comprehensible, distinct, lucid, understandable.

la moodo. seem *vb* appear, assume, look, pretend.

la qaadi karo. portable *adj* handy, light, movable.

la yahay. beloved *n* dear, honey, love, lover, sweetie, sweetheart.

la'aan. failing *prep* lacking, needing, wanting.

la'aan. lack *n* dearth, deficit, need, scarcity, shortcoming.

la-talin. advise *vb* admonish, counsel, commend, recommend, suggest, urge; acquaint, apprise, inform, notify; confer, consult, deliberate.

la-taliye. adviser *n* counsellor, director, guide, instructor.

la-tegid. elope *vb* abscond, bolt, decamp, disappear, leave.

la-wareegid. confiscate *vb* appropriate, forfeit, seize.

la-xaday. stolen *adj* filched, pilfered, purloined.

laab ku qabasho. embrace *vb* clasp, encircle, enclose, encompass, enfold, hold, include. *n* clasp, hug.

laab ku qabasho. snuggle *vb* cuddle, nestle, nuzzle.

laab. fold *n* flap, pleat.

laabid. fold *vb* bend, cover, double, wrap; embrace; collapse, fail. *n* gather, plait, pleat.

laad. kick *n* force, punch; excitement, pleasure, thrill.

laadid. kick *vb* boot, resist, spurn.

laakin. but *conj* except, excepting, further, moreover, still, unless, yet.

soo laaladin. suspend *vb* hang, sling, swing; adjourn, defer, interrupt, withhold.

laalush siin. bribe *vb* buy, corrupt, influence, pay off.

laalush. bribe *n* enticement, pay-off.

laamadoodsi. doze *vb* drowse, nap, sleep, slumber. *n* forty-winks, nap.

laan. branch *n* bough, limb, twig; department, part, portion, section, subdivision.

laan. branch *n* offshoot, scion, shoot, sprout, twig.

laangadhe. lame *adj* crippled, disabled, halt, hobbling, limping.

laba jeer. double *adj* dual, twice, twofold. *adv* twice, twofold.

laba-wajiilenimo. hypocritical *adj* false, insincere, two-faced.

labood. masculine *adj* manlike, manly, mannish, virile; powerful, robust, strong;

lacag dhigasho. bank *vb* deposit, keep, save. stockpile.

lacag la'aan. penniless *adj* destitute, poor, needy, poverty-stricken.

lacag. finances *npl* funds, resources, revenues, treasury; income, property.

aad u ladan. prosperous *adj* blooming, flourishing, fortunate, rich, successful, thriving.

laga yaabaa. perhaps *adv* possibly.

lagam'a maarmaan. inevitable *adj* certain, necessary, unavoidable.

lagama marmaan. necessary *adj* inevitable, unavoidable, essential, indispensable, requisite, compulsory.

lagu daalaayo. trying *adj* fatiguing, irksome, tiresome, wearisome.

lahaanshi. possess *vb* control, have, hold, keep, occupy, own, seize.

lahaansho. possession *n* ownership, proprietorship, control; (*pl*) assets, effects, estate, property, wealth.

lama filaan ah. abrupt *adj* blunt, brusque, curt, discourteous; cramped, harsh, jerky, stiff.

lama filaan. unexpected *adj* abrupt, sudden, unforeseen.

lambar. number *n* digit, figure, numeral, sum, total.

lamma degaan. desert *adj* barren, desolate, forsaken, lonely, solitary, uncultivated, uninhabited, unproductive, untilled, waste, wild.

lammane. pair *n* brace, couple, double, duo.

lammane. couple *n* brace, pair, two; bond.

laxaad leh. magnitude *n* bulk, dimension, extent; consequence, greatness, importance.

laxaad leh. substantial *adj* bulky, heavy, large, sizable, solid, sound, well-made.

layaabid. amaze *vb* astonish, astound, bewilder, confound, confuse, dumbfound, perplex, stagger, stupefy.

layli. exercise *n* action, activity, effort, exertion, drill; lesson, task, test.

leefid. lap *vb* drink, lick, tongue.

leeg. fit *n* convulsion, fit, paroxysm, qualm, seizure, spasm, spell; mood, tantrum, turn.

leexaysi. swing *vb* oscillate, sway, vibrate, wave; brandish, flourish, whirl.

leexo. swing *n* fluctuation, oscillation.

legdamid. tussle *n* conflict, contest, fight, scuffle, struggle.

legdan. tussle *vb* scuffle, struggle, wrestle.

legdan. wrestle *vb* contend, contest, grapple, strive, struggle.

leh. have *vb* cherish, keep, hold, own, possess; acquire, gain, get, obtain, receive.

libdhid. vanish *vb* disappear, dissolve, fade, melt.

lid isku ah. adverse *adj* conflicting, contrary, opposing; antagonistic, harmful, hostile, hurtful, inimical, unfavourable, unpropitious; calamitous, disastrous, unfortunate, unlucky, untoward.

lid ku ah. opposite *adj* facing, different, diverse, incompatible. * *n* contradiction, contrary, reverse.

lid ku ah. rival *adj* competing, contending, opposing.

lid ku ah. against *prep* adverse to, contrary to, resisting, opposite to.

lid. opponent *n* adversary, antagonist, competitor, contestant, enemy, foe, rival.

liigid. leak *vb* drip, exude, ooze, percolate.

liigid. ooze *vb* drip, exude, leak.

liis qorid. list *vb* alphabetize, catalogue, chronicle, codify, enumerate, file, index, inventory, record, register, tabulate, tally.

liis. catalogue *n* inventory, invoice, list, record, register, schedule.

liisan. licence *n* authorization, leave, liberty, permission, privilege, right; certificate, charter, dispensation, permit, warrant.

liqid. gobble *vb* bolt, devour, gorge, gulp, swallow.

liqid. swallow *vb* consume, devour, drink, eat, gulp, imbibe.

lugad. language *n* dialect, speech, tongue, vernacular; conversation, expression, idiom, jargon, parlance, phraseology, slang, speech, style, terminology.

lulid. wave *vb* brandish, flaunt, flourish, swing; beckon, signal.

lulid. sway *vb* fluctuate, rock, roll, swing, wave. * n authority, command, control.

M

ma-dhalaysnimo. barren *adj* childless, sterile; (*botanical*) bare, infertile, unproductive, unfruitful.

ma-dhalaysnimo. infertility *n* barrenness, sterility, unfruitfulness, unproductivity.

ma-dhallays. sterile *adj* barren, empty, unfruitful, unproductive, unprolific.

ma-dhinte. immortal *adj* abiding, enduring, eternal, imperishable, indestructible, lasting, permanent; ceaseless, continuing.

maad. humour *n* mood, temper; fun, jocularity, pleasantry, wit.

maadi. material *adj* nonspiritual, physical, temporal; essential, important, relevant;

maadi. worldly *adj* ambitious, irreligious, selfish, proud, sordid, unspiritual.

maado. material *n* stuff, substance.

ka maagid. shirk *vb* avoid, dodge, evade, slack.

ka maagid. hesitate *vb* delay, pause, shilly-shally, vacillate, waver; falter, stammer, stutter.

ka maagid. halt *vb* hesitate, pause, stammer, waver.

maah-maah. saying *n* adage, aphorism, maxim, proverb, saw.

maahmaah. proverb *n* adage, aphorism, maxim, saying.

maahsan. preoccupied *adj* absentminded, abstracted, dreaming, engrossed, inattentive, lost, musing, unobservant.

maahsan. oblivious *adj* careless, inattentive, mindless, negligent.

maahsan. musing *n* absent-mindedness, daydreaming, meditation, reflection.

maal-gelin. investment *n* money invested; endowment.

maal. treasure *n* jewels, money, riches, wealth.

maal. riches *npl* abundance, affluence, fortune, money, wealth.

maal. resources *npl* capital, funds, income, money, property, supplies, wealth.

maal. wealth *n* fortune, money, possessions, property, riches, treasure; affluence, plenty, profusion.

maalgelin. fund *vb* endow, finance, invest, provide, subsidise, support.

maalin kasta. everyday *adj* common, commonplace, customary, habitual, routine, usual.

maalin. dawn *n* day, daybreak, sunrise; brightness, luminosity, radiance, ray; candle, lamp, lantern, lighthouse, taper, torch.

maalin. day *n* daylight, sunlight, sunshine; time.

maalqabeen. rich *adj* affluent, flush, moneyed, opulent, prosperous, wealthy; luxurious, splendid, sumptuous, superb, valuable; abundant, ample, copious, plentiful, sufficient; fertile, luxuriant, productive, prolific.

maalqabeen. opulent *adj* affluent, flush, luxurious, moneyed, plentiful, rich, sumptuous, wealthy.

maalqabeyn. affluent *adj* abounding, abundant, bounteous, plenteous; moneyed, opulent, rich, wealthy.

maamul. management *n* administration, government, guidance, supervision.

maamulid. regulate *vb* control, direct, govern, guide, manage.

maamulid. minister *n* agent, assistant; administrator, executive, envoy; chaplain, churchman, clergyman, parson, vicar.ministry

maamulid. administer *vb* contribute, deal out, dispense, supply; conduct, control, direct, govern, manage, oversee, superintend.

maamulid. govern *vb* administer, manage, regulate, reign, rule, supervise.

maamuule. princial *n* chief, head, leader; head teacher, master.

maareeye. manager *n* comptroller, conductor, director, executive.

la maareyn karo (fudud). manageable *adj* controllable, docile, easy, governable.

maareyn. handle *vb* feel, finger, manhandle, paw, touch; manage, manipulate, wield.

maareyn. manage *vb* administer, conduct, direct, guide, handle.

maaweelo. treat *n* entertainment, gratification, pleasure.

maaweelo. diversion *n* amusement, distraction, enjoyment, entertainment, game, pastime; detour, digression.

maaweelo. recreation *n* amusement, diversion, entertainment, game, leisure, pastime, relaxation, sport.

mab'da. principle *n* basis, element, essence, axiom, law, maxim; precept, rule, tenet, theory.

aan mabda lahayn. unscrupulous *adj* dishonest, ruthless, unprincipled, unrestrained.

mabda. precept *n* commandment, decree, edict, injunction, instruction, law, order, regulation; direction, doctrine, maxim, principle, teaching, rule.

mabsuud ah. jubilant *adj* exultant, exulting, rejoicing, triumphant.

macaamilaad. deal *n* bargain, transaction.

macaan. delicious *adj* luscious, nice, palatable, choice.

macaan. sweet *n* delicacy, titbit.

macaan. sweet *adj* candied, cloying, honeyed, sugary; agreeable, charming, delightful.

macaan. lush, luscious *adj* delicious, delightful, pleasing; honeyed, sugary, fresh, juicy, luxuriant, moist, sappy, succulent, watery.

macaash leh. gainful *adj* advantageous, beneficial, profitable; lucrative, remunerative.

macaash. profit *n* advantage, benefit, interest.

macaashid. profit *vb* advance, benefit, gain, improve.

macallin. teacher *n* coach, instructor, master, schoolteacher, tutor.

macallin. tutor *n* coach, instructor, master, teacher.

machad. institute *n* academy, college, foundation, guild, institution, school.

macluumaad. information *n* advice, intelligence, knowledge, notice; advertisement, message, tip, word, warning.

macne yar. insignificant *adj* immaterial, inconsequential, paltry, petty, small, trivial, unimportant.

macno yar. trifling *adj* frivolous, inconsiderable, insignificant, petty, shallow, trivial, unimportant.,

macno-daran. pointless *adj* futile, meaningless, vague, stupid.

madaale. untiring *adj* persevering, indefatigable, patient, tireless, unceasing, unflagging, unwearied.

madaalo leh. fun *adj* amusing, diverting, droll, entertaining.

madadaalin. tickle *vb* amuse, delight, divert, please, titillate.

madadaalo. fun *n* amusement, diversion, merriment, mirth, pranks, sport.

ugu madan. pre-eminent *adj* chief, distinguished, excellent, paramount, peerless, predominant, renowned, surpassing, unequalled.

madax adag. obstinate *adj* headstrong, inflexible, self-willed, stubborn, unyielding.

madax adag. intractable *adj* cantankerous, contrary, dogged, inflexible, obdurate, obstinate, perverse, pig-headed, stubborn.

madax adag. unyielding *adj* indomitable, inflexible, resolute, staunch, steadfast; intractable, obstinate, stiff, stubborn, wilful.

madax adag. dogmatic *adj* authoritative, dictatorial, opinionated, overbearing.

madax adag. self-willed *adj* headstrong, obstinate, stubborn, wilful.

madax adag. unbending *adj* inflexible, rigid, stiff; firm, obstinate, resolute, stubborn.

madax adagy. uncompromising *adj* inflexible, obstinate, orthodox, rigid, stiff, unyielding.

madax adayg. obdurate *adj* inflexible, obstinate, pigheaded, stubborn, unbending, unyielding.

madax adayg. headstrong *adj* obstinate, self-willed, stubborn, ungovernable, unruly.

madax adayg. opinionated *adj* conceited, dictatorial, dogmatic, stubborn.

madax bannaani. sovereignty *n* authority, dominion, empire, power, rule, supremacy, sway.

madaxa hab maamuska. marshal *n* conductor, director, master of ceremonies, regulator;

madaxa. head *adj* chief, first, highest, leading, main, principal.

madaxadag. inflexible *adj* rigid, stiff, unbending; intractable, obdurate, obstinant, stubborn, unyielding, unbending.

maddadaalo. entertainment *n* hospitality; banquet, feast, festival, reception, treat; amusement, diversion, pastime, recreation, sport.

madhan. empty *adj* blank, unoccupied, vacant, void; unfilled, unfurnished; deserted, desolate, free; foolish, frivolous, senseless, silly, stupid, trivial, weak.

madhan. shallow *adj* trivial, empty, simple, superficial.

madhan. vacant *adj* blank, empty, unfilled; thoughtless, unthinking, unreflective; uninhabited, untenanted.

madhin. empty *vb* deplete, drain, evacuate, exhaust.

madhinte. undying *adj* deathless, endless, immortal, imperishable.

madhnaan. vanity *n* emptiness, foolishness, hollowness, triviality, worthlessness; conceit, egotism, ostentation.

madhnaan. void *n* abyss, chasm, emptiness.

madoobeyn. blur *vb* darken, dim, obscure.

madow. black *adj* dark, ebony, inky, jet; dingy, dusky, murky; dark, depressing, disastrous, gloomy, sombre.

mafiiq. brush *n* broom; collision, encounter.

mafiiq. scope *n* compass, range, reach.

magaalo madax. capital *n* chief city, metropolis; money, investments, shares.

magac kaliya. nominal *adj* minimal, ostensible, professed, so-called, titular.

magac la'. anonymous *adj* nameless, unacknowledged.

magac u samayn. christen *vb* baptise, name.

magac. name *n* designation, nickname, surname, title.

magacaabid. nominate *vb* appoint, choose, designate, name.

magacaabid. ordain *vb* appoint, call, consecrate, elect, order, prescribe.

magacaabid. appoint *vb* determine, establish, fix, prescribe; allot, assign, delegate, depute, detail, settle; name, nominate.

magoojin. dash *vb* bolt, dart, fly, run, rush.

mahad celin. grateful *adj* appreciative, indebted, obliged, thankful.

mahad naq. gratitude *n* goodwill, indebtedness, thankfulness.

mahadcelin. recognition *n* acknowledgement, appreciation.

majaajiliste. wag *n* humorist, jester, joker, wit.

majnuun. eccentric *adj* cranky, erratic, odd, outlandish, peculiar, strange, unnatural, whimsical. *n* crank, curiosity, original.

majuujin. pinch *vb* compress, nip, squeeze.

makhrib. evening *n* eve, even, eventide.

mala awaalid. speculate *vb* conjecture, muse, ponder, reflect, think; gamble, hazard, risk.

mala'awaal. meditation *n* cogitation, contemplation, musing, pondering, reflection.

malayn. guess *vb* conjecture, surmise, suspect; believe, imagine, reckon, suppose, think.

malayn. conjecture *vb* guess, hypothesis, imagine, suppose. surmise.

malayn. presumption *n* guess, hypothesis, inference, opinion, understanding; arrogance, assurance, effrontery, probability.

malayn. imagine *vb* dream, fancy, pretend; invent, suppose, hypothesize, guess, think.

malayn. gauge *vb* assess, estimate, guess, reckon.

male-awaal. imagination *n* fantasy, invention, unreality.

malo. thought *n* conjecture, guess, idea, notion, supposition.

malqabeen. moneyed, monied *adj* affluent, opulent, rich, well-off, well-to-do.

wax la mamnuucay. taboo *adj* banned, forbidden, prohibited, proscribed.

mamnuucid. veto *vb* ban, embargo, forbid, interdict, prohibit.

mamnuucid. outlaw *vb* ban, banish, condemn, exclude, forbid, make illegal, prohibit.

mamnuucid. forbid *vb* ban, disallow, embargo, prohibit, proscribe, taboo, veto.

mamnuucid. prohibit *vb* debar, hamper, hinder, preclude, prevent; ban, disallow, forbid, inhabit, interdict.

mansab. status *n* position, rank, standing, station.

mansab. post *n* employment, office, place, position, situation, station.

maqan. away *adv* absent, not present.

maqan. absent *adj* abroad, away, elsewhere, gone, not present; abstracted, dreaming, inattentive, lost, musing, napping, preoccupied.

maqlid. hear *vb* eavesdrop, hearken, listen, overhear.

maqlid. obey *vb* comply, conform, heed, submit, yield.

maqnaansho. absence *n* nonappearance, nonattendance; abstraction, distraction, inattention, musing, preoccupation, reverie; default, defect, deficiency, lack, privation.

mar mar. infrequent *adj* occasional, rare, scarce, sporadic, uncommon, unusual.

marag. evidence *n* confirmation, corroboration, grounds, indication, proof, testimony, witness.

marawaxad. fan *n* blower, cooler, ventilator.

marawaxadin. fan *vb* agitate, move, blow, cool, refresh, ventilate; excite, fire, rouse, stimulate.

margin. strangle *vb* choke, smother, squeeze, stifle, suffocate, throttle, tighten.

marin habaabid. deviate *vb* err, go astray, stray, swerve, wander; differ, diverge.

marin. entry *n* access, approach, avenue, entrance, passage, way; admission, admittance, audience, interview.

marin. passage *n* voyage; corridor, gallery, hall.

marin. route *n* course, direction, journey, march, road, path, way.

marinhabaabin. mislead *vb* deceive, delude, misdirect, misguide.

markaati. witness *n* attestation, conformation, corroboration, evidence, testimony; bystander, corroborator, eyewitness, onlooker, spectator, testifier.

markale. again *adv* afresh, anew, another time, once more; besides, further, in addition, moreover.

markhaati. testimony *n* affirmation, attestation, declaration, deposition, evidence, proof, witness.

isla markiiba. at once *adv* directly, forthwith, immediately, straightaway, straightway, without delay.

marmar. seldom *adv* infrequently, occasionally, rarely.

marmar. occasional *adj* infrequent, irregular, uncommon.

ka maroojin. wring *vb* contort, twist, wrench; extort, force, wrest.

maroojin. wrench *vb* distort, twist, wrest, wring; extort, extract.

maroojin. squeeze *vb* clutch, constrict, crush, grip, nip, press, squash.

maroojin. screw *vb* force, squeeze, tighten, twist, wrench.

marti-galiye. host *n* entertainer, innkeeper, landlord, master of ceremonies, presenter, proprietor, owner, receptionist.

marxalad. stage *n* degree, point, step.

ka mas'uul ah. accountable *adj* amenable, answerable, duty-bound, liable, responsible.

mas'uul. responsible *adj* accountable, amenable, answerable, liable, trustworthy.

masaafo. distance *n* farness, remoteness.

masaxid. rub *vb* clean, massage, polish, scour, wipe; apply, put, smear, spread.

masaxid. wipe *vb* clean, dry, mop, rub.

mashin. machine *n* tool; machinery, engine.

mashruuc. enterprise *n* activity, effort, endeavour, project, undertaking, scheme, venture.

mashruuc. undertaking *n* affair, business, endeavour, engagement, enterprise, venture.

mashruuc. project *n* design, intention, plan, proposal, scheme.

masiibo ah. tragic *adj* calamitous, catastrophic, disastrous, dreadful, grievous, heart-breaking, mournful, sad.

masiibo. tragedy *n* adversity, calamity, catastrophe, disaster, misfortune.

masiibo. calamity *n* adversity, affliction, catastrophe, disaster, misfortune, mishap.

masiibo. disaster *n* accident, adversity, blow, calamity, catastrophe, misadventure, misfortune, mishap.

masiibo. catastrophe *n* adversity, blow, calamity, disaster, misfortune, mishap, trouble.

masixid. erase *vb* blot, cancel, delete, expunge, obliterate, scratch out.

maskax bedelid. indoctrinate *vb* brainwash, initiate, instruct, teach.

maskax fayow. sane *adj* lucid, normal, rational, reasonable.

maskax fiican. intelligent *adj* acute, alert, apt, astute, brainy, bright, clear-headed, clear-sighted, clever, discerning, knowing, quick, sagacious, sensible, shrewd, understanding.

maskax fiicni. intelligence *n* brains, intellect, mentality, sense, spirit; imagination, insight, quickness, understanding, wit.

maskax furan. wit *n* genius, intellect, intelligence, reason, sense, understanding; banter, humour, jest, joke, repartee, satire.

maskax furan. liberal *adj* broad-minded, catholic, magnanimous, tolerant, unbiased, unbigoted; ample, bounteous, plentiful.

maskax furnaan. witty *adj* bright, clever, droll, funny, humorous, jocular.

maskax. brain *n* brains, intellect, reason.

maskax. reason *n* intellect, judgement, mind, understanding; common sense, reasonableness.

masuul. guardian *n* custodian, defender, guard, keeper, preserver, protector, trustee, warden.

mataan. twin *n* double, duplicate, match.

mataano. twin *adj* duplicate, identical, matching.

maxakamad. court *n* tribunal, palace.

maxbuus. convict *n* criminal, culprit, felon, malefactor, prisoner.

maxsuul. product *n* outcome, proceeds, returns, yield; consequence, effect, result.

maydk dadka. corpse *n* body, carcass, remains.

meel bannaan. space *n* expanse, extent, spread; capacity, room, place.

meel ka dhac. wrong *vb* abuse, injure, maltreat, oppress.

meel ka dhicid. offend *vb* affront, annoy, chafe, displease, irritate.

meel walba jooga. ubiquitous *adj* omnipresent, pervasive, universal.

meel wax iska galaan. joint *n* connection, junction, juncture, hinge.

meel yar oo bannaan. gap *n* breach, break, chasm, chink, cleft, crack, hiatus, interval, opening, pass, ravine, rift, space, vacancy.

meel. place *n* area, district, locale, locality, location, premises, region, site, spot, whereabouts; abode, building, dwelling, residence; city, town, village.

meel. position *n* place, site, situation, spot, station; rank, standing, status; post, situation.

meel. site *n* location, place, plot, position, spot.

meel. locality *n* location, neighbourhood, place, position, site, situation, spot.

meesha ugu fog. utmost *adj* extreme, farthest, highest, last, most distant, remotest; greatest, uttermost.

micnaha. content *n* essence, gist, meaning, substance.

micne. substance *n* content, core, drift, essence, gist, meaning, sense.

micno lahayn. paltry *adj* inconsiderable, insignificant, petty, trivial, unimportant.

micno leh. expressive *adj* meaningful, significant; eloquent, strong, vivid.

micno darro. nonsensical *adj* absurd, foolish, irrational, senseless, silly, stupid.

midab. tint *n* colour, dye, hue, shade, tinge, tone.

midab. hue *n* colour, complexion, dye, shade, tinge, tint, tone.

midab. dye *n* colour, hue, shade, stain, tinge, tint.

midab. colour *n* hue, shade, tint, tone; pigment, stain.

midabayn. stain *vb* blot, smirch, soil, spot, sully; colour, dye. *n* blot, defect, flaw, spot.

midabayn. dye *vb* colour, stain, tinge.

midabyn. colour *vb* dye, paint, stain, tint.

midho. fruit *n* crop, harvest, produce; consequence, effect, outcome, result; issue, offspring, young.

midow. coherence *n* consistency, harmony, intelligibility, meaning, rationality, unity.

mihnad. vocation *n* business, calling, employment, occupation, profession, pursuit, trade.

miisaamid. offset *vb* balance, counteract.

miisaaniyad. budget *n* account, estimate, funds, resources.

miisanid. weigh *vb* consider, deliberate, examine, study.

milatari. military *n* army, militia, soldiers.

milid. thaw *vb* dissolve, liquefy, melt, soften, unbend.

milid. dissolve *vb* liquefy, melt; disappear, fade, vanish, disintegrate.

aan milmi karin. insoluble *adj* indissoluble, indissolvable, irreducible; inexplicable, insolvable.

milmid. melt *vb* dissolve, fuse, liquefy, thaw.

mindi. knife *n* blade, jackknife, lance.

miskiin ah. lowly *adj* humble, meek, mild, modest, plain, poor, simple, unassuming, unpretentious.

miskiin. unassuming *adj* humble, modest, unobtrusive, unpretentious.

miskiin. naive *adj* artless, candid, ingenuous, simple, unaffected, unsophisticated.

mitid ah. militant *adj* belligerent, combative, fighting.

miyi. rural *adj* agrarian, country, pastoral, rustic.

moodo. fashion *n* appearance, cut, form; fad, mode, style, usage, vogue.

mowdhuuc. text *n* copy, composition, essay, subject, theme, thesis, topic, treatise.

mowdhuuc. topic *n* business, question, subject, text, theme, thesis.

mowduuc. subject *n* affair, matter, point, theme, topic.

moyee. but *prep* except, excepting, excluding, save.

mucaarid. opposition *n* antagonism, hostility, resistance; hindrance, obstacle, obstruction, prevention.

mucjiso ah. phenomenal *adj* marvellous, miraculous, prodigious, wondrous.

mucjiso. miracle *n* marvel, wonder.

mudanaan. noble *adj* dignified, elevated, eminent, exalted, generous, great, honourable, illustrious.

mudane. noble *n* aristocrat, grandee, lord, nobleman, peer.

muddo-muddo ku bixin. instalment *n* payment, portion.

mudid. inject *vb* force in, insert, introduce.

mudnaaan. precedence *n* pre-eminence, preference, priority, superiority, supremacy.

mug. volume *n* book, tome; amplitude, bulk, dimension, fullness, power, quantity.

mug. capacity *n* volume; brains, calibre, power, talent; ability, cleverness, competency, skill.

mugdi ah. sombre *adj* dark, dismal,drab, dull, doleful, mournful, sad, sober.

mugdi ah. murky *adj* cloudy, dark, dim, gloomy, hazy, lurid, obscure, overcast.

mugdi ka dhigid. dull *vb* blunt; deaden, dim, tarnish.

mugdi. dark *adj* black, cloudy, dim, dusky, inky, lurid, moonless, murky, opaque, overcast, shadowy, starless, sunless; cheerless, despondent, disheartening, gloomy, joyless.

mugdis. obscure *adj* dark, dim, gloomy, shadowy, sombre; difficult, unintelligible, vague.

mugdiyeen. obfuscate *vb* cloud, darken, obscure, confuse, muddle.

la mugdiyeeyo. darken *vb* dim, eclipse, obscure, shade.

mugdiyeyn. cloud *vb* darken, dim, obscure, shade.

muhiim ah. paramount *adj* chief, pre-eminent, principal, supreme.

muhiim ah. strategic *adj* critical, decisive, key, vital.

muhiim ah. key *adj* basic, crucial, essential, important, major, principal.

muhiim ah. vital *adj* essential, indispensable, necessary.

muhiimah. significant *adj* important, material, meaningful, emphatic, expressive, telling.

muhim ah. momentous *adj* grave, important, serious, significant.

muhim ah. prominent *adj* embossed, jutting, projecting, protuberant, raised; celebrated, distinguished, eminent, famous, foremost, leading; conspicuous, important, salient.

muhim ah. main *adj* capital, cardinal, principal; essential, important, indispensable; enormous, huge.

muhim ah. essential *adj* fundamental, indispensable, important, intrinsic, necessary, requisite, vital.

muhim ah. important *adj* grave, serious, significant, urgent, valuable, weighty; esteemed, influential, prominent, substantial.

ugu muhimsan. principal *adj* cardinal, chief, essential, first, foremost, highest, leading, main, pre-eminent, prime.

ugu muhimsan. predominant *adj* controlling, dominant, overruling, prevailing, prevalent, supreme.

mukhajil. modest *adj* bashful, coy, reserved, shy, unpretentious; chaste, proper, pure; decent, moderate.

mukhajil. self-conscious *adj* awkward, bashful, diffident, embarrassed.

mukharib. vandal *n* barbarian, destroyer, savage.

muqaal. image *n* effigy, likeness, picture, representation, shape, reflection.

muqaamaraad leh. adventurous *adj* bold, chivalrous, courageous, daring, doughty; foolhardy, headlong, precipitate, rash, reckless; dangerous, hazardous, perilous.

muqaamaraad. adventure *n* chance, contingency, experiment, fortuity, hazard, risk, venture; crisis, contingency, event, incident, occurrence, transaction.

muqadas ah. holy *adj* blessed, consecrated, dedicated, devoted, sacred, sanctified; devout, godly, pious, pure, religious, righteous, saintlike, saintly, sinless, spiritual.

muraad. destination *n* end, object, journey's end, resting-place, terminus.

muraayad. mirror *n* looking-glass, reflector.

muran badan. quarrelsome *adj* argumentative, cross, irritable.

muran. quarrel *n* brawl, clash, contest, difference, disagreement, dispute, row, tiff.

muran. dispute *n* controversy, debate, discussion, disputation; altercation, argument, disagreement, dissension, spat, squabble, tiff, wrangle.

muran. controversy *n* argument, contention, debate, dispute, quarrel, strife; lawsuit.

muran. brawl *n* dispute, feud, fracas, fray, quarrel, row, scuffle, squabble.

muran. squabble *n* dispute, quarrel, row, rumpus.

murgid. sorrow *vb* grieve, lament, mourn, weep.

murgid. mourn *vb* grieve, lament, sorrow, wail.

sii murgin. complicate *vb* confuse, entangle, involve.

murgin. tangle *vb* complicate, perplex, snarl, twist; ensnare, entrap, involve.

murmid. quarrel *vb* clash, dispute, fight.

murmid. brawl *vb* bicker, dispute, quarrel, squabble.

murmid. dispute *vb* argue, debate; challenge, contradict, deny, contest.

murmid. squabble *vb* argue, bicker, quarrel, wrangle.

murmid. argue *vb* plead, reason upon; debate, dispute; denote, evince, imply, indicate, mean, prove; contest, debate, discuss, sift.

murmid. row *vb* argue, dispute, fight, quarrel, squabble.

murmid. feud *vb* argue, bicker, clash, contend, dispute, quarrel.

murugaysan. dejected *adj* crestfallen, depressed, despondent, disheartened, dispirited, downcast, down-hearted, gloomy, miserable, sad, wretched.

murugaysan. sad *adj* grave, serious; sombre, dejected, depressed, gloomy, mournful, sorrowful.

murugeysan. gloomy *adj* dark, depressing, dim, dusky, obscure; cheerless, dismal; dejected, depressed, despondent, disheartened, dispirited, downcast, downhearted, glum, melancholy, morose, sad, sullen.

murugo. misery *n* distress, grief, heartache, misfortune, sorrow, suffering, unhappiness, woe, wretchedness.

murugo. grief *n* anguish, bitterness, distress, heartbreak, misery, regret, sadness, sorrow, suffering, tribulation, woe.

murugo. sorrow *n* affliction, grief, heartache, sadness, trouble, woe.

murugo. woe *n* affliction, grief, heartache, melancholy, misery, sorrow, tribulation, trouble, unhappiness, wretchedness.

murugsan. miserable *adj* distressed, forlorn, heartbroken, unhappy, wretched; poor, valueless, worthless;

murugsan. dispirited *adj* dejected, depressed, discouraged, disheartened, down-cast, down-hearted.

murugsan. wretched *adj* afflicted, distressed, forlorn, sad, unfortunate, unhappy; deplorable, depressing, pitiable, sad, shocking, sorrowful.

arrin murugsan. inextricable *adj* entangled, intricate, perplexed, unsolvable.

murugsan. mournful *adj* lamentable, sad, woeful; melancholy, sorrowful, tearful.

murugsan. melancholy *adj* blue, dejected, depressed, despondent, gloomy, glum, sad, sombre bisil. mellow *adj* mature, ripe; rich, silvery, smooth, soft; intoxicated, tipsy.

murugsan. blue *adj* dejected, depressed, dispirited, downcast, gloomy, glum, melancholy, sad.

musaafurin. exile *vb* banish, expatriate, expel, ostracize.

mushahaaro. wages *npl* allowance, earnings, emolument, hire, pay, payment, remuneration, salary, stipend.

mushaxaar. pay *n* allowance, remuneration, salary, wages.

mushkalad. dilemma *n* difficulty, fix, plight, predicament, problem, quandary, strait.

mushkilo. difficulty *n* dilemma, fix, hindrance, impediment, knot, obstacle, obstruction, pickle, predicament, trouble.

mushkilo. matter *n* difficulty, trouble; material, stuff; subject, subject matter, topic; discharge, pus.

mushkulad. problem *n* dilemma, dispute, doubt, puzzle, riddle, theorem.

mustaqbal. future *n* hereafter, outlook, prospect.

mustaqbal. outlook *n* future, prospect, view; lookout, watch-tower.

musuqid. embezzle *vb* appropriate, filch, misappropriate, pilfer, purloin, steal.

musuqmaasuq. corruption *n* demoralization, immorality, sinfulness, wickedness; bribery, dishonesty.

musuqqid. corrupt *vb* debase, falsify; bribe, entice.

mutacasab. bigoted *adj* dogmatic, intolerant, obstinate, narrow-minded, opinionated, prejudiced.

muunad. sample *n* illustration, instance, piece, specimen.

muuqaal. appearance *n* advent, arrival, apparition, coming; form, shape; colour, face, fashion, feature, guise, pretence, pretext; air, aspect, complexion, demeanour, manner, mien.

aan muuqan. opaque *adj* dark, dim, hazy, muddy, obscure, unclear.

muuqda, caan. notable *adj* distinguished, memorable, conspicuous, evident, noticeable, prominent, striking; well-known.

muuqda. manifest *adj* apparent, clear, conspicuous, visible.

si fiican u muuqda. vivid *adj* bright, brilliant, clear, expressive, graphic, intense, lucid, striking.

muuqda. ostensible *adj* apparent, declared, visible.

muuqda. evident *adj* apparent, clear, conspicuous, distinct, manifest, obvious, patent, plain, unmistakable.

muuqda. conspicuous *adj* apparent, clear, glaring, noticeable, striking, visible.

muuqda. apparent *adj* discernible, perceptible, visible; conspicuous, evident, legible, manifest, obvious, open, patent, plain, unmistakable.

muuqda. plain *adj* even, flat, level, certain, clear, conspicuous, evident, explicit, unambiguous, candid, direct, open, artless, natural, simple, unaffected, unlearned; unadorned.

muwaadin. native *n* aborigine, inhabitant, national, resident.

muwadin. citizen *n* inhabitant, resident, subject, townsman.

muxtarim ah. deferential *adj* respectful, reverential.

muxtarim. respectful *adj* courteous, deferential, dutiful, formal, polite.

muxtarim. respectable *adj* considerable, honourable, proper, upright, worthy.

muyusig. music *n* harmony, melody, symphony.

N

naadir. rare *adj* infrequent, scarce, uncommon, unusual.

naadir. scarce *adj* infrequent, rare, uncommon.

naafayn. maim *vb* cripple, disable, disfigure.

naafayn. disable *vb* cripple, enfeeble, hamstring, impair, paralyse.

naafayn. incapacitate *vb* cripple, disable; disqualify, make unfit.

naafaysan. lame *adj* crippled, disabled, halt.

naafo ah. crippled *adj* disabled, game, injured, lame.

naafo. maim *n* crippling, disfigurement, mutilation;

naaxaris leh. pitiful *adj* compassionate, kind, merciful, sympathetic.

nabad. peace *n* calm, quiet, accord, harmony; agreement, armistice.

nabadgelyo. farewell *n* adieu, leave-taking, departure, leave, parting, valedictory.

nabadgelyo. security *n* guard, protection, safeguard, safety, shelter.

nabadgelyo. goodbye *n* adieu, farewell, parting.

ku naban. adjacent *adj* adjoining, bordering, contiguous, near, near to, neighbouring, touching.

nabar bugsaday. scar *n* disfigurement, flaw, mark.

nabar u yeelid. scar *vb* hurt, mark, wound.

nabar. cut *n* gash, incision, nick, slit.

nabar. incision *n* cut, gash, notch, opening.

nabar. prick *n* mark, perforation, point, puncture; prickle, sting, wound.

nabcaysi. disapprove *vb* blame, censure, condemn, dislike.

la nabcaysto. resentful *adj* angry, bitter, hurt, irritable, revengeful, sore, touchy.

nacas. idiot *n* blockhead, booby, dunce, fool, ignoramus, imbecile, simpleton.

nacas. fool *n* blockhead, dolt, idiot, imbecile, nincompoop, ninny, nitwit, simpleton; buffoon, clown, harlequin, jester, punch, scaramouch, zany.

nacas. oaf *n* blockhead, dolt, dunce, fool, idiot, simpleton.

nacasnimo. idiotic *adj* fatuous, foolish, irrational, senseless, stupid.

nacasnimo. absurd *adj* extravagant, fantastic, fatuous, foolish, idiotic, incongruous, ill-advised, ill-judged, irrational, ludicrous, nonsensical, preposterous, ridiculous, senseless, silly, stupid, unreasonable.

nacasnimo. foolish *adj* brainless, daft, fatuous, idiotic, inane, inept, senseless, shallow, silly, simple, thick-skulled, witless; absurd, ill-judged, nonsensical, preposterous, ridiculous, unreasonable, unwise; childish, trivial.

nacayb. malice *n* animosity, bitterness, enmity, grudge, hate, ill will, malevolence.

nacladid. damn *vb* condemn, doom, kill, ruin.

nadal. villain *n* blackguard, reprobate, rogue, ruffian, scapegrace, scoundrel.

nadiif. clean *adj* immaculate, spotless, unsoiled, unspotted, unstained, unsullied, white.

nadiifa. tidy *adj* clean, neat, orderly, shipshape, spruce, trim.

nadiifan. clean *adj* hygienic, sanitary, wholesome.

nadiifin. tidy *vb* clean, neaten, straighten.

nadiifin. clean *vb* cleanse, purge, purify, rinse, scour, scrub, wash, wipe.

naf la'aan. inanimate *adj* dead, inert, lifeless.

nafaqayn. nourish *vb* feed, nurse, nurture, promote, succour.

nafaqo leh. nutritious *adj* invigorating, nourishing, strengthening, supporting, sustaining.

nafaqo leh. fertile *adj* fruitful, luxuriant, plenteous, productive, rich, teeming.

nafaqo. nourishment *n* diet, food, nutrition, sustenance.

nafaqo. nutrition *n* diet, food, nourishment.

nafayn. mutilate *vb* cripple, disfigure, injure, maim, mangle, mar.

nafayn. cripple *vb* lame, maim, mutilate, paralyse.

nafleh. live *adj* alive, animate, living; active, animated, wide-awake.

nafta. soul *n* mind, spirit; being, person..

najiijto. consequence *n* effect, result; conclusion, outcome.

nakhtiin. revise *vb* reconsider, re-examine, review; alter, amend, correct, edit.

naqdin. criticize *vb* appraise, evaluate, examine, judge.

naqli. imitation *adj* artificial, fake, man-made, mock, reproduction.

nasasho. pause *n* break, rest, suspension, hesitation.

nasasho. leisure *n* recreation, vacation.

nasasho. rest *vb* pause, repose, stop; sleep, slumber. *n* lull, pause, siesta, sleep.

nasid. pause *vb* rest, stay, stop, wait, hesitate.

nasiib badan leh. lucky *adj* auspicious, favourable, fortunate, propitious, prosperous.

nasiib darro. misfortune *n* adversity, affliction, bad luck, catastrophe, disaster, hardship,

nasiib leh. fortunate *adj* favoured, lucky, propitious, prosperous, successful.

nasiib. random *adj* casual, chance, haphazard.

nasiib. chance *n* accident, luck; possibility; opening, opportunity; risk.

nasiib. fortune *n* chance, luck, success; affluence, opulence, prosperity, riches, wealth; destiny, fate, lot, star.

nasiib. luck *n* chance, fate, fortune, hazard, serendipity, success.

nasiib. luck *n* destiny, doom, fate, fortune, lot.

natiijo. outcome *n* conclusion, consequence, result, upshot.

natiijo. result *n* conclusion, consequence, outcome; consequence, effect, end, fruit, outcome, product; decision, finding, verdict.

si naxariis ah. kindly *adj* benevolent, considerate, friendly, humane, well-disposed.

naxariis daran. unfeeling *adj* callous, cold-blooded, heartless, hard, stony, unkind, unsympathetic.

naxariis daran. pitiless *adj* cruel, hardhearted, merciless, relentless, unfeeling.

naxariis leh. obliging *adj* accommodating, civil, considerate, kind, friendly, polite.

naxariis leh. sympathetic *adj* commiserating, compassionate, kind, pitiful.

naxariis leh. compassionate *adj* gracious, kind, merciful, sympathetic, tender.

naxariis leh. kind *adj* amiable, benevolent, brotherly, charitable, compassionate, gentle, good, generous, humane, indulgent, lenient, obliging, sympathetic, tender-hearted.

naxariis leh. indulgent *adj* humouring, kind, lenient, pampering, tolerant.

naxariis leh. gentle *adj* humane, kind, lenient, mild, soft, tender, tender-hearted; docile, peaceable, placid, quiet, tame; chivalrous, courteous, refined.

naxariis leh. heartfelt *adj* cordial, deep-felt, profound, sincere, warm.

naxariis leh. motherly *adj* affectionate, kind, maternal, tender.

naxariis. compassion *n* kind-heartedness, kindness, mercy, pity, sympathy, tenderness.

naxariis. kindness *n* benevolence, charity, generosity, goodness, grace, humanity.

naxariis. sympathy *n* accord, affinity, agreement, fellow-feeling, kindliness.

naxaris daran. merciless *adj* barbarous, callous, cruel, hard-hearted, unfeeling.

naxaris leh. considerate *adj* thoughtful; charitable, patient.

naxaris leh. mild *adj* gentle, kind; bland, gentle, pleasant; calm, placid, pleasant, tranquil.

naxaris. badan. merciful *adj* compassionate, forgiving, gracious, lenient, pitiful.

naxaris. mercy *n* benevolence, clemency, compassion, leniency, pity, tenderness; blessing, favour, grace; forgiveness, pardon.

naxdin leh. terrible *adj* appalling, dire, dreadful, frightful, gruesome, horrible.

naxdin. shock *n* agitation, consternation, distress.

ka naxin. overawe *vb* frighten, intimidate, scare, terrify.

ka naxin. startle *vb* alarm, frighten, scare, shock; amaze, astonish, astound.

ka naxin. shock *vb* appal, horrify, offend, scandalize, stun.

naxin. menace *vb* alarm, frighten, intimidate, threaten.

firka naxsan. hysterical *adj* frantic, frenzied, overwrought, uncontrollable; comical uproarious.

necbaansho. dislike *n* aversion, disgust, distaste, loathing, repugnance.

necbaysi. animosity *n* bitterness, enmity, grudge, hatred, hostility, rancour, rankling, spleen, virulence.

neef qadasho. breathe *vb* live, exist; exhale, give out.

neef-tuurid. gasp *vb* blow, choke, pant, puff.

neefgurasho. pant *vb* gasp, puff.

neefjeedid. inhale *vb* breathe in, draw in, inbreathe, inspire.

neefsasho. breath *n* pant, sigh, respiration, whiff; pause, respite, rest; breathing space, instant, moment.

nicid. dislike *vb* detest, disapprove, hate, loathe.

nidaam la'aan. anarchy *n* chaos, confusion, disorder, misrule, lawlessness, riot.

nidaam. order *n* arrangement, method, system; law, regulation, rule; brotherhood, community, class, fraternity, society; sequence, succession.

nidaamin. arrange *vb* array, class, classify, dispose, distribute, group, range, rank; adjust, determine, fix upon, settle; concoct, construct, devise, plan, prepare, project.

nidaamin. order *vb* arrange, systematize; command, direct, instruct, require.

nidaamin. grade *vb* classify, group, order, rank, sort.

nidaamsan. shipshape *adj* neat, orderly, tidy, trim, well-arranged.

nidaamsan. systematic *adj* methodical, orderly, regular.

nidaamsan. neat *adj* clean, nice, orderly, tidy, trim, unsoiled.

nidaamsan. methodical *adj* exact, orderly, regular, systematic.

nidaamsan. orderly *adj* methodical, regular, systematic; peaceable, quiet, well-behaved; neat, shipshape, tidy.

si aan nidaamsanayn. slapdash *adv* haphazardly, messily, carelessly, hurriedly.

aan nidaamsanayn. disorderly *adj* chaotic, confused, intemperate, irregular, unmethodical, unsystematic, untidy, ungovernable, unmanageable, unruly.

aan nidaamsanayn. untidy *adj* disorderly, slatternly, slovenly, unkempt.

nin. man *n* adult, being, body, human, individual; humanity, humankind, mankind;

si niyad ah. solemn *adj* earnest, grave, serious, sober.

niyad jab. discouragement *n* dissuasion; deterrent, hindrance, impediment, obstacle.

niyad jab. depression *n* dent, dimple, dint, excavation, hollow, indentation, pit; blues, dejection, despondency, downheartedness, gloom, melancholy, sadness.

niyad jab. despair *n* dejection, desperation, despondency, hopelessness.

niyad jabid. despair *vb* despond, give up, lose hope.

niyad jabin. discourage *vb* deter, dissuade, hinder.

niyad ka jaban. depress *vb* dampen, deject, discourage, dishearten, dispirit, sadden.

niyad kac. unstrung *adj* overcome, shaken, unnerved, weak.

niyad kac. emotion *n* excitement, feeling, passion, sentiment, sympathy.

niyad kicin. excite *vb* animate, arouse, awaken, evoke, incite, inflame, instigate, kindle, move, provoke, rouse, spur, stimulate.

niyad wacni. goodwill *n* benevolence, kindness, good nature, patronage.

niyad. spirit *n* disposition, frame of mind, mood; cheerfulness, courage, energy, enthusiasm, resolution.

nolol dheeri. outlive *vb* last, live longer, survive.

nolol leh. lively *adj* active, agile, alert, brisk, energetic, nimble, quick, smart, stirring, supple, vigorous, vivacious; animated, blithe, gleeful, jolly, merry, spirited, sportive, sprightly, spry.

nolol leh. alive *adj* animate, breathing, live; aware, responsive, sensitive, susceptible; brisk, cheerful, lively, sprightly.

nolol. life *n* animation, energy, sparkle, verve, vigour; biography, curriculum vitae, memoirs, story.

nolosha. vitality *n* animation, life, strength, vigour, virility.

nooc. kind *n* brand, breed, class, genus, race, set, species, strain, style, type.

nooc. type *n* character, form, kind, nature, sort.

noocyo. variety *n* diversity, medley, miscellany, mixture, multiplicity, variation; kind, sort.

nool. live *vb* be, exist; continue, endure, last, remain, survive.

noolaan. subsist *vb* be, breathe, continue, endure, exist, live.

ku noolaan. lodge *vb* abide, dwell, inhabit, live, reside, rest, stay, stop.

ka noqosho. withdraw *vb* abstract, disengage, recall, remove, resign, retire, retract, revoke; decamp, depart, retire.

nugul. copy *n* duplicate, facsimile, off-print, replica, reproduction; model, pattern.

u nugul. susceptible *adj* impressionable, prone, receptive, sensitive.

nuqsaan. inferiority *n* mediocrity; deficiency, imperfection, inadequacy, shortcoming.

ka nuugid. extract *vb* extort, pull out, remove, withdraw. *n* excerpt, passage, quotation, selection; distillation, essence, infusion, juice.

nuugid. engross *vb* absorb, engage, occupy.

nuugis. absorb *vb* assimilate, drink in, imbibe, soak up; consume, devour, swallow up, take up; arrest, engage, engross, fix, immerse, occupy, rivet.

O

ogaansho. aware *adj* acquainted, apprised, conscious, conversant, informed, knowing, mindful, sensible.

ogalaan. consent *vb* agree, allow, assent, concur, permit.

ogeysiin. notify *vb* advertise, announce, inform, publish, promulgate.

ogeysiis. notice *n* advice, announcement, news, notification.

oggalaansho. permission *n* authorization, consent, permit, warrant.

ogglaan. concession *n* allowance, privilege.

u oggolaan. let *vb* admit, allow, authorize, permit.

oggolansho. admit *vb* let in, receive; agree to, accept, acknowledge, concede, confess; allow, bear, permit, suffer, tolerate.

ogolaansho. approve *vb* appreciate, commend, like, praise, recommend, value.

u ogolaansho. allow *vb* acknowledge, admit, concede, confess, grant, own; authorize, grant, let, permit; bear, endure, suffer, tolerate; grant, yield, relinquish, spare; approve, justify, sanction; abate, deduct, remit.

ogolaansho. authorization *n* confirmation, support.

ogolaasho siin. sanction *vb* authorize, support; confirm.

olole. expedition *n* campaign, excursion, journey, march, quest, voyage.

oohin dheer. bawl *vb* cry, howl, roar, shout, yell.

oohin. cry *n* exclamation, outcry, lament, weeping.

ooyid. wail *vb* bemoan, deplore, lament, mourn; cry, howl, weep. oohin. wail *n* complaint, cry, lamentation, moan.

ooyid. weep *vb* bemoan, bewail, complain, cry, lament, sob.

ooyid. cry *vb* call, exclaim; blubber, snivel, sob, wail, weep, whimper; scream, screech, squawk, yell; proclaim, publish.

ordid. race *vb* compete, run.

ordid. course *n* road, route, track, way; process, sequence.

ku ordid. rush *vb* attack, charge, dash, drive, gush, hurtle, surge, sweep, tear.

ordid. run *vb* bolt, career, gallop, hasten, hurry, race, scamper, scuttle; flow, glide, proceed, stream; liquefy, melt; flee; manage. flow, rill, rivulet, runlet, runnel, streamlet.

orod. rush *n* advance, dash, onslaught, flourish.

— Q —

qaab. means *npl* method, mode, way; income, resources, wealth, wherewithal.

qaab. shape *n* aspect, figure, form, outline, pattern.

qaab. form *n* contour, mould, outline, pattern, shape.

qaabayn. mould *vb* carve, form, make, model, shape.

qaabayn. shape *vb* form, make, fashion, mould.

u qaadasho. presume *vb* assume, believe, infer, surmise, suppose, think.

u qaadasho. assume *vb* take, undertake; affect, counterfeit, feign, pretend, sham; arrogate, usurp; beg, hypothesize, imply, postulate, posit, presuppose, suppose, simulate.

qaaddid. pick *vb* gather, pluck; choose.

kor u qaadid. enhance *vb* augment, elevate, heighten, increase, raise.

qaadid. take *vb* accept, grasp, seize, snatch; filch, pilfer, steal; arrest, capture, conquer, gain, win; choose, select; carry, conduct, convey.

ka qaadid. remove *vb* displace, shift, transfer; extract, withdraw; banish, destroy, suppress, depose, dismiss, eject, expel, oust.

kor u qaadid. elevate *vb* erect, hoist, lift, raise; exalt, promote; dignify, ennobl.

qaadid. shoulder *vb* bear, carry, hump, support,

qaadid. transport *vb* carry, convey, ship, take.

qaadid. bear *vb* support, uphold; carry, transport; endure, stand, suffer, tolerate, undergo.
dabeecadda. bearing *n* behaviour, deportment, conduct, carriage.

qaadid. carry *vb* bear, convey, transport; bear up, support, sustain.

qaajo. hungry *adj* famished, greedy, starved, starving.

qaali ah. expensive *adj* costly, dear, high-priced.

qaali ah. dear *adj* costly, expensive, high-priced; beloved, cherished, darling, precious, treasured.

qaali. costly *adj* dear, expensive, high-priced; luxurious, precious, sumptuous, valuable.

qaali. precious *adj* costly, priceless, prized, valuable; adored, beloved, cherished, dear, idolized, treasured.

qaangaar. mature *adj* full-grown, ripe; completed, ready, well-considered.

qaawan. bare *adj* exposed, naked, nude, stripped, unclothed, uncovered, undressed, unsheltered; plain, unadorned, uncovered, unfurnished; empty, destitute, poor.

qaawan. naked *adj* bare, nude, unclothed, uncovered, undressed; defenceless, exposed, unprotected; plain, stark, unconcealed, unvarnished.

qaawan. nude *adj* bare, exposed, naked, uncovered, unclothed, undressed.

qaawin. divest *vb* disrobe, strip, unclothe, undress; deprive, dispossess, strip.

qabasho. seize *vb* capture, grab, grasp, snatch; confiscate, arrest, capture.

qabasho. grip *vb* clasp, clutch, grasp, hold, seize.

qabasho. grapple *vb* catch, clutch, grasp, grip, hold, hug, seize, tackle, wrestle.

qabasho. hold *vb* clasp, clinch, clutch, grasp, grip, seize; have, keep, occupy, possess, retain; arrest, control, detain, imprison, restrain, restrict; bind, connect, fasten, fix, lock; keep up, maintain, sustain; cherish, embrace; adhere, cleave, cling, cohere, stick. *n* anchor, foothold, grasp, grip; prop, stay, support; claim, footing, vantage point; locker, storage, storehouse.

qabatid. grasp *vb* catch, clasp, clinch, clutch, grapple, grip, seize; comprehend understand.

la qabatimo. adopt *vb* appropriate, assume; accept, approve, avow, espouse, maintain, support; affiliate, father, foster.

qabo. catch *vb* apprehend, arrest, capture; overtake; enmesh, ensnare, entangle, entrap.

qabooji. cool *vb* chill, refrigerate; allay, calm, quieten.

qaboojin aad ah. freeze *vb* congeal, glaciate, harden, stiffen; chill.

qaboojin. quieten *vb* lull, pacify, soothe, tranquillize.

qabow. cold *adj* arctic, biting, bleak, chilly, cutting, frosty, icy, raw, wintry; frost-bitten, shivering; apathetic, frigid, indifferent, passionless, stony, unconcerned, unfeeling.

la qabsasho. adapt *vb* adjust, conform, coordinate, fit, qualify, proportion, suit, temper.

la qabsasho. acclimatize *vb* accustom, adapt, adjust, condition, familiarize, habituate, inure, naturalize, season.

qabsasho. occupy *vb* capture, hold, keep, possess.

qabsasho. conquer *vb* defeat, master, overcome, overpower, overthrow, rout, subdue, subjugate, vanquish; overcome, surmount.

la qabto. capture *vb* apprehend, arrest, catch, seize.

lagu qabto. nab vb catch, clutch, grasp, seize.

qabweyni. imperious *adj* arrogant, authoritative, haughty, overbearing, tyrannical.

qadarin. homage *n* allegiance, devotion, fidelity, loyalty, respect, reverence, service; adoration, devotion, worship.

qafis. cage *n* coop, pen, pound.

qalaad. stranger *n* foreigner.

qalaad. outlandish *adj* alien, exotic, foreign, strange; barbarous, bizarre, queer, strange, uncouth.

qalaad. strange *adj* alien, bizaare, curious, exotic, far-fetched, foreign, novel, odd, outlandish, peculiar, queer, remote, surprising, uncommon, unfamiliar, unknown, unusual.

qalab. equipment *n* apparatus, baggage, gear, outfit, rigging.

qalab. tackle *n* apparatus, equipment, gear, harness, implements.

qalab. implement *n* appliance, instrument, tool, utensil.

qalabeyn. equip *vb* appoint, arm, furnish, provide, rig, supply.

qalad. fault *n* blemish, defect, error, flaw, imperfection, spot, weakness.

qalafsan. rough *adj* bumpy, craggy, irregular, jagged, uneven; discourteous, gruff, harsh, impolite, rude, uncivil, unrefined; stormy, tempestuous, turbulent, violent, wild; disorderly, riotous, rowdy, uncivil.

qalbi furan. benign *adj* amiable, amicable, friendly, gentle, kind, kindly, obliging.

qalbi jaar. downhearted *adj* crestfallen, dejected, depressed, despondent, discouraged, disheartened, dispirited, downcast, low-spirited, sad, unhappy.

qalbi jab. heartbroken *adj* broken-hearted, comfortless, desolate, disconsolate, forlorn, inconsolable, miserable, woebegone, wretched.

qalcad. castle *n* citadel, fortress, stronghold.

qalcad. tower *n* dungeon, stronghold, tower, castle keep.

qalibaad. invert *vb* capsize, overturn; reverse, transpose.

qallafsan. stern *adj* austere, dour, forbidding, grim, severe, uncompromising.

qallafsan. presumptuous *adj* arrogant, assuming, brash, forward, irreverent, insolent.

qallalan. dry *adj* desiccated, dried; arid, parched; thirsty; barren, dull, plain, tedious, uninteresting; cutting, keen, sarcastic, sharp.

qallalid. wither *vb* dry, sear, shrivel, wilt, wizen; decline, droop, languish, waste.

qallalid. shrivel *vb* dry, dry up, wither, wrinkle.

qallibid. upset *vb* capsize, overturn, spill, topple; agitate, distress, disturb, fluster, shock, trouble.

qallibid. capsize *vb* overturn, upset.

qalloocan. indirect *adj* circuitous, devious, oblique, roundabout, tortuous.

qalloocan. oblique *adj* slanting, indirect, obscure.

qalloocin. bend *vb* bow, curve, deflect, turn; deviate, swerve, lower, stoop.

qalloocin. slant *vb* incline, lean, lie obliquely, list, slope.

qalloocin. tweak *vb, n* jerk, pinch, pull, twinge, twitch.

qalloocsami karo. flexible *adj* lithe, pliable, pliant, supple, willowy, yielding.

qalloocsan. bent *adj* angled, angular, bowed, crooked, curved, twisted; (*with* on) determined, fixed on, resolved. * *n* bias, inclination, leaning, partiality, propensity.

u qalma. worth *n* credit, excellence, importance, merit, worthiness, virtue; cost, estimation, price, value.

u qalmid. worthy *adj* deserving, fit, suitable; estimable, excellent, good, honest, honourable, reputable, upright.

u qalmid. deserve *vb* earn, gain, merit, procure, win.

aan u qalmin. unsuited *adj* unadapted, unfitted, unqualified.

qandaraas. contract *n* agreement, arrangement, bargain, bond, covenant, treaty.

qaniinid. sting *vb* hurt, nettle, prick, wound.

qaniinyo. morsel *n* bite, mouthful, titbit; bit, fragment, morceau, part, piece, scrap.

qanniinid. bite *vb* chew, crunch, gnaw.

qaraacid. knock *vb* beat, cuff, rap, slap.

qaraar. decision *n* adjudication, pronouncement, sentence, resolution.

qaraar. verdict *n* answer, decision, finding, judgement, opinion, sentence.

qarasho. understanding *n* intellect, intelligence, judgement, knowledge, sense.

qarax. eruption *n* explosion, outbreak, outburst; rash.

qarin. disguise *vb* conceal, cover, hide, mask, shroud, veil.

iska qarin. evade *vb* avoid, dodge, shun, elude, prevaricate.

qarin. cloak *vb* conceal, cover, hide, mask, veil.

qarin. hide *vb* bury, conceal, cover, secrete, suppress, withhold; cloak, disguise, eclipse, mask, screen, shelter, suppress, veil.

qarin. conceal *vb* bury, cover, hide; disguise, mask.

qaris. obscure *vb* cloud, darken, eclipse, shade; conceal, cover, hide.

qarka. rim *n* brim, border, edge, margin.

qarka. bank *n* embankment, knoll, mound; border, brink, margin, rim.

qarqid. drench *vb* dowse, drown, saturate, soak, souse, steep, wet.

qarqid. drown *vb* deluge, engulf, flood, immerse, inundate, overflow, sink, submerge, swamp; overcome, overpower, overwhelm.

qarraqan. wreck *n* crash, destruction, ruin, shipwreck, smash, undoing.

sir ku qarsi. confide *vb* entrust, trust.

qarsoodi. clandestine *adj* concealed, covert, furtive, hidden, private, secret.

qarsoodi. privacy *n* concealment, secrecy; seclusion, solitude.

qarsoodi. private *adj*confidential, hidden, secret.

qarsoodi. confidential *adj* private, secret.

qarsoodi. furtive *adj* clandestine, hidden, secret, sly, skulking, sneaking, sneaky, stealthy, stolen, surreptitious.

qarsoomid. disappear *vb* depart, fade, vanish; cease, dissolve.

qarsoomid. fade *vb* disappear, die, perish, vanish; decay, decline, droop, fall, languish, wither; bleach, pale.

qarsoon. mysterious *adj* dim, enigmatic, hidden, incomprehensible, inexplicable, obscure, puzzling, secret, unfathomable, unknown.

qarsoon. inscrutable *adj* hidden, impenetrable, incomprehensible, inexplicable, mysterious.

qarsoon. secret *adj* concealed, hidden, mysterious, unknown; confidential, private.

qarsoon. hidden *adj* clandestine, concealed, covered, masked, secret, veiled; dark, mysterious, mystic, obscure.

qarxid. explode *vb* burst, detonate, discharge, shatter.

qarxid. burst *vb* break open, explode, shatter, split open.

qas. mess *n* confusion, hotchpotch, jumble, muddle; pickle, plight, predicament.

qas. confusion *n* disorder, disturbance, jumble, tumult.

qas. confusion *n* confusion, disorder, medley, mess, mixture, muddle.

qas. commotion *n* agitation, disturbance, ferment; ado, disorder, disturbance, turbulence, turmoil.

qas. muddle *n* mess, plight, predicament.

qas. turmoil *n* agitation, commotion, confusion, ferment, flurry, hubbub, trouble, uproar.

qas. fuss *n* ado, agitation, bother, bustle, commotion, disturbance, pother, stir, worry.

qasab ah. compulsory *adj* binding, enforced, necessary, obligatory, unavoidable.

qasab. compulsion *n* force, forcing, pressure, urgency.

ku qasab. compel *vb* constrain, force, coerce, necessitate, oblige.

wax qashin ah. junk *n* rubbish, trash, waste.

qashin. waste *n* expenditure, extravagance, loss, squandering; debris, junk, refuse, rubbish, trash.

qashin. litter *n* confusion, disarray, disorder, mess, untidiness; fragments, rubbish, shreds. bedding; couch, palanquin, sedan, stretcher

qashin. rubbish *n* debris, refuse, waste; garbage, litter, trash.

qasid. muddle *vb* confuse, disarrange, disorder.

isku qasid. jumble *vb* confuse, mix, muddle.

ka qaxid. desert *vb* abandon, abscond, forsake, leave, quit, vacate.

qayaxan. stark *adj* absolute, bare, downright, pure, sheer.

qayaxan. distinct *adj* clear, defined, definite, obvious, plain, unmistakable.

ka qayb galid. participate *vb* engage in, partake, perform, share.

ka qayb qadasho. implicate *vb* include, involve.

qayb wax kamid ah. ingredient *n* component, constituent, element.

qayb. category *n* class, division, heading, order, rank.

qayb. segment *n* bit, part, piece, portion, section.

qayb. part *n* piece, portion, remnant, scrap, section, segment; component, constituent.

qayb. proportion *n* part, portion, quota, ratio, share.

qayb. portion *n* bit, fragment, morsel, part, piece, scrap, section; lot, measure, quota, ration, share.

qayb. ration *n* portion, share.

qayb. component *n* constituent, element, ingredient, part.

qayb. split *n* crack, fissure; breach, division, separation.

qayb. section *n* fraction, part, piece, segment, slice.

qayb. division *n* category, class, compartment, section, segment; breach, difference, disagreement, discord, feud, rupture, variance.

qaybin. distribute *vb* allocate, allot, apportion, assign, deal, dispense, divide, dole out, give, share.

qaybin. split *vb* rend, splinter; divide, part, separate.

qaybin. deal *vb* dispense, distribute, divide, give, share.

qaybin. circulate *vb* disseminate, promulgate, publish, spread.

qaybin. divide *vb* bisect, cleave, cut, dismember, disunite, open, part, rend, segregate, separate, sever, split; allot, apportion, assign, distribute, dole, mete, portion, share; demarcate, partition.

qaybin. ration *vb* apportion, distribute, restrict.

qaybin. part *vb* divide, sever, detach, separate.

qaybinaaya. parting *adj* dividing, separating; departing.

qaybsasho. share *vb* divide, parcel out, split; participate.

qaylin. clatter *vb* rattle; babble, jabber, prattle.

qaylin. shout *vb* bawl, cheer, roar, whoop, yell.

qaylin. scream *vb* screech, shriek, squeal.

qaylin. yell *vb* bawl, bellow, cry out, roar, screech, shriek, squeal.

qaylin. clamour *vb* shout, vociferate.

qaylin. squeal *vb* scream, screech, shriek, squawk, yell.

qaylin. mouth *n* chaps, jaws; aperture, opening, orifice, entrance, inlet;

qaylo dheer. uproar *n* clamour, din, hullabaloo, noise, outcry, uproar.

qaylo. racket *n* clamour, clatter, din, hubbub, noise, uproar; game, scheme.

qaylo. squeal *n* scream, screech, shriek, squawk, yell.

qaylo. din *n* clamour, clatter, crash, hubbub, hullabaloo, noise, racket, row, shout, uproar.

qaylo. tumult *n* agitation, flurry, fracas, hubbub, melee, noise, racket, turmoil, uproar.

qaylo. outcry *n* clamour, noise, shout, tumult.

qaylo. cry *n* cry, screech, shriek.

qayo dheer oo dhuuban. yell *n* cry, howl, roar, scream, screech, shriek.

qayrel caadi. monstrous *adj* colossal, enormous, extraordinary, huge, immense; dreadful, flagrant, frightful, terrible.

aan qeexnayn. vague *adj* ambiguous, doubtful, indefinite, ill-defined, indistinct, uncertain, undetermined, unfixed, unsettled.

qeyaxan. unvarnished *adj* candid, plain, simple, true, unadorned, unembellished.

qeydhin. raw *adj* inexperienced, unseasoned, untried; crude, green, immature, unfinished, unripe; uncooked.

qiimaha. charge *n* responsibility, trust; order, instruction; cost, expense, outlay; price, sum; assault, attack.

qiimayn hoose. underestimate *vb* belittle, underrate, undervalue.

qiimayn. value *vb* appraise, assess, estimate; esteem, prize, treasure. qiime leh *n* importance, usefulness, utility, worth; cost, price;

qiime leh. remarkable *adj* distinguished, eminent, extraordinary, noteworthy; rare, strange, striking, unusual.

qiime leh. valuable *adj* advantageous, precious, useful; costly, expensive, rich; admirable, estimable, worthy.

qiime. cost *n* amount, charge, expenditure, expense, outlay, price.

qiimeyn. treasure *vb* cherish, prize, value.

qiimeyn. appreciate *vb* appreciate, esteem, estimate, rate, realize, value.

qiimeyn. rate *vb* estimate, value. * *n* cost, price.

qiimeyn. price *vb* assess, evaluate, rate, value.

qiimeyn. prize *vb* appreciate, cherish, esteem, treasure, value.

qiimo lahayn. base *adj* cheap, inferior, low, sorry, worthless.

wax qiimo-daran. tawdry *adj* flashy, gaudy, garish, meretricious, ostentatious, showy.

qiimolahayn. worthless *adj* futile, paltry, poor, trifling, useless, valueless, wretched; base, ignoble, low, mean, vile.

qiiq leh. steamy *adj* misty, moist, vaporous.

qiiq. smoke *n* fume, mist, vapour.

qiiraysan. ardent *adj* burning, fiery, hot; eager, earnest, fervent, impassioned, keen, passionate, warm, zealous.

qirid. acknowledge *vb* recognize; accept, admit, accept, allow, concede, grant; avow, confess, own, profess.

qirid. profess *vb* acknowledge, affirm, allege, avow, confess, declare, proclaim, state.

qirird. confess *vb* admit, own up.

qirrid. certify *vb* attest, notify, testify, vouch, verify.

qiyaas. criterion *n* gauge, measure, standard, test, touchstone.

qiyaas. size *n* amount, bulk, dimensions, extent, mass, volume.

qiyaas. estimation *n* estimation, judgement, valuation; calculation, computation.

qiyaas. measure *n* gauge, meter, rule; degree, extent, length, limit; metre, rhythm, tune, verse.

qiyaas. estimation *n* estimate, valuation;judgement, opinion; honour, regard, respect, reverence.

qiyaasid. time *vb* control, measure, regulate.

qiyaasid. estimate *vb* assess, calculate, gauge, judge, reckon.

qiyaasid. measure *vb* estimate, gauge, value.

qod. mine *n* colliery, pit, shaft.

qodid. dig *vb* delve, excavate, hollow out, quarry, scoop, tunnel.

qodid. mine *vb* dig, excavate, quarry, unearth;

qof iska adag. self-control *n* restraint, willpower.

qof sharciga ka baxsaday. fugitive *n* émigré, escapee, evacuee, fleer, outlaw, refugee, runaway.

qof. guy *n* boy, man, person; dowdy, eccentric, fright, scarecrow.

qof. mortal *n* human, man, person, woman.

qof. body *n* carcass, corpse, remains; torso, trunk, mass; being, individual, mortal person; company, corporation, party, troop.

qofaan waxba isku falayn. scoundrel *n* cheat, rascal, rogue, swindler, trickster, villain.

qofka iska dhiga waxaanu ahayn. impostor *n* charlatan, cheat, deceiver, mountebank, pretender, trickster.

qofka jago haya. incumbent *n* holder, occupant.

qol. room *n* accommodation, capacity, latitude, scope, space; place, apartment, chamber, lodging.

qol. hut *n* cabin, cottage, lodge, shed; association club, group, society.

qolof. frame *n* framework, shell, skeleton; form, structure.

qoqobid. segregate *vb* detach, disconnect, part, separate.

qoraal. memorandum *n* minute, note, record.

qori-xarfid. xylograph *n* cut, woodcut, wood engraving.

qorid. write *vb* compose, copy, inscribe, pen, scrawl, scribble, transcribe.

aan la qorin. unwritten *adj* oral, traditional, unrecorded.

qoris. note *n* account, bill, epistle, letter, promissory note; (of music).

qorshayn. project *vb* plan, delineate, draw, exhibit; bulge, extend, jut, protrude.

qorshayn. scheme *vb* design, plan, plot, project.

qorshayn. manoeuvre *vb* contrive, intrigue, manage, plan, plot, scheme.

qorshe. strategy *n* plan, policy, stratagem, tactics.

qorshe. plan *n* diagram, sketch; arrangement, programme, project, scheme.

qorshe. design *n* plan, system; conspiracy, intrigue, plot.

qosal. chuckle *n* giggle, laughter, snigger, titter.

qoslid. laugh *vb* cackle, chortle, chuckle, giggle, guffaw, snicker, snigger, titter.

lagu qoslo. laughable *adj* amusing, comical, droll, farcical, funny, ludicrous, mirthful, ridiculous.

wax lugu qoslo. farcical *adj* absurd, comic, droll, funny, laughable, ludicrous, ridiculous.

wax qosol leh. funny *adj* amusing, comic, comical, diverting, droll, facetious, farcical, humorous, jocose, jocular, laughable, ludicrous, sportive, witty; curious, odd, queer, strange. *n* jest, joke; cartoon, comic.

qosol leh. comical *adj* amusing, farcical, funny, humorous, laughable, ludicrous.

qosol leh. humorous *adj* comic, comical, droll, funny, jocular, laughable, ludicrous, playful, witty.

qosol. laugh, *n* chortle, chuckle, giggle, guffaw, laughter, titter.

qosol. smile *n* grin, simper, smirk.

wax lugu qosolo. ridiculous *adj* absurd, amusing, comical, droll, eccentric, farcical, funny, laughable, ludicrous, nonsensical, preposterous.

qoxooti. refugee *n* refugee, exile.

qoyaan. wet *n* dampness, humidity, moisture, wetness.

qoyan. humid *adj* damp, dank, moist, wet.

qoyan. sodden *adj* drenched, saturated, soaked, wet.

qoyan. damp *adj* dank, humid, moist, wet.

qoyn. steep *vb* saturate, soak.

qoyn. wet *vb* damp, dampen, drench, moisten, saturate, soak, sprinkle, water.

qoyn. soak *vb* drench, saturate, wet.

qoys. family *n* household, people; ancestors, blood, clan, dynasty, kindred, lineage, race, stock, strain, tribe; class, genus, group, kind, subdivision.

qubaysi. bathe *vb* immerse, wash, drench, flood.

ka qubid. spill *vb* effuse, pour out, shed.

qudh ka jarid. assassinate *vb* butcher, destroy, kill, massacre, murder, slaughter, slay.

qudhgoye. murder *n* assassination, homicide, killing, manslaughter, massacre.

qudhgoye. murderer *n* assassin, butcher, cut-throat, killer, slayer.

qudhmay. dilapidated *adj* decadent, decayed, ruined, run down, wasted.

qudhmay. rotten *adj* corrupt, decomposed, putrid, rank, stinking; defective, unsound; corrupt, deceitful, immoral, unsound, untrustworthy.

qudhmay. rancid *adj* bad, fetid, foul, sour, stinking.

qudhmay. musty *adj* fetid, mouldy, sour, spoiled, stale.

qudhmid. rot *vb* decay, decompose, degenerate, putrefy, spoil.

qudhmid. decay *vb* deteriorate, disintegrate, fail, perish, wither; decompose, putrefy, rot.

qudhun. rot *n* corruption, decay, decomposition, putrefaction.

quful. lock *n* bolt, fastening, padlock; embrace, grapple, hug.

qufulid. lock *vb* bolt, fasten, padlock, seal; confine, impede, restrain, stop.

qullad. jar *n* can, crock, ewer, jug.

qulqul. flow *n* current, discharge, flood, gush, rush, stream, trickle; abundance, copiousness.

qulqulid. flow *vb* pour, run, stream; come, emanate, issue, spring.

quman. vertical *adj* erect, perpendicular, plumb, steep, upright.

qunyar socod. conservative *adj* preservative, unprogressive.

qunyar. slow *adj* deliberate, gradual; dull, sluggish, stupid.

qunyarid. slow *vb* decelerate, moderate, ease up, relax, slacken.

qurix leh. stylish *adj* chic, elegant, fashionable, polished, smart.

qurob. cut *n* gash, slash, slit.

qurux. beauty *n* attractiveness, comeliness, loveliness.

qurxin. embellish *vb* adorn, beautify, decorate, emblazon, enhance, enrich, garnish, grace, ornament.

dahab ku qurxin. gild *vb* adorn, beautify, bedeck, decorate, embellish, illuminate.

qurxin. flowery *adj* embellished, ornate.

qurxin. ornament *vb* adorn, beautify, bedeck, decorate, grace.

qurxin. enrich *vb* endow; adorn, deck, decorate, embellish, ornament.

qurxin. decorate *vb* adorn, beautify, bedeck, deck, embellish, garnish, grace, ornament.

la qurxiyey. ornate *adj* decorated, elaborate, elegant, embellished, flowery, ornamental.

qurxoon. handsome *adj* comely, fine-looking; becoming, graceful; generous, gracious, magnanimous.

qurxoon. lovely *adj* beautiful, charming, delightful, enchanting, exquisite, graceful, pleasing, sweet, winning.

qurxoon. sunny *adj* bright, brilliant, cheerful, genial, optimistic, smiling, unclouded.

qurxoon. fancy *adj* elegant, fine, nice, ornament; extravagant, fanciful.

qurxoon. beautiful *adj* charming, exquisite, handsome, lovely, pretty.

qurxoon. pretty *adj* attractive, beautiful, bonny, comely, elegant, pleasing, trim.

qurxoon. graceful *adj* beautiful, becoming, comely, easy, elegant.

qurxoon. splendid *adj* brilliant, imposing, magnificent, sumptuous, superb; grand, heroic, noble, sublime.

qurxoon. elegant *adj* beautiful, graceful, handsome, courtly, cultivated, fashionable, polished, refined.

quudin, cunto. feed *vb* cherish, eat, nourish, sustain.

quudin. nourish *vb* feed, nurse, nurture, promote, succour.

quudin. nurture *vb* feed, nourish, nurse, tend, train.

quusid. dive *vb* plunge.

quusid. sink *vb* droop, drop, fall, founder, go down, submerge.

quusid. duck *vb* dip, dive, immerse, plunge, submerge; bend, bow, dodge, stoop.

R

ra'yi. opinion *n* idea, impression, judgment, view.

ra'yi. standpoint *n* point of view, viewpoint.

ra'yi. impression *n* fancy, idea, instinct, notion, opinion, recollection; effect, influence, sensation; brand, imprint, mark, stamp.

ku raacid. concur *vb* agree, approve, consent, cooperate.

ku raacid. endorse *vb* approve, back, confirm, ratify, sanction, support, vouch for, warrant;.

raacid. accompany *vb* attend, chaperon, convoy, escort, follow, go with.

raacsan. moreover *adv, conj* also, besides, further, furthermore, likewise, too.

raad. trace *n* evidence, mark, record, sign, vestige.

raad. track *n* footmark, footprint, footstep, mark, trace; course, pathway, road, way.

raad. footstep *n* footmark, footprint, trace, track.

raadin. trace *vb* detect, follow, track, unearth.

raadin. seek *vb* hunt, look, search; attempt, try.

raadin. search *vb* explore, ferret, hunt, look, probe.

raadis. hunt *n* exploration, inquiry, inspection, investigation.

raajito. X-ray *n* roentgen ray, röntgen ray.

raajo. desire *n* passion; hope, want, wish.

raali ah. willing *adj* amenable, compliant, disposed, inclined, minded; eager, forward, prompt, ready.

raalinimo. content *adj* agreeable, contented, happy, pleased, satisfied.

raaliyeyn. apology *n* defence, justification, vindication; acknowledgement, excuse, explanation, plea, reparation.

raalli gelin. satisfy *vb* content, please, suffice; convince, persuade; answer, fulfil, meet.

raalli ka noqosho. satisfaction *n* comfort, contentment, ease, enjoyment, pleasure.

u raaxayn. comfort *vb* cheer, console, encourage, gladden, soothe.

u raaxayn. relieve *vb* aid, comfort, free, help, succour, support, sustain; release, rescue.

ku raaxaysi. gusto *n* enjoyment, gust, liking, pleasure, relish, zest.

raaxaysi. comfort *n* help, support, succour; consolation, relief.

raaxo lahayn. uneasy *adj* apprehensive, edgy, nervous, restive, uncomfortable, unquiet, worried.

raaxo leh. snug *adj* comfortable, compact, cosy, sheltered

raaxo leh. cosy *adj* comfortable, easy, snug.

raaxo leh. luxurious *adj* opulent, pampered, self-indulgent, sensual, voluptuous.

raaxo. pleasure *n* comfort, delight, enjoyment, joy, gladness, amusement, diversion, entertainment.

raaxo. enjoyment *n* delight, delectation, gratification, happiness, pleasure, satisfaction.

raaxo. luxury *n* enjoyment, gratification, indulgence, opulence, pleasure.

rabash. nuisance *n* annoyance, bore, bother, infliction, pest.

rabayn. domesticate *vb* tame.

aan la rabayn. untamed *adj* fierce, unbroken, wild.

rabbaayad. tame *adj* docile, domesticated; commonplace, dull, flat, uninteresting.

rabbayn. rear *vb* nurse, nurture, train; breed, grow.

rabbayn. tame *vb* domesticate, subdue, train.

rabid. wish *vb* desire, hanker, long; direct, intend, mean, want. rabitaan. wish *n* behest, desire, intention, want, will; desire, hankering, inclination, liking, longing, want, yearning.

rabid. long (for) *vb* crave, desire, hanker, lust, pine, wish, yearn.

rabid. need *vb* demand, lack, require, want.

rabid. lust *vb* covet, crave, desire, want, yearn.

rabitaan. whim *n* caprice, fancy, humour, quirk, vagary, whimsy, wish.

rabitaan. will *n* determination, resoluteness, self-reliance; desire, intent, purpose, volition, wish; command, decree, order, request.

rabitaan. longing *n* craving, desire, hankering, hunger, pining, yearning.

rabitaan. desire *n* longing, lust; carnality, lasciviousness, lechery, lewdness, wantonness.

rabshad badan. troublesome *adj* distressing, disturbing, painful; irksome, tiresome; importunate, intrusive.

rabshad. disturbance *n* ado, confusion, excitement; commotion, disorder, tumult, uproar.

rabshad. hurly-burly *n* bustle, commotion, confusion, disturbance, tumult, turmoil.

rabshayn. trouble *vb* agitate, annoy, concern, disturb, distress, molest, perplex.

rabsheen. perturb *vb* agitate, disturb, trouble, unsettle, vex.

rabshid. interrupt *vb* break, check, disturb, hinder, intercept, interfere with, obstruct, stop.

rabsho. chaos *n* anarchy, confusion, disorder.

rabsho. trouble *n* adversity, distress, misfortune; fuss, inconvenience, vexation.

rabshoole. knotty *adj* complex, difficult, hard, involved, perplexing, troublesome.

racfaan. application *n* entreaty, invocation, solicitation, suit.

rafcaan qaadasho. appeal *vb* address, entreat, implore, invoke, refer, request, solicit. rafcaan.

rag ah. virile *adj* forceful, manly, masculine, robust, vigorous.

rajayn. hope *vb* anticipate, await, expect, long; believe, rely, trust.

rajo gelin. inspire *vb* animate, enliven, stimulate.

rajo la'aan. hopeless *adj* abject, crushed, depressed, despondent, despairing, desperate, disconsolate, downcast, forlorn, pessimistic, woebegone; abandoned, helpless, incurable; impossible, unachievable, unattainable.

rajo la'aan. desperation *n* despair, hopelessness; fury, rage.

rajo leh. promising *adj* auspicious, encouraging, hopeful, likely, propitious.

rajo xumi. pessimistic *adj* depressed, despondent, downhearted, gloomy, morose, sad.

rajo. hopeful *adj* anticipatory, confident, expectant, optimistic, sanguine; cheerful, encouraging, promising.

rajo. anticipation *n* apprehension, contemplation, expectation, hope, prospect, trust; expectancy, forecast, foresight, foretaste, preconception, presentiment.

rajo. hope *n* confidence, belief, faith, trust; anticipation, desire, expectancy, expectation.

rajo. expectation *n* anticipation, hope, prospect, reliance, trust.

rakaab. passenger *n* traveller, voyager.

randhiis. durable *adj* abiding, constant, enduring, lasting, permanent.

rarid. saddle *vb* burden, encumber, load.

rarrid. pack *vb* compress, fill; load.

rasayn. pile *vb* amass, collect, heap, load.

rasmi. formal *adj* official, strict; exact, precise, prim, punctilious, rigid, starched, set, strict.

raxan. swarm *n* crowd, horde, host, multitude, throng.

raxoleh. comfortable *adj* agreeable, enjoyable, pleasant; convenient, snug; painless.

ka reebid. exclude *vb* ban, bar, blackball, debar, ostracize, preclude, reject.

reer aduun. earthly *adj* terrestrial; worldly; material, natural, secular, temporal.

reer guuranimo. nomadic *adj* migratory, pastoral, vagrant, wandering.

reerguuraa. itinerant *adj* nomadic, peripatetic, roaming, roving, travelling, unsettled, wandering.

ridid. depose *vb* dethrone, displace, oust.

ridis. topple *vb* fall, overturn, tumble, upset.

riixid. propel *vb* drive, force, impel, push, urge; hurl, throw.

riixid. shove *vb* jostle, propel, push, push aside.

riixid. thrust *vb* drive, force, impel, jam, plunge, poke, push, ram, run.

riixid. push *vb* elbow, jostle, shove, thrust; advance, drive, urge;

riixid. pull *vb* drag, haul, tow, tug; gather, pick, pluck, detach.

riyo. dream *n* day-dream, delusion, fancy, fantasy, hallucination, illusion, imagination, vision.

riyoon. dream *vb* fancy, imagine, think.

rogid. tumble *vb* roll, toss, wallow; fall, topple, trip; disarrange, rumple, tousle.

rogid. overturn *vb* overthrow, reverse, subvert, upset.

roob da'did. hail *vb* bombard, rain, shower, storm, volley.

roob. rain *n* cloudburst, downpour, shower.

isku roodid. shrink *vb* contract, dwindle, shrivel; draw back, flinch, quail, recoil, wince.

rooxaan. ghost *n* apparition, phantom, spectre, spook, sprite.

aan la rumaysan. incredible *adj* absurd, inadmissible, nonsensical, unbelievable.

rumaysnaan. faith *n* belief, confidence, reliance, trust; creed, doctrines, dogmas, persuasion, religion.

run ah. genuine *adj* authentic, honest, proper, real, right, true, veritable.

run ah. true *adj* actual, authentic, genuine, real; accurate, correct, exact, straight.

run ah. frank *adj* candid, direct, open, outspoken, plainspoken, sincere, straightforward, truthful, unreserved.

run ah. real *adj* actual, authentic, genuine, true.

run badan. truthful *adj* correct, reliable, true, trustworthy, veracious.

run-sheeg. aboveboard *adj* candid, frank, honest, open, straightforward, truthful, upright.

run-sheeg. outspoken *adj* blunt, candid, frank, plainspoken, unreserved.

run. fact *n* occurrence, performance; actuality, certainty, existence, reality, truth.

run. truth *n* fact, certainty, honesty, probity, reality.

run. reality *n* fact, truth.

runlow. candid *adj* unbiased, unprejudiced; frank, honest, open, sincere, straightforward.

runtii. indeed *adv* absolutely, actually, certainly, in fact, in truth, in reality, positively, really, strictly, truly, verily, veritably. *interj* really! you don't say! is it possible!

ruugid. chew *vb* crunch, masticate, munch; bite, champ, gnaw.

ruxid. flap *vb* beat, flutter, shake, vibrate, wave.

ruxid. wag *vb* nod, shake, waggle.

ruxid. rock *vb* cradle, soothe, still, tranquillize; reel, shake, sway.

ruxis. shake *vb* quake, quiver, shiver, tremble; agitate, jar, jolt, frighten.

ruxitaan. wag *n* flutter, nod, oscillation, vibration.

S

saadaal. forecast *n* plan, prophecy.

saadaal. forecast *vb* anticipate, foresee, predict.

saadaalin. predict *vb* forecast, foresee, foretell, forewarn, portend, prophesy, soothsay.

saadaalin. divine *vb* foretell, predict, prophesy.

saafi. fair *adj* blond, light, white; beautiful, comely; clear, cloudless, pleasant, unclouded; equitable, just; average, indifferent, ordinary, passable, reasonable, tolerable.

saafi. pure *adj* immaculate, spotless, stainless, unadulterated, unblemished, unpolluted; chaste, holy, incorrupt, innocent,virgin, virtuous.

saafinimo. purity *n* cleanness, clearness, correctness, faultlessness, honesty, innocence, integrity, piety.

saaflabood. radical *adj* essential, fundamental, uncompromising, total.

saahidnim. pious *adj* devout, godly, holy, religious.

saamax. forgiveness *n* absolution, acquittal, amnesty, exoneration, pardon, remission, reprieve.

ka saamaxnaan. immunity *n* exemption, freedom, release.

saami. part *n* part, portion, allotment, share.

saamixid. forgive *vb* absolve, acquit, condone, excuse, exonerate, pardon, remit.

saamixid. excuse *vb* absolve, acquit, exonerate, forgive, pardon, remit; overlook.

saamixid. pardon *vb* forgive, remit; acquit, excuse.

saaqid ah. delinquent *adj* negligent, offending.

ka saarid. eject *vb* disgorge, emit, evacuate, spew, spit, spout, spurt, vomit; reject, throw out.

ka saarid. evict *vb* dispossess, eject, thrust out.

soo saarid. emit *vb* breathe out, discharge, eject, exhale, outpour, spurt, squirt.

saaxib shaqo. colleague *n* ally, assistant, associate, collaborator, companion, helper, partner.

saaxib. partner *n* associate, colleague.

saaxib. friend *adj* advocate, ally, associate, benefactor, chum, companion, comrade, crony, confidant, defender, intimate, patron, supporter, well-wisher.

saaxib. mate *n* associate, companion, consort, crony, friend; husband, spouse, wife.

aad u saaxiib ah. intimate *adj* close, near; familiar, friendly; bosom, chummy, dear, special; confidential, personal, private, secret; cosy, friendly, warm.

la saaxiib leh. sociable *adj* affable, companionable, friendly, genial.

saaxiib. fellow *n* associate, companion, comrade; counterpart, mate, match, partner; member; boy, character, individual, man, person.

saaxiib. crony *n* ally, associate, chum, friend, mate, pal.

saaxiib. friend *n* chum, confidant, companion, crony, intimate.

saaxiib. pal *n* buddy, chum, companion, comrade, friend.

la saaxiibid. befriend *vb* aid, assist, help, patronize.

saaxiibtinimo ah. friendship *n* affection, attachment, fondness, love, regard; fellowship, familiarity, fraternization, intimacy.

si saaxiibtinimo ah. friendly *adj* affectionate, amiable, kind, well-disposed; amicable, cordial, fraternal, neighbourly; conciliatory, peaceable, unhostile.

si saaxiibtinimo ah. amicable *adj* amiable, cordial, friendly, harmonious, kind, kindly, peaceable.

sabab. motive *n* cause, purpose, reason, stimulus.

aan sababsanayn. arbitrary *adj* absolute, autocratic, despotic, domineering, imperious, overbearing, unlimited; capricious, discretionary, fanciful, voluntary, whimsical.

sabbayn. float *vb* drift, glide, hang, ride, sail, soar, swim, waft.

sabbayn. waft *vb* carry, convey, drift, float, transmit, transport.

sabool. poor *adj* indigent, impecunious, penniless, poverty-stricken; barren, paltry, slight, small, valueless, worthless; frail, weak; miserable, unfortunate, unhappy, unlucky, wretched; deficient, insufficient, meagre, scant.

saboolnimo. needy *adj* destitute, poor.

saboolnimo. poverty *n* destitution, distress, impecuniousness, indigence, penury, privation, straits, want; beggary, pauperism; dearth, lack.

sacab tumid. clap *vb* applaud, cheer. *n* bang, burst, explosion.

sacbin. applaud *vb* acclaim, approve, cheer, clap, commend, compliment, encourage, extol, magnify.

sadaqo. philanthropy *n* alms-giving, altruism, benevolence, charity, kindness.

sadhayn. infect *vb* contaminate, corrupt, defile, poison, pollute, taint, vitiate.

saf. row *n* file, line, queue, series, string, tier; alley, street, terrace.

safar badda ah. voyage *n* crossing, cruise, journey, passage, sail.

safar gaaban. excursion *n* drive, expedition, jaunt, journey, ramble, ride, sally, tour, trip, voyage, walk.

safar-gaaban. jaunt *n* excursion, ramble, tour, trip.

safar. quest *n* expedition, journey, search, voyage.

safar. journey *n* excursion, expedition, jaunt, pilgrimage, tour, trip, voyage.

safayn. refine *vb* clarify, purify; improve, polish.

safayn. polish *vb* buff, burnish, shine, smooth; civilize, refine.

aan safaysnayn. earthy *adj* coarse, material, unrefined.

safid. rank *vb* arrange, classify.

safrid. travel *vb* journey, roam, rove, tour, voyage, go.

bad ku safrid. voyage *vb* cruise, journey, navigate, sail.

safrid. tour *vb* journey, travel, visit.

safrid. journey *vb* roam, rove, travel.

sagaxadda guriga. floor *n* storey; bottom, deck, pavement, stage.

sahamin. survey *vb* examine, inspect, review, scan, study, view.

sahan. survey *n* examination, inspection, retrospect.

sahlan. informal *adj* easy, familiar, natural, simple.

u sahlid. facilitate *vb* expedite, help.

sakhraan. drunk *adj* inebriated, intoxicated, tipsy.

aan sakhransanayn. sober *adj* temperate, unintoxicated; cool, reasonable, serious, steady.

salaad. prayer *n* beseeching, entreaty, adoration, devotion(s)

salaamid. greet *vb* accost, address, complement, hail, salute, welcome.

salaamid. hail *vb* greet, salute; accost, address, call, hallo, signal.

salaan. greeting *n* compliment, salutation, salute, welcome.

salaaxid. fondle *vb* caress, coddle, cosset, pet.

salbabakh. panic *n* alarm, fear, fright, terror.

salbabakhid. panic *vb* alarm, scare, terrify; become terrified, overreact.

sallad. basket *n* box, crate, hamper, picnic basket.

samafal. charity *n* benevolence, goodwill, kindness, generosity.

samafale. benevolent *adj* charitable, generous, humane, kind, kind-hearted, obliging, philanthropic, tender, unselfish.

samayn. make *vb* create; fashion, figure, form, frame, mould, shape;

samayn. form *vb* fashion model, mould, shape; make, produce; discipline, educate, teach, train.

samayn. constitute *vb* compose, form, make, set up.

samayn. perform *vb* accomplish, do, fulfil, satisfy; act, play.

samays. texture *n* character, composition, constitution, fabric, grain, make-up, structure.

samir la'aan. impatient *adj* restless; eager, hasty, impetuous, irritable.

sanam. idol *n* deity, god, icon, image, symbol; beloved, darling, favourite, pet.

sarbeeb ah. metaphorical *adj* allegorical, figurative, symbolic.

sarir. couch *n* bed, divan, seat, settee, sofa.

sarraysa. lofty *adj* elevated, haughty, high, imposing, majestic, proud, stately, tall, towering.

ugu sarreeya. supreme *adj* chief, dominant, first, highest, paramount, pre-eminent, principal.

ugu sarreeya. top *adj* chief, finest, first, highest, leading, principal, uppermost.

sarreeya. high *adj* elevated, lofty, tall, towering; costly, dear, pricey; high-pitched, high-toned, piercing, sharp, shrill.

ugu sarreeya. sovereign *adj* chief, commanding, highest, principal, supreme.

sarreya. superior *adj* better, greater, higher, finer, first-class, foremost, principal.

ugu sarreysa. uppermost *adj* foremost, highest, loftiest, supreme, topmost, upmost.

halka ugu sarreysa. climax *n* crown, culmination, head, peak, summit, top.

sawir. facsimile *n* copy, duplicate, fax, reproduction.

sawir. effigy *n* figure, image, likeness, portrait, representation, statue.

sawir. picture *n* illustration, image, likeness, portrait.

sawirid. outline *vb* draft, draw, silhouette, sketch.

sawirid. duplicate *vb* copy, double, repeat, replicate, reproduce. *n* copy, counterpart, facsimile, replica, transcript.

sawirid. film *vb* darken, fog, mist, obscure, veil; photograph, shoot, take.

sawirid. mirror *vb* copy, echo, emulate, reflect, show.

sawirid. map *vb* chart, draw up, plan, plot, set out, sketch.

sawiro leh. graphic *adj* descriptive, diagrammatic, figurative, pictorial, striking, telling, vivid, well-drawn.

sax ah. legitimate *adj* genuine, valid; correct, justifiable, logical, reasonable.

sax ah. precise *adj* accurate, correct, definite, exact, strict, unequivocal, well-defined; careful, exact.

sax ah. proper *adj* defensible, justifiable, right.

sax. precision *n* accuracy, correctness, exactitude, exactness, preciseness.

sax. accurate *adj* careful, close, correct, exact, faithful, nice, precise, regular, strict, true, truthful.

saxah. correct *adj* accurate, equitable, exact, faultless, just, precise, proper, regular, right, true, upright.

saxid. rectify *vb* amend, correct, mend, straighten.

saxmad. crowd *n* block, crush, pack.

sayid. lord *n* director, governor, manager, master, ruler; head, leader, principal.

se. but *adv* even, notwithstanding, still, yet.

seef labood. fanatic *n* bigot, devotee, enthusiast, visionary, zealot.

seexasho. sleep *vb* catnap, doze, nap, slumber.

seexasho. snooze *vb* catnap, doze, drowse, nap, sleep, slumber.

shaabad. stamp *n* brand, impression, print; character, description, kind, sort.

shaabadayn. stamp *vb* brand, imprint, mark, print.

shaac ka qaadid. impart *vb* communicate, disclose, divulge, relate, reveal, tell.

shactiroole. jolly *adj* blithe, cheerful, funny, gay, jocular, jovial, joyous, merry, mirthful.

shakhsi. individual *n* being, character, person, personage, somebody, someone.

shaki badan. dubious *adj* doubtful, uncertain, questionable.

shaki badan. doubtful *adj* dubious, sceptical, undecided; ambiguous, unsure; questionable, undecided.

shaki badan. problematic *adj* doubtful, dubious, enigmatic, puzzling, questionable, suspicious, uncertain.

shaki leh. suspect *adj* distrustful, suspecting, wary; doubtful, dubious, questionable, suspicious.

shaki leh. questionable *adj* ambiguous, controversial, debatable, doubtful, problematic, suspicious.

shaki-qaba. sceptical *adj* doubtful, hesitating, incredulous, questioning, unbelieving.

shaki. misgiving *n* doubt, hesitation, suspicion, uncertainty.

shaki. doubt *n* question, uncertainty, misgiving, scepticism, suspicion.

shaki. suspicion *n* conjecture, guess, inkling, surmise, distrust, doubt, mistrust.

ka shakiyid. doubt *vb* distrust, mistrust, query, question, suspect.

ka shakiyid. suspect *vb* conjecture, guess, surmise, think; distrust, doubt, mistrust.

ka shalayn. grieve *vb* mourn, lament, regret, sorrow, suffer.

shali la'aan. doubtless *adv* certainly, unquestionably; clearly, indisputably, precisely.

shandad. box *n* case, chest, container, crate, packet, parcel, trunk.

shandad. case *n* box, cabinet, container, holder, receptacle.

ka shanlayn. regret *vb* bemoan, repent, mourn, rue. * *n* disappointment, grief, sorrow, trouble; remorse, repentance.

shanlaysi. comb *vb* groom, rake, untangle; ransack, rummage, search.

shaqaale. staff *n* employees, personnel, team, workers, workforce.

ka shaqayn. manipulate *vb* handle, operate, work.

shaqayn. toil *vb* drudge, labour, strive, work.

shaqayn. work *vb* act, operate; drudge, labour, slave, toil.

shaqayn. busy *vb* devote, work.

ka shaqayn. strive *vb* aim, attempt, endeavour, labour, struggle, toil.

shaqayn. labour *vb* drudge, strive, toil, travail, work.

loo shaqeeye. boss *n* employer, foreman, master, overseer, superintendent.

shaqo siin. employ *vb* busy, engage, enlist, commission, use.

shaqo. occupation *n* business, calling, craft, employment, job, post, profession, trade, vocation.

shaqo. task *n* chore, duty, employment, mission, undertaking, work

shaqo. employment *n* business, calling, occupation, profession, pursuit, trade, vocation, work.

shaqo. work *n* exertion, drudgery, grind, labour; business, employment, function, occupation, task; action, accomplishment, achievement, deed, feat, product.

shaqo. business *n* calling, employment, occupation, profession, pursuit, vocation; affair, concern, matter, transaction, undertaking; duty, function, office, task, work.

shaqo. profession *n* business, calling, employment, occupation, trade, vocation.

shaqo. service *n* duty, employment, office.

sharaf daran. dishonourable *adj* disgraceful, disreputable, infamous, scandalous, shameful; base, false, shameless.

sharaf darro. stigma *n* disgrace, shame.

sharaf leh. dignified *adj* majestic, noble, stately.

sharaf-xumi. disgraceful *adj* discreditable, dishonourable, disreputable, scandalous, shameful.

sharaf. prestige *n* credit, distinction, importance, influence, reputation, weight.

sharaf. honour *n* dignity, distinction, elevation, nobleness; consideration, credit, esteem, fame, glory, reputation; high-mindedness, honesty, integrity, probity, uprightness.

sharatan. bet *vb* gamble, wager.

sharax. description *n* account, explanation, narration, portrayal, report.

sharax. explanation *n* account, answer, clarification, interpretation, justification, meaning, solution.

sharax. elaborate *adj* complicated, decorated, detailed, ornate.

sharaxid. portray *vb* depict, describe, represent.

sharci ah. valid *adj* binding, cogent, efficient, good, important, logical, powerful, solid, sound, strong, substantial, sufficient, weighty.

sharci ah. permissible *adj* admissible, allowable, lawful.

sharci. regulation *n* law, order, precept, rule.

sharci. law *n* act, code, command, commandment, decree, edict, order, principle, statute, regulation, rule; jurisprudence; litigation, process, suit.

sharciga. rule *n* command, direction, order, guide, law, regulation.

sharciyaysan. lawful *adj* constitutional, legal, legitimate; allowable, authorized, permissible, rightful, just, proper, valid.

sharfid. honour *vb* respect, revere, venerate; keep, observe.

sharrax. decoration *n* adornment, enrichment, embellishment, ornament.

sharxid. illustrate *vb* clarify, demonstrate, explain; depict, draw.

sharxid. represent *vb* depict, describe, portray, portray, symbolize.

sharxid. explain *vb* demonstrate, elucidate, expound, illustrate, interpret, unravel; account for, justify.

sharxid. describe *vb* explain, narrate, portray, recount, relate.

shay. item *n* article, detail, entry, particular, point.

shaydaan. sprite *n* spook, devil.

sheegid. divulge *vb* communicate, declare, disclose, discover, exhibit, expose, impart, proclaim, promulgate, publish, reveal, tell, uncover.

sheegid. name *vb* call, christen, dub, term, mention, designate, indicate, nominate, specify.

sheegid. express *vb* assert, declare, enunciate, utter, speak, state, voice.

sheegid. report *vb* mention, narrate, publish, relate, state, tell; minute, record.

wax sheegid. remark *vb* comment, express, mention, say, state, utter.

sheegid. mention *vb* acquaint, allude, cite, disclose, divulge, impart, inform, name.

sheegid. utter *vb* articulate, disclose, emit, express, give forth, pronounce, speak, talk, tell, voice.

aan la sheegin. unsaid *adj* tacit, unmentioned, unspoken, unuttered.

sheekayn. narrate *vb* describe, detail, enumerate, recite, recount, tell.

ka sheekayn. relate *vb* narrate, report, tell; connect, correlate.

wada sheekeysi. conversation *n* chat, colloquy, communion, confabulation, conference, dialogue, discourse, intercourse, parley, talk.

sheeko. parable *n* allegory, fable, story.

sheeko. novel *n* fiction, romance, story, tale.

sheeko. tale *n* account, fable, legend, narration, novel, story, yarn.

sheeko. yarn *n* anecdote, boasting, fabrication, narrative, story, tale, untruth.

sheeko. story *n* fable, fiction, novel, legend, tale.

shidaarah. elusive *adj* deceptive, deceitful, delusive, evasive, fallacious, fraudulent, illusory.

shidid. light *vb* ignite, inflame, kindle; illuminate.

shidid. spark *vb* begin, fire, incite, kindle, set off, stimulate. abuur. spark *n* beginning, germ, seed.

shidid. light *vb* ignite, inflame, kindle.

shiidid. grate *vb* rub, scrape, rasp; creak, grind, jar, vex.

shiidid. grind *vb* crush, grate, pulverize; sharpen, whet.

shiidid. jam *vb* block, crowd, crush, press.

shil. mishap *n* accident, calamity, disaster, misfortune.

shil. casualty *n* accident, catastrophe, disaster, mishap, misfortune.

shil. misadventure *n* accident, calamity, catastrophe, misfortune, mishap, reverse.

shil. accident *n* calamity, casualty, condition, contingency, disaster, fortuity, incident, misadventure, miscarriage, mischance, misfortune, mishap; alteration, chance, contingency.

shir. conference *n* consultation, parley; meeting.

shir. meeting *n* encounter, interview; assembly, audience, company, conference; intersection, junction.

shirkad. company *n* assembly, band, body, collection, communication, congregation, crowd, flock, gang, gathering, group, herd, set; guests, visitor, visitors; corporation, firm, house, partnership.

shirkad. firm *n* association, business, company, concern, corporation, house, partnership.

shirqool. intrigue *n* conspiracy, deception, plot, ruse, scheme, stratagem, wile.

shirqool. conspiracy *n* intrigue, plot, scheme.

shirqool. plot *n* connivance, conspiracy, intrigue, plan.

shirqoolid. plot *vb* conspire, intrigue, scheme; plan, project.

ka shisheeya. beyond *prep* above, before, farther, over, past, yonder.

shisheeye. foreigner *n* stranger.

shisheeye. stranger *n* alien, foreigner, newcomer, immigrant, outsider, visitor.

ku shubid. pour *vb* cascade, flood, flow, rain, shower, stream.

shumin. cuddle *vb* caress, embrace, fondle, hug, pet.

shumin. caress *vb* cuddle, embrace, fondle, hug, kiss, pet.

shumis. caress *n* cuddle, embrace, hug, kiss.

shumis. cuddle *n* caress, embrace, hug,.

shuruud la'aan. unconditional *adj* absolute, complete, full, unlimited, unrestricted.

shuruud. terms *npl* conditions, provisions, stipulations.

shuux. drizzle *n* mist, mizzle, rain, shower, sprinkling.

si adag. severe *adj* hard, harsh, rigorous, stern, strict, critical.

si derisnimo ah. neighbourly *adj* attentive, civil, friendly, kind, obliging, social.

si fudud. readily *adv* easily, promptly, cheerfully, willingly.

si kastaba. nevertheless *adv* however, nonetheless, notwithstanding, yet.

si qarsoon. underhand *adj* clandestine, deceitful, hidden, sly, stealthy.

si sax ah. exact *adj* precise, true; accurate, correct.

si xun u isticmaal. misuse *vb* abuse, ill-treat, squander, waste.

si-kaalmayn. further *vb* advance, aid, assist, encourage, help, promote, strengthen.

sibibaxasho. slide *vb* glide, move smoothly, slip.

shubka sibidhka. cement *n* mixture; cement.

sida ay u badan tahay. likely *adv* doubtlessly, presumably, probably.

sida badan. mostly *adv* chiefly, especially, generally, mainly, particularly, principally.

sidoo kale. even *adv* exactly, just, likewise.

sii deyn. **vent** *vb* emit, express, release.

sii kasta ahaate. however *adv* but, nevertheless, notwithstanding, still, though, yet.

sii sheegid. foretell *vb* predict, prophesy; forecast, foreshadow, portend, presage.

siin. supply *vb* equip, furnish, give, provide, stock.

siin. provide *vb* contribute, furnish, produce, supply.

siiro. memoir *n* account, autobiography, biography, narrative, record.

silsilad. chain *n* bond, fetter, manacle, shackle.

siman. flat *adj* horizontal, level; even, smooth, unbroken; dull, lifeless, monotonous, uninteresting.

la siman. peer *n* equal, equivalent.

siman. smooth *adj* even, flat, level, polished, unwrinkled, sleek.

siman. even *adj* flat, level, smooth; equal, regular, uniform, unruffled.

siman. level *adj* equal, even, flat, horizontal, smooth.

la siman. parallel *adj* abreast, concurrent, equal.

isku simid. level *vb* equalize, flatten, smooth; demolish, destroy, raze.

simid. smooth *vb* flatten, level, plane.

la simid. match *vb* equal, rival; marry, join, sort;

sinji. race *n* ancestry, clan, nation, people, tribe, stock.

sinji. species *n* breed, class, group, kind, sort, variety.

sir. secret *n* confidence.

sirlow. wily *adj* artful, crafty, cunning, foxy, intriguing, sly, subtle, tricky.

sirlow. secretive *adj* close, reticent, uncommunicative, wary.

sixid. correct *vb* adjust, amend, improve, mend, rectify, regulate, remedy; discipline, punish.

sixid. right *vb* correct, regulate, settle, straighten. *adj* direct, straight; lawful, legal, legitimate; appropriate, correct, proper, reasonable, suitable; actual, genuine, real, true. *adv* fairly, justly, lawfully, properly; actually, really, truly.

sixir. witchcraft *n* enchantment, magic, necromancy, sorcery, spell.

sixir. charm *n* magic, sorcery, spell; amulet, talisman.

sixir. magic *n* conjuring, sorcery, witchcraft; *adj* bewitching, enchanting, fascinating,

sixiroole. sorcerer *n* charmer, diviner, enchanter, magician, soothsayer, witch, wizard.

sixiroole. magician *n* conjurer, enchanter, shaman, wizard; diviner, conjurer, magician, necromancer, seer, soothsayer, sorcerer.

sixni. dish *n* bowl, plate, saucer, vessel.

sixran. spellbound *adj* bewitched, enchanted, entranced, enthralled, fascinated.

sixrid. bewitch *vb* captivate, charm, enchant, enrapture, entrance, fascinate, spellbind.

sixun u fasir. misconstrue *vb* misread, misinterpret, mistake, misunderstand.

siyaasad. policy *n* plan, strategy, tactics.

skaki. doubt *n* misgiving, suspicion.

so-dhawayn wacan. hospitable *adj* attentive, bountiful, kind; cordial, generous, liberal, open, sociable.

socdaal gaaban oo ujeeddo leh. errand *n* mission, purpose.

socdaal. traveller *n* explorer, passenger, pilgrim, rover, trekker, voyager, wanderer, wayfarer.

socdaal. tour *n* circuit, excursion, expedition, journey, round.

kala socid. classify *vb* arrange, categorize, class, group. pigeonhole, rank, tabulate.

socod, dhaqaaq. motion *n* action, movement, gait, gesture; suggestion; proposal, proposition.

socod. walk *vb* go, march, move, pace, saunter, step, stride, stroll.

socod. movement *n* change, motion; crusade, organisation.

socod. walk *n* constitutional, excursion, hike, ramble, saunter, stroll, tramp, turn.

socod. stalk *vb* march, pace, stride, strut, swagger; follow, hunt, shadow, track.

socodsiin, socod. move *vb* dislodge, push, shift; rouse, stir, touch, agitate.

soconaaya. continuous *adj* connected, continued, extended, prolonged, unbroken, uninterrupted.

aan soconayn. stationary *adj* fixed, motionless, permanent, stable, standing, still.

soo baxaaya. protrude *vb* bulge, extend, jut, project.

soo bixi. occur *vb* appear, arise, offer; befall, chance, eventuate, happen, result, supervene.

soo bixid. arise *vb* ascend, mount, soar, tower; appear, emerge, rise, spring; begin, originate; rebel, revolt, rise; accrue, come, emanate, ensue, flow, issue, originate, proceed, result.

soo saarid. mint *vb* fabricate, forge, invent, make, produce.

soo saarid. yield *vb* bear, produce, supply; give up, let go, resign, submit, surrender.

soo-dejin. import *vb* bring in, introduce, transport.

soo-dhaweyn. welcome *vb* embrace, greet, hail, receive.

soo-dhoweyn. warmth *n* animation, ardour, cordiality, eagerness, enthusiasm, excitement, fervour, heat, passion.

soo-dhoweyn. usher *vb* conduct, direct, escort, shepherd, show.

soo-saarid. manufacture *vb* build, compose, construct, create.

soocid. sort *vb* arrange, assort, class, classify, order.

soocid. single (out) *vb* choose, pick, select.

kala soocid. sift *vb* separate, sieve, sift; analyse, examine, fathom, inquire into, probe.

soodhaweyn. reception *n* entertainment, greeting, welcome; party.

isu soodhwaan. reconcile *vb* appease, conciliate, pacify, placate, reunite; harmonize, heal, settle.

soohid. knit *vb* connect, interlace, join, unite, weave.

soomid. fast *vb* abstain, go hungry, starve.

soon. fast *n* abstention, abstinence, diet, fasting, starvation.

soonoqosho. recur *vb* reappear, return.

wax soosaar. yield *n* output, produce, profit, return, revenue.

ka soosaar. tap *vb* broach, draw off, extract, pierce; draw on, exploit, mine, use, utilize.

soosaarid. issue *vb* come out, flow out, flow forth, gush, spout, spring, spurt; arise, come, emanate, ensue, flow, follow, originate, proceed, spring; appear, come out, deliver, emerge, send out; distribute, give out; publish, utter.

soosarid. produce *vb* exhibit, show; bear, beget, procreate, yield; accomplish, make, originate, fabricate, manufacture. * *n* crop, fruit, harvest, product, vegetables, yield.

sootoosin. revive *vb* resuscitate; invigorate, reawaken, recover, refresh, renew, rouse.

su'aal. question *n* enquiry, inquiry, query, puzzle.

su'aalid. interrogate *vb* ask, examine, inquire of, question.

su'aalid. question *vb* ask, enquire, examine, inquire, interrogate, quiz, sound out; doubt, query; challenge, dispute.

subax. morning *n* aurora, daybreak, dawn, morn, morningtide, sunrise.

sugid. wait *vb* delay, linger, pause, remain, rest, stay, tarry; await, expect, look for.

sugitaan. wait *n* delay, halt, holdup, pause, respite, rest, stay, stop.

sumad-xun. infamous *adj* abominable, disreputable, heinous, odious, scandalous, vile.

sumad. emblem *n* badge, mark, representation, sign, symbol.

sumayn. poison *vb* contaminate, corrupt, envenom, pollute, taint, vitiate.

sumcad xumayn. slander *vb* backbite, defame, libel, traduce, vilify.

sumcad xummo ah. slanderous *adj* defamatory, false, libellous, malicious.

sumcad xumo. notorious *adj* celebrated, conspicuous, famed, famous, flagrant, infamous, renowned.

sumcad. fame *n* celebrity, eminence, glory, greatness, honour, illustriousness, kudos, lustre, notoriety, renown, reputation, repute.

sumcad. reputation *n* character, fame, honour, prestige, renown.

sumcad. notoriety *n* fame, publicity, reputation.

sun leh. venomous *adj* deadly, poisonous, toxic; malicious, noxious, spiteful.

sun. poison *n* toxin, venom.

sun. venom *n* poison, virus; bitterness, gall, hate, ill-will, malice, malignity, rancour, spite, virulence.

suubanaasho. meek *adj* gentle, humble, lowly, mild, modest.

suubin. commit *vb* do, enact, perform, perpetrate; imprison; pledge.

suufi. zealous *adj* devoted, eager, earnest, enthusiastic, fervent, keen, prompt, ready.

aan suuragal ahayn. impossible *adj* hopeless, impracticable, unattainable; unthinkable.

suurtagal ah. practicable *adj* achievable, attainable, feasible, possible, workable.

suurtagal. possible *adj* conceivable, potential; accessible, feasible, likely, practical, practicable, workable.

suuxid. faint *vb* swoon; fade, fail, weaken. *adj* drooping, exhausted, feeble, languid, listless, sickly, weak; cowardly, faint-hearted, timid, dispirited. *n* blackout, swoon.

suuxid. numb *adj* deadened, dulled, insensible, paralysed.

suyuc aah. dank *adj* damp, humid, moist, wet.

T

la taaban karo. tangible *adj* actual, evident, obvious, open, perceptible, real, solid, substantial.

la taaban karo. palpable *adj* tangible; evident, manifest, obvious, plain, unmistakable.

taabasho. touch *vb* feel, handle, pat, tap; affect, impress, move, stir.

taabasho. stroke *vb* caress, feel, massage, rub, touch.

taagan. upright *adj* erect, perpendicular, vertical; fair, good, honest, incorruptible, just, straightforward.

taagan. erect *adj* upright; vertical, perpendicular, straight.

taageere. fan *n* admirer, devotee, enthusiast, follower, supporter.

taageere. follower *n* adherent, admirer, discipline, partisan, pupil.

taageerid. uphold *vb* aid, champion, defend, justify, maintain, support, sustain, vindicate.

taageerid. support *vb* back, promote, second, support.

taageerid. back *vb* aid, favour, second, support; go back, move back, retreat.

taageero. support *n* assistance, backing, encouragement, favour.

taagerid. support *vb* approve, back, encourage, maintain, nurture, prop, sustain.

taagid. erect *vb* build, construct, raise.

taagid. install *vb* inaugurate, induct, introduce; establish, place, set up.

taagid. hoist *vb* elevate, heave, lift, raise, rear.

taah. groan *n* cry, moan, whine; complaint; grouse, grumble.

taah. moan *n* groan, lament, lamentation, sigh, wail.

taahid. moan *vb* deplore, groan, lament, mourn, sigh, weep.

taahid. groan *vb* complain, lament, moan, whine; creak.

taallo. monument *n*, memorial, pillar, tomb, tombstone.

taallo. memorial *n* commemoration, monument, plaque.

taalo jeedin. propose *vb* offer, recommend, suggest.

taalo. proposal *n* offer, proposition, recommendation, suggestion, tender.

taariikh. date *n* age, day, generation, time: epoch, era, period.

tababar. instruction *n* schooling, teaching, training, tuition; advice, counsel, direction, order.

tababar. drill *n* discipline, exercise, training.

tababare. instructor *n* educator, master, schoolteacher, teacher, tutor.

tababarid. tutor *vb* coach, educate, instruct, teach.

tababarid. qualify *vb* empower, entitle, equip, fit; limit, modify, restrict.

tababarid. train *vb* discipline, drill, educate, exercise, instruct, prepare.

tabarucid. subscribe *vb* approve, agree, assent, consent; contribute, donate, give, offer, promise.

u tacsiyeen. pity *vb* commiserate, condole, sympathize.

u tacsiyeen. console *vb* calm, cheer, comfort, encourage, soothe.

tafaasiil. details *npl* minutiae, particulars, parts.

tafiir. posterity *n* descendants, offspring, progeny, children, family, heirs, issue.

tagan. immobile *adj* fixed, immovable, motionless, rigid, stationary.

tageerid buuxda. unanimous *adj* agreeing, concordant, solid, united.

wax tagey. foregoing *adj* antecedent, former, preceding, previous, prior.

wax tagey. foregone *adj* bygone, former, past, previous.

ka tagid. discard *vb* abandon, cast off, lay aside, reject.

ka tagid. abandon *vb* desert, drop, evacuate, forsake, leave, quit, relinquish, yield; cede, forgo, give up, let go, renounce, resign, surrender, vacate, waive.

ka tagid. resign *vb* abandon, abdicate, leave, quit, relinquish, renounce.

ka tagid. jilt *vb* break, deceive, discard, flirt.

isku tagid. club *vb* combine, unite; beat, bludgeon, cudgel.

ka tagid. leave *vb* abandon, decamp, go, quit, vacate, withdraw; desert, forsake, relinquish, renounce.

ka tagid. forsake *vb* abandon, desert, leave, quit; forswear, relinquish, renounce.

tagid. go *vb* advance, move, pass, proceed; journey, roam, travel, walk, wend; depart, disappear.

ka tagid. omit *vb* drop, eliminate, exclude, miss, neglect, overlook, skip.

aan tagnayn. unsteady *adj* changeable, unstable, wavering; tottering, wavering, wobbly.

takhtar. doctor *n* general practitioner, GP, healer, medic, physician.

takiid. assertion *n* affirmation, allegation, asseveration, averment, declaration, position, predication, remark, statement, word; defence, emphasis, maintenance, pressing, support, vindication.

takooran. outcast *n* exile, expatriate; castaway, pariah, reprobate, vagabond.

takooran. exile *n* outcast, refugee.

takoorid. ostracize *vb* banish, boycott, exclude, excommunicate, exile, expatriate, expel, evict.

takrifal. abuse *vb* dishonour, misapply, misuse, wrong; harm, hurt, ill-use, ill-treat, injure, maltreat, mishandle

talantaali. alternative *adj* another, different, second, substitute.

ku talin. recommend *vb* approve, commend, endorse, praise, sanction; commend, commit; advise, counsel, prescribe, suggest.

la-taliye. counsel *n* advice, caution, instruction, opinion, suggestion; advocate, barrister, counsellor, lawyer.

taliye. commander *n* captain, chief, chieftain, head, leader.

ka tallaabid. cross *vb* intersect, pass over, traverse; hinder, interfere: ill-tempered, irritable, peevish, petulant, sulky, sullen, surly, touchy, waspish.

tallaabo. footstep *n* footstep, footprint, footfall, gait, pace, step, track, stride, walk.

tallaabsi. step *vb* pace, stride, tread, walk.

tallaabsi. pace *vb* go, hasten, hurry, move, step, walk. * *n* amble, gait, step, walk.

talo. advice *n* admonition, caution, counsel, exhortation, persuasion, suggestion, recommendation; information, notification; care, counsel, deliberation, forethought.

tamar. energy *n* activity, dash, drive, efficacy, efficiency, force, go, impetus, power, strength, verve, vim, vigour, zeal.

tamar. stamina *n* energy, force, power, strength, sturdiness, vigour.

tamashlayn. stroll *vb* ramble, saunter, wander.

tamshale. excursion *n* promenade, ramble, walk.

ka tanaasulid. waive *vb* defer, forego, surrender, relinquish, remit, renounce.

tannaasulid. defer *vb* bow to, give way, submit, yield.

tarjumaad. version *n* interpretation, reading, rendering, translation.

tarjumaad. interpretation *n* meaning, sense; explanation, explication, rendition, translation, version.

tarjumid. interpret *vb* decipher, decode, explain, solve, unfold, unravel; translate.

tartame. candidate *n* applicant, competitor.

tartame. competitor *n* adversary, antagonist, contestant, opponent.

tartamid. compete *vb* contend, contest, rival, strive, struggle, vie.

la tartan. challenge *vb* dare, dispute.

tartan. match *n* competition, contest, game, trial.

tartan. competition *n* contest, emulation, rivalry.

la tartan. contest *vb* argue, contend, dispute, question; strive, struggle; compete, vie.

tartiib. gradual *adj* approximate, continuous, gentle, progressive, slow, successive.

la tashi. counsel *vb* advise, caution, recommend, warm.

la tashi. consult *vb* ask, confer, question.

la tashi. confer *vb* advise, consult, talk; bestow, give, grant.

tashiil. thrift *n* economy, frugality, parsimony, saving, thriftiness.

tashiil. sparing *adj* economical, frugal, parsimonious, thrifty.

taxadar badan. provident *adj* careful, cautious, considerate, prudent; economical, frugal, thrifty.

taxadar la'aan. reckless *adj* careless, devil-may-care, heedless, remiss.

taxadir. care *n* caution, foresight, providence, prudence, safeguard.

taxan. succession *n* chain, continuation, progression, run, sequence, series.

taxan. series *n* chain, progression, sequence, succession.

taxan. sequence *n* progression, succession; chain, series.

tayo leh. quality *n* attribute, characteristic, feature, nature, property; condition, grade, kind, sort.

tayoleh. classical *adj* first-rate; Greek, Latin, Roman; elegant, refined.

tegid. depart *vb* go, leave, migrate, quit; die.

ka tegid. quit *vb* depart from, leave, withdraw from; abandon, desert, forsake.

tif. trickle *n* dribble, drip, seepage.

tifid. trickle *vb* dribble, drip, drop, ooze, seep.

tiir. post *n* column, pier, pillar, stake, support.

tiiro ah. steep *adj* sheer, sloping, sudden.

tiiro. slope *n* gradient, incline, slant, tilt, ramp.

tiiro. inclination *n* slope, steep, tilt.

ku tiirsane. dependant *n* hanger-on, retainer, subordinate, vassal.

ku tiirsani. rely *vb* depend, lean, trust.

ku tiirsani. depend *vb* hang, hinge, rely, turn.

ku tiirsi. lean *vb* incline, slope; recline, repose; depend, rely, trust.

tijaabin. experiment *vb* investigate, test, try.

tijaabin. sample *vb* test, try.

tijaabo ah. tentative *adj* essaying, experimental, provisional, testing.

tijaabo ah. trial *adj* experimental, exploratory.

tijaabo. trial *n* experiment, test; affliction, hardship, sorrow, tribulation; action, case, cause, hearing, suit.

tijaabo. experiment *n* investigation, practice, proof, test, trial.

tilmaam ah. symbolic, symbolical *adj* allegorical, emblematic, figurative, representative.

tilmaamid. point *vb* aim, direct, indicate, show.

tilmaamid. hint *vb* allude, imply, insinuate, intimate, mention, refer, suggest.

tilmaamid. intimate *vb* allude to, express, hint, indicate, insinuate, signify, suggest, tell.

tilmaamid. gesture *vb* indicate, motion, signal, wave.

tilmaamid. direct *vb* guide, lead, point, show.

tilmaamid. insinuate *vb* hint, infer, intimate, suggest.

tilmaamid. indicate *vb* denote, mark, point out, show, signify, specify, tell.

timo la'aan. bald *adj* bare, naked, uncovered, hairless.

tirid. delete *vb* cancel, erase, obliterate, remove.

aan la tirin karin. innumerable *adj* countless, numberless.

tirin. count *vb* enumerate, number, score; calculate, compute, reckon.

tiro alaabo isku nool ah. set *n* assortment, batch, collection; band, company, group.

tiro badan. many *adj* legion, myriad, numerous.

tiro. quantity *n* extent, measure, number, portion, share, size.

tirtirid. abolish *vb* abrogate, annul, cancel, eliminate, invalidate, nullify, quash, repeal, rescind, revoke; annihilate, destroy, end, eradicate, extirpate, extinguish, obliterate, overthrow, suppress, terminate.

tirtirid. eliminate *vb* eradicate, exclude, expel, remove, omit, reject.

tirtirid. obliterate *vb* cancel, delete, destroy, eradicate, erase.

tirtirid. repeal *vb* abolish, annul, cancel, rescind, revoke.

tirtirid. invalidate *vb* annul, cancel, nullify, quash, reverse, undo.

tixgelin. privilege *n* advantage, favour, licence, permission, prerogative, right.

tixgelin. ponder *vb* consider, contemplate, deliberate, meditate, muse, reflect.

tolid. mend *vb* darn, patch, repair, restore, retouch; ameliorate, amend, correct.

toogasho. shoot *vb* discharge, fire, let off; extend, jut, project.

tookh. inclination *n* aptitude, bent, bias, proneness, propensity, tendency; desire, fondness, liking, partiality, predilection.

toos ah. point-blank *adj* direct, downright, explicit.

si toos ah. directly *adv* forthwith, immediately, instantly, quickly, promptly, soon, speedily.

toos. point-blank *adv* directly, plainly.

toos. direct *adj* immediate, straight, frank, sincere, straightforward, unequivocal.

toosan. downright *adj* absolute, categorical, clear, explicit, plain, positive, undisguised, unequivocal.

toosan. straight *adj* direct, undeviating, unswerving; erect, perpendicular, upright, vertical.

toosan. unswerving *adj* direct, straight, undeviating; constant, determined, firm, resolute, steadfast.

toosan. virtuous *adj* good, honest, moral, upright; chaste, innocent, pure, undefiled.

toosan. perfect *adj* complete, entire, full, whole; faultless, pure, spotless, unblemished.

toosid. wake *vb* arise, awake, awaken; animate, arouse, awaken, kindle, stimulate.

toosid. raise *vb* erect, lift, rear; improve, promote; assemble, collect, get, levy.

toosin. correction *n* amendment, improvement; discipline, punishment.

toosin. awaken *vb* arouse, excite, incite, kindle, provoke, spur, stimulate; wake, waken; begin, be excited.

toosnaan. virtue *n* chastity, goodness, morality, purity

aan toosnayn. tortuous *adj* crooked, serpentine, sinuous, twisted, winding; circuitous, indirect, perverse, roundabout.

tumid. hammer *vb* beat, forge, form, shape.

tumis. blow *n* bang, knock, punch, thump, wallop, impact; calamity, disaster, misfortune, setback.

ka turid. draw *vb* drag, haul, tow, tug, pull; extract, extort; allure, entice, induce; sketch, draft, prepare.

turjubaan. interpreter *n* translator.

tusaalayn. typify *vb* denote, embody, exemplify,image, indicate, represent, signify.

tusaale. example *n* copy, model, pattern, piece, prototype, representative, sample, specimen.

tusaale. specimen *n* copy, example, model, pattern, sample.

tusaale. example *n* criterion, ideal, model, standard.

tusaale. quotation *n* extract, excerpt, reference, selection; estimate, tender.

tusid. show *vb* display, exhibit, present; indicate, mark, point out; explain, reveal, guide.

tusid. display *vb* spread, unfold; exhibit, show; flaunt, parade.

tusid. sign *vb* indicate, signal, gesticulate.

tuug. thief *n* burglar, embezzler, housebreaker, pickpocket, poacher, robber, swindler.

tuug. rogue *n* cheat, knave, rascal, scamp, scoundrel, swindler, thief, trickster, villain.

tuugo. theft *n* embezzlement, fraud, larceny, pilfering, robbery, stealing, swindling, thieving.

wax tuulan. heap *n* accumulation, collection, huddle, lot, mass, mound, pile, stack.

tuulid. heap *vb* accumulate, amass, collect, pile up, store.

la tuurey. abandoned *adj* depraved, derelict, deserted, discarded, dropped, forsaken, left, outcast, rejected, relinquished.

tuurid. toss *vb* cast, fling, hurl, pitch, throw; agitate, rock, shake.

tuurid. fling *vb* cast, chuck, heave, hurl, pitch, shy, throw, toss.

tuurid. hurl *vb* cast, dart, fling, pitch, project, send, sling, throw, toss.

tuurid. throw *vb* cast, chuck, fling, hurl, launch, overturn, pitch, sling, toss.

tuurid. cast *vb* fling, hurl, pitch, sling, throw, toss.

ku tuurid. pelt *vb* bombard, pepper, stone, hurl, throw.

tuusale. model *n* dummy, example, mould; copy, facsimile, imitation, representation.

tuusale. suggestion *n* hint, indication, insinuation, proposal, recommendation.

U

u badan tahay. probably *adv* apparently, likely, maybe, perchance, perhaps, presumably, possibly, seemingly.

u dhashay. native *adj* aboriginal, domestic, indigenous, natural.

u dhawaan. nearly *adv* almost, approximately, closely, well-nigh.

u digid. warn *vb* caution, forewarn; admonish, advise.

u eeg. similar *adj* analogous, like, resembling.

u eeg. like *adj* alike, equal, resembling, same, similar.

u leexasin. verge *vb* approach, border, skirt.

aan u-qalmin. unfit *adj* ill-equipped, incapable, incompetent, unqualified, unsuitable; unhealthy, unsound.

u-sheeg. tell *vb* describe, narrate, recount, relate, report; betray, confess, own, reveal.

ubax. flower *n* bloom, blossom.

ubax. bloom *n* blossom, flower, rose.

ubaxbixin. flower *vb* bloom, blossom, develop; thrive, prosper.

udgoon. essence *n* odour, perfume, scent.

udhiibid. hand *vb* deliver, give, present, transmit.

ufiirsasho la'aan. headlong *adv* hastily, headfirst, helter-skelter, hurriedly, precipitately, rashly, thoughtlessly.

ugaadhsasho. hunt *vb* chase, drive, follow, hound, pursue, stalk, trap, trail; poach, shoot; search, seek.

ugaadhsi. hunt *n* chase, field-sport, pursuit.

ugeyn. add *vb* adjoin, affix, annex, append, attach, join, tag; sum, sum up, total.

ugu dambeyn. lastly *adv* conclusively, eventually, finally, ultimately.

ugu-dheer. innermost *adj* deepest, inmost.

aan ujeeddo lahayn. haphazard *adj* aimless, chance, random.

ujeeddo. meaning *n* drift, intention, purpose, sense.

ujeeddu. inducement *n* allurement, enticement, persuasion; motive, reason, spur, stimulus.

ujeedid. mean *vb* intend, signify, symbolize.

ujeedid. aim *vb* direct, level, point, train; design, intend, mean, purpose, seek.

ujeedo. aim *n* bearing, course, direction, tendency; design, object, view, reason.

ujuuro. fee *n* account, bill, charge, compensation, honorarium, remuneration, reward, tip.

ul. stick *n* bat, bludgeon, cane, club, cudgel, cue, pole, rod, staff, stake, switch, walking stick.

ula kac. deliberate *adj* purposeful, methodical, well-considered; intentional, premeditated.

ula kac. intentional *adj* deliberate, intended, premeditated, wilful.

umalayn. suppose *vb* believe, conclude, consider, conjecture, imagine, presume.

umibixid. evaporate *vb* distil, dehydrate, dry, vaporize, fade, vanish.

ummad. nation *n* commonwealth, realm, state; people, population, race, tribe.

ur xun. bad smell *n* offensive odour, stench.

ur-udgoon. scent *n* aroma, fragrance, odour, perfume, smell.

ur. odour *n* aroma, fragrance, perfume, scent, smell.

ur. smell *n* aroma, fragrance, odour, perfume, scent, stench, stink..

urid. stink *vb* emit a stench, reek, smell bad.

urin. smell *vb* scent, sniff, stink.

urur. collection *n* cluster, crowd, gathering, group, pack; heap, hoard, lot, mass.

urur. party *n* alliance, association; gathering.

urur. league *n* alliance, association, coalition, combination, confederacy, consortium, union.

urur. organization *n* business, constitution, structure, system.

urur. association *n* combination, company, confederation, connection, partnership, society.

isku ururid. congregate *vb* assemble, collect, convene, gather, meet, swarm, throng.

ururin. accumulate *vb* agglomerate, aggregate, amass, bring together, collect, gather, grow, heap, hoard, increase, pile, store.

ururin. compile *vb* compose, prepare, write; arrange, collect, select.

isu ururin. flock *vb* collect, congregate, gather, group, herd, swarm, throng.

isu ururin. gather *vb* assemble, collect, convene, muster, rally; accumulate, amass, hoard; fold, pleat, pucker, shirr, tuck.

isu ururin. troop *vb* crowd, flock, muster, throng.

ururin. mass *vb* assemble, collect, gather, rally, throng.

ururin. huddle *vb* cluster, crowd, gather; crouch, curl up, nestle, snuggle.

ururin. collect *vb* assemble, compile, gather, muster; accumulate, amass.

isku ururin. assemble *vb* call, collect, congregate, convene, convoke, gather, levy, muster; congregate, forgather.

uumi. vapour *n* cloud, exhalation, fog, mist, smoke, steam.

uurxun. malevolent *adj* evil-minded, hateful, hostile, ill-natured.

uyeerid. call *vb* designate, entitle, name; bid, invite, summons; cry, exclaim, proclaim, shout, waken.

W

waaberi. dawn *n* daybreak, dawning, cockcrow, sunrise, sun-up.

waaji gabxid. blush *vb* flush, glow, redden.

waajib. obligation *n* responsibility, contract, covenant; debt, liability.

waajib. liability *n* duty, obligation, responsibility.

waalan (qof). crazy *adj* delirious, demented, insane, irrational, mad

qof waalan. lunatic *n* madman, maniac, psychopath.

waalan. insane *adj* abnormal, crazed, crazy, demented, deranged, distracted, lunatic, mad, maniacal, unsound.

waali. mania *n* aberration, craziness, delirium, dementia, fanaticism.

waali. crazy *adj* demented, deranged, distracted, idiotic, insane, lunatic, mad, silly.

waallan. rascal *n* blackguard, knave, rogue, scallywag, scamp, scoundrel, villain.

waalli. frenzy *n* fury, insanity, lunacy, madness, mania, paroxysm, rage, raving.

waalli. insanity *n* craziness, delirium, dementia, derangement, lunacy, madness.

waalli. insanity *n* lunacy, delirium, madness, rage.

waalli. lunacy *n* aberration, craziness, crack, derangement, insanity, madness, mania.

ku waanin. persuade *vb* induce, influence, prevail upon, urge; advise, counsel; convince, satisfy.

waaqici ah. pragmatic *adj* earthy, hard-headed, matter-of-fact, practical, realistic, sensible.

waaqici. practical *adj* hardheaded, matter-of-fact, pragmatic, pragmatical; able, proficient, qualified

waaraaya. lasting *adj* abiding, durable, enduring, permanent, perpetual, stable.

waax. department *n* district, division, part, portion, province; bureau, function, office, province, sphere, station; branch, division, subdivision.

waayid. forfeit *vb* lose.

la waayid. miss *vb* fail, fall short, mistake, overlook, trip.

waayo arag la'aan. inexperienced *adj* callow, green, raw, unpractised, unskilled, untrained, untried, young.

waayo arag la'aan. unversed *adj* inexperienced, raw, unpractised, unprepared, unskilful.

waayo-arag. veteran *adj* aged, experienced, seasoned, old.

waayo-arag. experienced *adj* able, accomplished, expert, knowing, practised, qualified, skilful, trained, versed, veteran, wise.

wacad. vow *n* oath, pledge, promise.

wacadqaadid. vow *vb* consecrate, dedicate, devote; asseverate.

wacdiyid. preach *vb* urge, exhort, lecture, moralize, sermonize.

wacid. summon *vb* call, convene, invite, invoke, rally, rouse.

wada hadal. dialogue *n* script, speech, text, words.

wada xaajood. negotiate *vb* arrange, bargain, deal, debate, sell, settle, transact, treat.

wada xiriir. intercourse *n* communication, communion, dealings, fellowship, intimacy.

wadaagid, ka dhexeeya. mutual *adj* common, interchangeable, reciprocal.

loo wadajiro. joint *adj* combined, concerted.

wadar. total *adj* complete, entire, full, whole.

wadar. sum *n* amount, total, totality, whole.

waddo-luggeed. path *n* footway, passage, route, track, trail, way.

wadid. drive *vb* go, guide, ride, travel; aim, intend.

wadid. operate *vb* act, function, work; manipulate, use, run, work.

wadigo. path *n* footway, passage, route, track, trail, way.

aan loo wadin. accidental *adj* casual, chance, contingent, fortuitous, undesigned, unintended; adventitious, dispensable, immaterial, incidental, nonessential.

wadne. heart *n* bosom, breast; centre, core, essence, interior, kernel, marrow; affections, ardour, emotion, feeling, love.

waji gabax. blush *n* bloom, flush, glow.

waji ururin. grimace *vb, n* frown, scowl, smirk, sneer.

waji-macbuus. sulky *adj* churlish, cross, grouchy, moody, morose, sullen.

wajib ah. imperative *adj* authoritative, commanding, urgent; binding, obligatory.

wajib. allegiance *n* duty, homage, fealty, fidelity, loyalty, obligation.

wakhti aad u gaaban. jiffy *n* instant, moment, second, twinkling, trice.

wakhti ilaalin. punctual *adj* early, prompt, ready, timely.

wakhti tagey. past *adj* ended, gone, ancient. *prep* after, beyond. *n* history, olden times.

wakhti yar oo nasasho. intermission *n* interval, lull, pause, remission, respite, rest, stop, suspension.

wakhti yar. moment *n* flash, instant, jiffy, second, trice, twinkling, wink: importance, significance, value.

wakhti. term *n* duration, period, season, semester, spell, time; expression, name, phrase, word.

wakhti. time *n* duration, season, spell, term, while; age, date, era, period.

wakhti. era *n* age, date, epoch, period, time.

wakhti. duration *n* period, time.

wakiil. agent *n* channel, instrument, means, medium, organ.

wakiil. deputy *n* agent, commissioner, envoy, legate, lieutenant, proxy, representative, substitute.

wakiil. representative *n* agent, delegate, deputy, emissary, envoy, messenger, proxy, substitute.

wakuti yar oo nasasho. interval *n* interlude, pause, recess, season, space, term.

walaal tinimo. brotherly *adj* affectionate, amicable, cordial, friendly, kind.

walaaqid. stir *vb* agitate, disturb, prod; arouse, awaken, excite, provoke, stimulate.

walax. thing *n* being, body, entity, object, something, substance; affair, circumstance, matter.

wallaac. hesitation *n* doubt, indecision, uncertainty, vacillation.

wallaac. concern *n* affair, business, matter, transaction; anxiety, worry.

wallaac. anxiety *n* apprehension, care, concern, disquiet, fear, foreboding, misgiving, perplexity, trouble, uneasiness, vexation, worry.

wallaacsan. anxious *adj* apprehensive, restless, solicitous, uneasy, unquiet, worried.
apologetic *adj* exculpatory, excusatory; defensive, vindictive.

wanaag. goodness *n* excellence, value, worth; honesty, integrity, morality, principle, probity, uprightness, virtue.

wanaag. integrity *n* goodness, honesty, principle, probity, rectitude, uprightness, virtue.

wanaagsan. good *adj* fit, proper, satisfactory, suitable, well-adapted; dutiful, honest, just, pious, reliable, religious, righteous, true, upright, virtuous, well-behaved; benevolent, favourable, friendly, gracious, humane, kind, merciful, obliging, well-disposed; cheerful, lively, genial, social; able, competent, dextrous, expert, qualified, ready, skilful, thorough, well-qualified; competent, credit-worthy; agreeable, pleasant. *n* interest, prosperity, welfare.

wanaagsan. virtuous *adj* good, honest, moral, upright; chaste, innocent, pure, undefiled.

wanaagsan. well-mannered *adj* civil, courteous, elegant, polished, polite, smooth, suave, urbane.

wanaagsan. admirable *adj* astonishing, striking, surprising, wonderful; excellent, fine, rare, superb.

aad u wanaagsan. exquisite *adj* delicate, choice, excellent, precious, rare, valuable; complete, matchless, perfect.

wanaajin. improve *vb* better, correct, enhance, mend, rectify, edify.

war keene. informant *n* adviser, informer, newsmonger, notifier.

waraaq laysu diro. letter *n* epistle, missive, note.

waran ku dilid. impale *vb* spear, spike, stab, transfix.

waraygsi. whirl *vb* gyrate, pirouette, turn, twirl, twist, wheel. *n* eddy, flurry, spin, swirl, twirl, vortex.

waraymid. savage *vb* attack, lacerate, mangle, maul.

warbixin. report *n* account, bulletin, statement; description, story, talk.

wareeg ah. spherical *adj* globular, rotund, round.

wareeg. twirl *n* convolution, revolution, turn, twist, whirling.

wareeg. round *adj* bulbous, circular, cylindrical, rotund, spherical; chubby, corpulent, plump, stout. *prep* about, around. *n* bout, cycle, rotation, turn; dance.

wareeg. ring *n* circle, hoop; clique, gang, set.

wareeg. cycle *n* age, circle, era, period, revolution, round.

wareeg. turn *n* rotation, round; deviation, swing, turning, twist, twirl; alteration, change, variation

wareeg. spin *n* gyration, roll, rotation, turn, whirl.

wareega goobada. circumference *n* boundary, girth, outline, perimeter, periphery.

wareegid. orbit *vb* encircle, revolve around.

ku wareegid. revolve *vb* circulate, rotate, turn.

wareegid. twirl *vb* revolve, rotate, spin, turn, twist, twirl.

ku wareegid. ring *vb* circle, encircle, enclose, surround.

wareegto. decree *n* act, edict, enactment, law, mandate, order, regulation, statute.

wareejin. spin *vb* revolve, turn, twirl, twist, whirl.

wareejin. twist *vb* rotate, spin, twine; complicate, distort, screw; encircle, wind, wreathe.

ku wareejin. enclose *vb* circumscribe, corral, encircle, encompass, fence in, hedge, pen, shut in, surround; box, cover, encase, envelop, wrap.

ku soo wareejin. surround *vb* beset, embrace, encircle, enclose, ring.

wareejin. turn *vb* revolve, rotate; bend, spin, swivel, twirl, twist, wheel; crank, wind; adapt, alter, change, transform, vary.

ku wareejin. wreathe *vb* encircle, festoon, garland, intertwine, surround, twine, twist.

wareer. medley *n* confusion, hotchpotch, jumble, mixture.

wareer. confusion *n* anarchy, chaos, clutter, disarray, disorder, jumble, muddle.

wareerid. daze *n* bewilderment, confusion; coma, stupor, swoon, trance.

wareerid. vertigo *n* dizziness, giddiness.

wareerin. baffle *vb* bewilder, confound, perplex.

wareerin. mystify *vb* bewilder, confound, confuse, perplex, puzzle.

wareersan. incoherent *adj* confused, illogical, irrational, rambling, unintelligible.

wargaliye. herald *n* announcer, crier, proclaimer, publisher; harbinger, precursor, proclaimer.

wargelin. inform *vb* advise, apprise, notify, tell, tip off, warn.

warshad yar. mill *n* factory, grinder.

warsheeg. informer *n* sneak, telltale.

warwarid. fuss *vb* bustle, fidget, fret, worry.

warwarreegid. wander *vb* ramble, range, roam, rove, stroll; deviate, digress, straggle, stray; moon, ramble, rave.

wasaarad. ministry *n* agency, government department.

wasakh ah. muddy *adj* dirty, impure, slimy, soiled; confused, incoherent, obscure, vague.

wasakh xun. nasty *adj* dirty, filthy, foul, loathsome, polluted, squalid, unclean; disagreeable, disgusting, offensive.

wasakh. foul *adj* dirty, filthy, impure, nasty, polluted, putrid, soiled, stained, squalid, sullied, rank, unclean; disgusting, hateful, loathsome, odious, offensive; dishonourable, underhand, unfair.

wasakh. filthy *adj* dirty, foul, mucky, nasty, obscene, pornographic, squalid, unclean.

wasakh. dirty *adj* filthy, foul, mucky, nasty, soiled, unclean; clouded, cloudy, dark, dull, muddy, sullied.

wasakh. pollution *n* contamination, corruption, defilement, impurity.

wasakhayn. smudge *vb* blur, daub, dirty, smear.

wasakhayn. muddy *vb* dirty, soil; confuse, obscure.

wasakhayn. soil *vb* contaminate, defile, dirty, pollute, stain, sully.

wasakhayn. pollute *vb* defile, taint; contaminate, corrupt, debase.

wasakhayn. tarnish *vb* defame, dim, dull, soil, stain, sully.

wasakhayn. adulterate *vb* alloy, contaminate, corrupt, debase, deteriorate, vitiate.

wasakhaysan. corrupt *adj* contaminated, impure, infected, rotten; dissolute, profligate, wicked.

wasiir. minister *n* administration, cabinet, council, government.

wax aan lagu tala galin. unintentional *adj* accidental, casual, irregular, occasional, random, unintentional.

wax garsiin. inflict *vb* bring, impose, lay on.

wax la hubo. incontrovertible *adj* certain, indisputable, indubitable, sure, undeniable.

wax lala simaa jirin. unequalled *adj* incomparable, inimitable, peerless, pre-eminent, unrivalled.

wax loo dhigaa jirin. unsurpassed *adj* matchless, peerless, unequalled, unmatched, unrivalled.

wax soo saar leh. prolific *adj* abundant, fertile, fruitful, productive, teeming.

wax yar. slight *adj* insignificant, small, unimportant, unsubstantial.

wax-soo-saar leh. fruitful *adj* productive; fertile; abundant, exuberant, plentiful, rich, teeming.

wax-yeelid. wreck *vb* blight, break, devastate, ruin, spoil.

waxba. naughty *adj* bad, corrupt, mischievous, perverse, worthless.

waxbarasho. schooling *n* education, instruction, teaching, training.

waxbarasho. education *n* instruction, schooling, teaching, training, tuition.

waxbarasho. tuition *n* education, instruction, schooling, teaching, training.

waxbarid. educate *vb* cultivate, develop, discipline, inform, instruct, nurture, rear, school, teach, train.

waxbayahay. nonentity *n* cipher, insignificance, nobody, nonexistence, nothingness.

waxqalaad. alien *adj* foreign, not native; differing, estranged, inappropriate.

waxtar la'an. inefficient *adj* feeble, ineffectual, ineffective, weak.

waxtar leh. helpful *adj* advantageous, beneficial, convenient, favourable, useful.

waxyeelaaya. affect *vb* act upon, alter, change, influence, modify, transform; concern, interest, regard, relate; improve, melt, move, overcome, subdue, touch; aim at, aspire to, crave, yearn for; adopt, assume, feign.

waxyeelayn. harm *vb* damage, hurt, injure, mistreat.

waxyeelid. damage *vb* harm, hurt, impair, injure, mar.

waxyeelid. spite *vb* annoy, offend, vex.

waxyeelid. mangle *vb* mutilate, rend, tear; cripple, crush, mutilate.

waxyeelid. mar *vb* blot, damage, harm, hurt, spoil.

waxyeelo badan. hurtful *adj* destructive, detrimental, harmful, injurious, mischievous, pernicious.

waxyeelo badan. harmful *adj* detrimental, hurtful, injurious, pernicious, prejudicial.

waxyeelo lahayn. innocuous *adj* harmless, innocent, inoffensive, safe.

waxyeelo leh. disastrous *adj* calamitous, catastrophic, ill-fated, ill-starred, ruinous, unfortunate, unlucky, untoward.

waxyeelo leh. destructive *adj* detrimental, hurtful, injurious, mischievous, ruinous.

waxyeelo leh. evil *adj* bad, base, corrupt, malicious, malevolent, malign, perverse, sinful, vile, wicked, wrong; destructive, harmful, hurtful, injurious.

waxyeelo. harm *n* damage, hurt, injury, wrong.

weerar ah. offensive *n* attack, onslaught.

weerar. assault *n* aggression, attack, charge, incursion, invasion, onset, onslaught; storm.

weerar. invasion *n* encroachment, incursion, infringement, inroad; aggression, assault, attack, foray, raid.

weerar. onset *n* assault, attack, charge, onslaught, storm, storming.

weerarid. raid *vb* assault, invade, pillage, plunder.

weerarid. attack *vb* assail, assault, charge, encounter, invade, set upon, storm, tackle; censure, criticise, impugn. * *n* aggression, assault, charge, offence, onset, onslaught, raid, thrust.

weerarid. invade *vb* encroach upon, infringe, violate; attack, enter in, march into.

weerarid. assault *vb* assail, attack, charge, invade.

wehel. companion *n* accomplice, ally, associate, comrade, consort, crony, friend, mate; partner, sharer.

wehel. escort *n* attendant, bodyguard, companion, guard, squire.

wehelin. escort *vb* accompany, conduct.

weji macbuus. wry *adj* askew, awry, contorted, crooked, distorted, twisted.

weji uruin. frown *vb* glower, lower, scowl.

weji. face *n* countenance, features, grimace, physiognomy, visage; audacity, boldness, confidence, effrontery, impudence.

wejihid. face *vb* confront.

weli. yet *adv* besides, further, however, so far, still, thus far. *conj* moreover, nevertheless, notwithstanding, now.

weli. still *adv, conj* till now, to this time, yet; however, nevertheless, notwithstanding; always, continually, ever, habitually, uniformly; after that, again, in continuance.

weligeed. forever *adv* always, constantly, continually, endlessly, eternally, ever, evermore, everlastingly, perpetually, unceasingly.

weligeedba. evermore *adv* always, constantly, continually, eternally, ever, forever, perpetually.

welinimo. saintly *adj* devout, godly, holy, pious, religious.

weyd. bony *adj* bony, emaciated, gaunt, lank, lean, meagre, skinny, slender, thin.

weydiin. query *vb* ask, enquire, inquire, question.

weydiin. question *n* demand, inquiry, interrogation.

weydiin. ask *vb* interrogate, inquire, question; adjure, beg, conjure, crave, desire, dun, entreat, implore, invite, inquire, petition, request, solicit, supplicate, seek, sue.

weydiisash. demand *vb* ask, inquire.

weydin. require *vb* demand, request, direct, enjoin, order, prescribe.

kan weyn. senior *adj* elder, older; higher, preceding, superior.

aad u weyn. mammoth *adj* colossal, enormous, gigantic, huge, immense, vast.

weyn. enormous *adj* colossal, elephantine, Herculean, huge, immense, monstrous, vast, gigantic, prodigious, titanic, tremendous.

ka weyn. elder *adj* older, senior. *n* ancestor, senior.

weyn. big *adj* bumper, bulky, great, huge, large, massive, monstrous; important, imposing.

aad u weyn. huge *adj* bulky, colossal, Cyclopean, elephantine, enormous, gigantic, herculean, immense, stupendous, vast,

aad u weyn. immense *adj* colossal, elephantine, enormous, gigantic, huge, large, monstrous, stupendous, titanic, tremendous, vast.

aad u weyn. spacious *adj* extensive, vast, wide; ample, capacious, large, roomy.

weyn. grand *adj* august, dignified, elevated, eminent, exalted, great, illustrious, lofty, lordly, majestic, noble, princely, stately, sublime.

weyn. great *adj* ample, big, bulky, Cyclopean, enormous, gigantic, Herculean, huge, immense, large, vast; celebrated, distinguished, eminent, exalted, famed, famous, illustrious, noted, prominent, renowned.

ugu weyn. capital *adj* chief, essential, important, leading, main, major, principal, prominent.

weyn. voluminous *adj* ample, big, bulky, full, great, large; copious, diffuse, discursive.

weyn. colossal *adj* enormous, gigantic, Herculean, huge, immense, monstrous, prodigious, vast.

weynayn. enlarge *vb* amplify, augment, broaden, extend, expand, increase, magnify, widen.

weyneyn. magnify *vb* amplify, augment, enlarge; bless, celebrate, elevate.

wicid. call *n* phone call, telephone call.

wiil. boy *n* lad, stripling, youth.

wiil. lad *n* boy, schoolboy, stripling, youngster, youth.

wixii guur la xiriira. marital *adj* connubial, conjugal, matrimonial.

X

ka xaadhid. skim *vb* brush, graze, scrape, sweep, touch lightly.

xaalad qallafsan. plight *n* dilemma, predicament, scrape, situation, state.

xaalad. condition *n* circumstances, plight, situation, state; proviso, stipulation, precondition, prerequisite.

xaalad. circumstance *n* event, fact, happening, occurrence, position, situation.

xaalad. situation *n* case, circumstances, predicament, state; employment, post.

xaalad. mood *n* disposition, temper.

xaaqid. brush *vb* clean, sweep, groom, rub down; graze, scrape, skim, touch.

xaasid. jealous *adj* distrustful, envious, suspicious.

xaasidnimo. jealousy *n* envy, suspicion, watchfulness.

xabaalaha. cemetery *n* burial-ground, churchyard, god's acre, graveyard, necropolis.

cod xabeebsan. hoarse *adj* harsh, husky, raucous, rough.

xabeebsan. raucous *adj* harsh, hoarse, husky, rough.

xabiibi. darling *n* dear, favourite, idol, love, sweetheart.

xad-dhaaf ah. exorbitant *adj* excessive, extravagant, inordinate, unreasonable.

xad-dhaaf ah. myriad *adj* innumerable, manifold, uncounted.

xad. border *n* edge, fringe, hem, margin, rim, skirt, verge; boundary, frontier, limit, outskirts.

xad. limit *n* boundary, frontier, hindrance, obstruction, restraint, restriction. termination, terminus.

xad. frontier *n* border, boundary, coast, limits.

xad. margin *n* border, brim, brink, edge, limit, rim

xaddaaf. excessive *adj* disproportionate, superabundant, superfluous, undue; extravagant, enormous, unreasonable; extreme, immoderate, intemperate; vehement, violent.

xaddayn. limit *vb* circumscribe, define, hinder, restrain, restrict.

xaddayn. hem *vb* border, edge, skirt; confine, enclose, surround, sew.

xaddhaaf. lavish *adj* excessive, extravagant, immoderate, profuse, unrestrained, wasteful.

xaddid. pilfer *vb* filch, purloin, rob, steal, thieve.

xadgudbid. trespass *vb* encroach, infringe, intrude.

xadgudub. intrusion *n* encroachment, infringement, transgression.

xadhig. imprisonment *n* captivity, confinement, duress, incarceration, restraint.

xadhig. captivity *n* confinement, imprisonment; bondage, slavery.

xadid. steal *vb* burgle, crib, embezzle, filch, pilfer, plagiarize, purloin, poach, shoplift, thieve.

xadid. thieve *vb* cheat, embezzle, pilfer, rob, steal, swindle.

xafidid. maintain *vb* keep, preserve, support, sustain; feed, provide, supply; allege, say.

xafiis. office *n* duty, function; bureau, room.

xaflad. ceremony *n* formality, observance, rite; parade, show.

xagal. angle *n* arc, bend, curve, elbow, turn.

xagga hore. front *n* anterior, brow, facade, face, frontage, forepart, vanguard; boldness, effrontery, face, impudence.

xagga kore. upward *adj* ascending, climbing, mounting, rising, uphill.

xal. solution *n* answer, clue, elucidation, explanation, key.

xallilid. solve *vb* answer, clear up, elucidate, explain, make plain.

xamaasad. verve *n* animation, ardour, energy, enthusiasm, force, rapture, spirit.

xamuul. burden *n* cargo, freight, load, weight; affliction, encumbrance, sorrow, trial, trouble.

xan. gossip *vb* chat, clack, gabble, prattle, tattle.

xan. rumour *n* gossip, hearsay, report, talk, story.

ka xanaajin. enrage *vb* anger, exasperate, incense, inflame, infuriate, irritate, madden, provoke.

ka xanaajin. tease *vb* annoy, badger, bother, irritate, pester, plague, tantalize, torment.

ka xanaajin. worry *vb* annoy, badger, beset, bother, disturb, fret, harass, irritate, molest, tease, torment, trouble, vex. welwel. worry *n* anxiety, apprehensiveness, care, concern, disquiet, trouble, uneasiness, vexation.

kaa xanaajiniya. galling *adj* chafing, irritating, vexing.

xanaaq. rage *n* frenzy, fury, madness.

xanaaq. huff *n* anger, passion, quarrel, temper, tiff.

xanaaqi. nervous *adj* irritable, fearful, shaky, timid.

xanaaqid. rage *vb* bluster, fret, fume.

xanaaqsan. irate *adj* angry, incensed, ireful, irritated, piqued.

xanlow. gossip *n* babbler, busybody, chatterer, gossipmonger, newsmonger, tattle-tale, tell-tale

xannaaneyn. nurse *vb* cherish, encourage, feed, foster, pamper; caress, dandle, fondle.

xannaano. conservation *n* preservation, protection

xannibo. barricade *vb* block up, fortify, protect, obstruct.

xannuujin. pain *vb* distress, hurt, torment, torture; afflict, trouble; sting, twinge.

xannuun badan. painful *adj* agonizing, sharp, tormenting, torturing; distressing, grievous, troublesome, unpleasant,

xannuun leh. sore *adj* painful, raw, tender, ulcerated; aggrieved, hurt, irritable, vexed.

xannuun. pang *n* anguish, distress, pain.

xannuunsan. unwell *adj* ailing, delicate, diseased, ill, indisposed, sick.

xanuun. agony *n* anguish, distress, pangs.

xanuun. pain *n* ache, agony, anguish, discomfort, distress, smart, soreness, sting, suffering, torture, twinge; affliction, misery, sorrow, trouble.

aan xaq ahayn. unfair *adj* biased, inequitable, one-sided, partial, unjust.

xaq. compensation *n* payment, recompense, remuneration, reward, salary; amends, reparation, equalization.

xaq. right *n* claim, privilege.

xaqiijin. accomplish *vb* achieve, acquire, attain, bring about, carry, carry through, complete, compass, consummate, do, effect, execute, fulfil, perform, perfect; conclude, end, finish, terminate.

xaqiijin. affirm *vb* allege, assert, asseverate, aver, declare, state; approve, confirm, establish, ratify.

xaqiiq. sure *adj* certain, confident, positive; assured, guaranteed, inevitable.

xaqiiqa raadin. inquiry *n* examination, investigation, research, scrutiny; interrogation, query, question, quiz.

wax xaqiiqada ka fog. untenable *adj* fallacious, illogical, indefensible, unjustifiable, weak.

xaqiiqo. nicety *n* accuracy, exactness, precision, truth.

xaqiraad badan. scornful *adj* contemptuous, disdainful, supercilious.

xaqiraad. contempt *n* derision, disdain, mockery, scorn.

xaqirid. snub *vb* cold-shoulder, cut, discomfit, humiliate, slight. * n check, rebuke, slight.

xaqirid. spurn *vb* cold-shoulder, disdain, disregard, reject, scorn.

xaraf. character *n* letter, mark, sign, symbol; individual, person.

xarayn. pen *vb* confine, coop, enclose.

xardhid. engrave *vb* carve, chisel, cut, etch, grave, hatch, sculpture.

xarif. deft *adj* adroit, clever, dextrous, handy, skilful.

xarig. twine *n* cord, string.

xariif ah. smart *adj* alert, brisk, clever, quick-witted, shrewd; elegant, fashionable, spruce, trim.

xariif. proficient *adj* able, accomplished, adept, competent, expert, masterly, practised, skilled, skilful.

xariif. clever *adj* able, apt, gifted, talented.

xariifnimo leh. masterly *adj* adroit, clever, dextrous, excellent, expert.

xariir ah. sleek *adj* glossy, silky, smooth, well-fed.

xarriijin. line *n* mark, streak, stripe; cable, cord, rope, string, thread; rank, row; ancestry, family, lineage, race, succession.

xasaasi ah. sensitive *adj* impressionable, delicate, tender, touchy.

xasad. grudge *n* aversion, dislike, enmity, grievance, hatred, ill-will, malice, pique, rancour, resentment.

xasdid. grudge *vb* envy, complain.

xashiish. debris *n* fragments, remains, rubbish, ruble, ruins, wreckage.

xashiish. trash *n* garbage, refuse, rubbish, waste; balderdash, nonsense, twaddle.

xasuuq. massacre *n* annihilation, butchery, carnage, extermination, pogrom.

xasuuqid. holocaust *n* carnage, destruction, devastation, genocide, massacre.

xasuuqid. massacre *vb* annihilate, butcher, exterminate, kill, murder, slaughter

xasuus reeb. souvenir *n* keepsake, memento, remembrance, reminder.

xasuus. recollection *n* memory, remembrance, reminiscence.

xasuus. memory *n* recollection, remembrance, reminiscence.

xasuusasho. recollect *vb* recall, remember, reminisce.

xasuusqor. record *n* account, diary, entry, file, list, minute, memorandum, note, register, report; memory, remembrance, history.

xasxusqor. chronicle *n* diary, journal, register, record.

xawaare. speed *n* celerity, haste, hurry, rapidity, swiftness, velocity.

xaydaan. fence *n* boundary.

xayiraad. restrict *vb* bound, circumscribe, confine, limit, restrain.

xayirid. block *vb* bar, blockade, check, choke, close, hinder, impede, jam, obstruct, stop.

xayn. flock *n* collection, group, multitude; bevy, company, convoy, drove, flight, gaggle, herd, pack, swarm, team, troupe; congregation.

xayn. herd *n* collection, crowd, drove, flock, multitude.

xeeb. coast *n* littoral, seaboard, sea-coast, seaside, shore, strand.

xeelad. subterfuge *n* artifice, dodge, evasion, mask, pretence, pretext, trick.

xeelan. tact *n* diplomacy, discretion, finesse, insight, understanding.

xeer. law *n* bill, decree, enactment, ordinance, statute, fact, reality.

xero. pen *n* coop, corral, hutch, enclosure, paddock.

xiddig. star *adj* leading, main, principal; celebrated, illustrious, well-known.

isku xidh. attach *vb* affix, annex, connect, fasten, join, hitch, tie; charm, captivate, enamour, endear, engage, win; (*legal*) distress, distrain, seize, take.

ku xidhasho. root *vb* anchor, embed, fasten, implant, establish.

xidhid. strap *n* thong, ligature, strip, tie.

xidhid. close *vb* seal, shut; conclude, finish, terminate.

xidhid. tie *vb* bind, fasten, knot; connect, join, link.

xidhid. imprison *vb* confine, jail, incarcerate, shut up.

xidhid. fix *vb* establish, fasten, place, plant, set; adjust, repair; fasten, lock, tie.

xidhid. detain *vb* arrest, delay, hinder, hold, keep, retain, stop; confine.

xidhid. arrest *vb* check, delay, detain, hinder, hold, interrupt, obstruct, restrain, stay, stop, withhold; apprehend, capture, catch, seize, take; catch, engage, engross, fix, occupy, secure, rivet.

xidhid. chain *vb* bind, confine, fetter, manacle, restrain, shackle; enslave.

isku xidhid. link *vb* connect, fasten, join, tie, unite.

xidhid. shut *vb* close, close up, fasten; (with in) confine, enclose. .

xidhiidhin. correspond *vb* agree, harmonize, match; answer, communicate.

xidhmo. bundle *n* bale, bunch, cluster; assortment, batch, collection, group, set; heap, pack, package, packet, parcel, pile, roll.

xidid-siibid. uproot *vb* eradicate, extirpate, root out.

xidmo. pack *n* bale, bundle, package, packet, parcel, burden, load, assortment, collection, set.

ku xiga. subsequent *adj* after, consequential, ensuing, later, following.

xigasho. quote *vb* cite, excerpt, name.

xigmad. wisdom *n* discernment, far-sightedness, insight, judgement, prudence, sagacity, sense, understanding; erudition, knowledge, learning, lore.

aad u xiisayn. eager *adj* earnest, enthusiastic, fervent, zealous.

xiisayn. interest *vb* attract, engage, enlist, excite, occupy.

xiiso badan. enchanting *adj* bewitching, blissful, captivating, charming, delightful, enrapturing, fascinating, rapturous, ravishing.

xiiso la'. nondescript *adj* characterless, commonplace, dull, ordinary, uninteresting, unremarkable.

xiiso la'aan. monotony *n* boredom, dullness, sameness, tedium.

aan xiiso lahayn. humdrum *adj* boring, dreary, dull, monotonous, tedious, tiresome, wearisome.

xiiso lahayn. monotonous *adj* boring, dull, tedious, tiresome, unvaried, wearisome.

xiiso leh. prepossessing *adj* alluring, amiable, attractive, charming, fascinating.

xiiso leh. interesting *adj* attractive, engaging, entertaining, pleasing.

xiiso leh. inviting *adj* alluring, attractive, bewitching, captivating, engaging, fascinating, pleasing, winning.

xiiso. enthusiasm *n* ardour, earnestness, devotion, eagerness, fervour, passion, warmth, zeal.

xijaab. pall *n* shroud, veil.

xijaab. veil *n* cloak, cover, disguise, mask, visor.

xilli. period *n* spell, season, term, time.

xilli. period *n* age, epoch, season, term, time.

xinjiraysi. coagulate *vb* clot, congeal, thicken.

isku xir. couple *vb* pair, unite; copulate, embrace.

isku xir. connect *vb* associate, join, link, unite.

ku xirasho. anchor *vb* fasten, fix, secure; cast anchor, take firm hold.

xirfad leh. skilful *adj* able, adept, adroit, clever, deft, expert.

xirfad leh. handy *adj* adroit, clever, dextrous, expert, ready, skilful, skilled; close, convenient, near.

xirfad. skill *n* ability, cleverness, deftness, expertise, facility, knack,

xirfad. knack *n* ability, adroitness, aptitude, dexterity, expertness, facility, skill.

xirfad. proficiency *n* accomplishment, aptitude, competency, dexterity, mastery, skill.

xirid. clip *vb* cut, snip, pare, prune, trim.

isku xirid. twin *vb* couple, link, match, pair.

xiriir. connection *n* alliance, association, junction, union.

xiriir. federation *n* alliance, confederation, leaguing, union, uniting; alliance, coalition, combination, confederacy, league, copartnership.

xiriir. knot *n* fastening, ligature; allegiance, bond, obligation.

xiriir. bond *n* connection, joint, juncture, link.

la xirir. contact *vb* approach, communicate with, reach.

xiro. enclosure *n* pen.

xirxirid. fasten *vb* bind, join, lash, moor, pinion, secure, strap, tie.

xisaab. account *n* bill, book, charge; inventory, record, register, score; calculation, computation, count, reckoning, score, tale, tally.

aan la xisaabin karin. incalculable *adj* countless, enormous, immense, inestimable, unknown, untold.

xisaabin. reckon *vb* calculate, compute, count; guess, estimate.

xisaabin. enumerate *vb* calculate, compute, count, reckon, specify.

xisaabin. compute *vb* calculate, count, enumerate, estimate, figure, reckon, sum up.

isku xisaabin. amount *n* aggregate, sum, total.

xisaabin. calculate *vb* compute, count, estimate, reckon.

xishood badan. bashful *adj* coy, diffident, shy, timid.

xishood daran. obscene *adj* immodest, indecent, lewd, loose, offensive, pornographic, shameless.

xishood daran. shameful *adj* disgraceful, dishonourable, scandalous.

xishood darro. shame *n* disgrace, dishonour; confusion, embarrassment.

xishood la'aan. shameless *adj* barefaced, brazen, hardened, immodest, unprincipled.

xishood leh. shy *adj* bashful, reserved, timid; cautious, wary, distrustful.

xishood. coy *adj* bashful, demure, diffident, modest, reserved, self-effacing, shrinking, shy, timid.

isku xishooda. ashamed *adj* abashed, confused.

ka xishoodsiin. embarrass *vb* distress, trouble, confuse, discomfit, shame.

ka xishoodsiin. shame *vb* abash, humble, humiliate.

xishoon. reserved *adj* coy, demure, modest, shy, taciturn.

xoog ah. strong *adj* energetic, firm, forcible, powerful, robust, sturdy.

xoog ah. intense *adj* ardent, earnest, fervid, passionate, vehement.

xoog badan. powerful *adj* mighty, potent, able-bodied, muscular, robust, strong, sturdy, vigorous, forceful, overpowering; influential.

xoog leh. robust *adj* able-bodied, athletic, brawny, energetic, firm, forceful, hardy, lusty, muscular, powerful, self-assertive, strong, sturdy, vigorous.

xoog leh. vehement *adj* furious, hot, impetuous, passionate, violent; forcible, mighty, powerful, strong.xijaabad. veil *vb* cloak, conceal, cover, hide, mask, screen.

xoog leh. sturdy *adj* dogged, firm; brawny, muscular, robust, stalwart, strong, thickset, vigorous.

xoog. hard *adv* forcibly, vehemently, violently.

xoog. strength *n* force, might, main, nerve, potency, power, vigour; brawn, grit, lustiness, muscle, robustness, stamina.

xoog. power *n* ability, competency, efficacy, faculty, might, potency, energy, force, strength, authority, command, control, government, influence.

xoog. force *n* energy, might, power, strength, vigour; coercion, compulsion, violence; army, battalion, legion, phalanx, posse, squadron, troop.

xoogan. violent *adj* fierce, frenzied, furious, hot, passionate,raging, stormy, tumultuous, turbulent, wild.

xooggan oo caafimaad qaba. lusty *adj* robust, stout, strong, vigorous; bulky, burly, corpulent, fat, large, stout.

xooggan. vigorous *adj* lusty, powerful, strong; active, energetic, virile, strenuous; hardy, robust, sturdy, healthy.

ka xoogid. wrest *vb* force, pull, strain, twist, wrench, wring.

ka xoogroonaan. overwhelm *vb* engulf, submerge, swallow up, swamp; conquer, crush, defeat, overpower, subdue, vanquish.

xoogsiin. arm *vb* array, equip, furnish; clothe, cover, fortify, guard, protect, strengthen.

xoojin. sustain *vb* bear, strengthen, support, uphold; assist, comfort, nourish.

xoojin. fortify *vb* brace, encourage, protect, reinforce, stiffen, strengthen.

xoojin. unite *vb*

ku xoomid. swarm *vb* abound, crowd, teem, throng.

ku xoomid. mob *vb* crowd, jostle, surround, throng.

ku xoomid. throng *vb* congregate, crowd, fill, flock, pack, press, swarm.

dad xoonsan. mob *n* crowd, rabble, multitude, throng.

xooog leh. potent *adj* intense, powerful, strong; mighty, influential, powerful.

xoqid. itch *vb* tingle.

xor ah. independent *adj* autonomous, free, unrestricted, voluntary; (*person*) self-reliant, unconstrained. unconventional.

xor ah. free *adj* independent, unattached, unimpeded, unrestrained; emancipated, liberated, released, self-governing; open, permitted; empty, open, unimpeded, unrestricted; available, easy, familiar, informal.

xorayn. liberate *vb* emancipate, free, release.

xorayn. free *vb* emancipate, enfranchise, liberate, release, rescue, save; extricate, rid, unbind, unchain, unfetter, unlock.

xorayn. emancipate *vb* deliver, discharge, disenthral, enfranchise, free, liberate, release, unchain, unfetter, unshackle.

xoriyad. freedom *n* emancipation, independence, liberation, liberty, release.

xoriyad. liberty *n* emancipation, freedom, independence, liberation, self-government; leave, licence, permission.

xorriyad. independence *n* freedom, liberty, self-direction.

xubin. member *n* arm, leg, limb, organ; component, part, portion; branch, clause.

xudduud. boundary *n* border, circumference, confine, limit, periphery.

xujeen. puzzle *vb* bewilder, confuse, mystify, perplex.

xukumid xabsi. convict *vb* condemn, imprison, sentence.

xukumid. master *vb* conquer, defeat, direct, govern, overcome, rule; acquire, learn.

xukumid. dominate *vb* control, rule, sway; command, overlook, surmount.

xukumid. sentence *vb* condemn, judge.

xukumidid. control *vb* command, direct, dominate, manage, oversee, sway, regulate, restrain.

xukun boobid. usurp *vb* appropriate, assume, seize.

xukun maxkamad. judgement *n* decision, condemnation, sentence.

xukun. mandate *n* charge, command, commission, requirement.

xumaaday. deteriorate *vb* spoil, degenerate, worsen.

xumaan ku dhiirin. seduce *vb* allure, deceive,dishonour, ensnare, entice.

ka xumaansho. sorry *adj* apologetic, contrite, regretful, remorseful, sad, vexed.

si xun u isticamaal. abuse *vb* dishonour, misapply, misuse, wrong; harm, hurt, ill-use, ill-treat, injure, maltreat, mishandle.

aad u xun. horrid *adj* abominable, disagreeable, disgusting, odious, offensive, repulsive, revolting, shocking, unpleasant, vile.

xun. bad *adj* detrimental, evil, harmful, hurtful, injurious; corrupt, immoral, sinful, wicked; defective, inferior, imperfect, poor, unsuitable.

aad xun. awful *adj* august, awesome, dread, grand, inspired; abashed, alarming, appalled, dire, frightful, portentous, tremendous.

xunbayn. foam *vb* cream, froth, lather, spume; boil, churn, seethe, simmer, stew.

xunbbo. froth *n* bubbles, foam, lather, spume; nonsense, trash, triviality.

xunbo. foam *n* bubbles, cream, froth, scum, spray, spume, suds.

xurguf. arguement *n* affray, broil, discord, dissension, enmity, feud, grudge, hostility, quarrel, vendetta.

xus. memento *n* memorial, remembrance, reminder, souvenir.

xusid leh. memorable *adj* celebrated, distinguished, extraordinary, famous, great.

xusid. memorial *adj* commemorative, monumental.

xuunbayn. froth *vb* bubble, cream, foam, lather, spume.

Y

yaab badan. wonderful *adj* amazing, astonishing, awe-inspiring, awesome, marvellous, miraculous, stupendous.

yaab leh. stupendous *adj* astonishing, marvellous, superb, wonderful; enormous, prodigious, tremendous.

yaab leh. stunning *adj* dumbfounding, stupefying.

yaab leh. freak *adj* bizarre, grotesque, monstrous, odd, unexpected, unforeseen.

yaab. wonder *n* amazement, astonishment, awe, bewilderment, curiosity, marvel, surprise, wonderment.

yaabid. marvel *vb* gape, gaze, goggle, wonder.

yaabid. astonish *vb* amaze, astound, confound, daze, dumbfound, overwhelm, startle, stun, stupefy, surprise.

ka yaabin. perplex *vb* bewilder, confuse, mystify, nonplus.

ka yaabin. stagger *vb* lurch, reel, sway, totter; amaze, astonish, astound, dumbfound, shock.

ka yaabin. surprise *vb* amaze, astonish, astound, disconcert, startle, stun.

ka yaabin. dumbfound *vb* amaze, astonish, astound, bewilder, confound, confuse, nonplus.

wax la yab leh. miraculous *adj* supernatural; amazing, extraordinary, incredible, marvellous, unbelievable, wondrous.

yacyacood. rare *adj* bloody, underdone.

yaqyaqsi. nauseous *adj* disgusting, distasteful, loathsome, offensive, repulsive, revolting, sickening.

ka yaqyaqsi. disgust *vb* nauseate, sicken; offend, repel, repulse.

waxaad u yar. infinitesimal *adj* infinitely small.

in yar. little *n* handful, jot, modicum, pinch, pittance, trifle.

yar. little *adj* diminutive, minute, small, tiny, wee; brief, short, small; slight, trivial, unimportant; mean, narrow, niggardly, paltry, selfish, stingy.

yar. minute *adj* diminutive, fine, little, microscopic, miniature.

yar. miniature *adj* diminutive, little, small, tiny.

yar. small *adj* diminutive, little, miniature, tiny, insignificant.

wax aad u yar. jot *n* atom, bit, iota, grain, mite, particle, scrap, whit.

yar. puny *adj* feeble, inferior, weak; insignificant, diminutive, little, small, stunted, tiny, underdeveloped, undersized.

yar. tiny *adj* diminutive, lilliputian, little, miniature, minute,pygmy, small, wee.

ugu yar. least *adj* meanest, minutest, smallest, tiniest.

yar. fine *adj* little, minute, small; delicate, thin; exquisite, nice, refined, subtle.

yar. petty *adj* insignificant, slight, small, unimportant.

ka yar. less *adv* barely, below, least, under; decreasingly. *prep* excepting, lacking, minus, short of, without.

yaraan. deficiency *n* lack, scarcity, shortage.

yarayn. reduce *vb* abbreviate, curtail, decrease, diminish, lessen, minimize, shorten; impoverish, ruin.

yarayn. lessen *vb* curtail, decrease, diminish, reduce, shrink.

yarayn. diminish *vb* belittle, decrease, lessen, reduce.

yarayn. dwindle *vb* decrease, diminish, lessen, shrink, waste away.

yarayn. contract *vb* abbreviate, abridge, condense, curtail, diminish, lessen, narrow, reduce, shorten; catch, get, make, take.

yarayn. decrease *vb* curtail, diminish, lessen, reduce.

yasid. detract *vb* belittle, decry, defame, disparage, diminish, lessen.

yeelid. agree *vb* accord, concur, harmonize, unite; accede, acquiesce, assent, comply, concur, subscribe; bargain, contract, covenant, engage, promise, undertake; compound, compromise; correspond, match, tally.

yool. object *n* thing, target; goal, intention, motive, purpose, use, view.

yool. goal *n* end, objective; aim, design, destination.

yuusid. nag *vb* carp, fuss, hector, henpeck, pester, torment, worry.